A COMPREHENSIVE
GUIDE TO SYDNEY

Where to go, what to do & what not to miss Where to find the best food (and the most reasonable prices) How to locate lodgings, from wild to mild (including alternative, low-cost stays) Your guide to the best beaches (and what to wear) Walking tours (complete with maps) Take a pub crawl for fun, entertainment and great beer! Waterfront guide, harbour cruises, sailing ships Guide to speaking Strine & understanding Sydney customs Where to find (and sample) the good wineries Weekend trips from Sydney Go walkabout And much more!

PLUS: OLYMPICS 2000 GUIDE

Here's just about everything
you'll need for a glorious,
low-cost stay in Sydney!

Marlor Press

TRAVEL
BOOKS

**THE OTHER SIDE
OF SYDNEY**

**LONDON FOR THE
INDEPENDENT TRAVELER**

**NEW YORK FOR THE
INDEPENDENT TRAVELER***

**STATE BY STATE GUIDE
TO BUDGET MOTELS**

COMPLETE TRIP DIARY

***Recipient of the
BEST TRAVEL GUIDE AWARD
from the Publishers Marketing Association**

The Other Side of SYDNEY

*An independent traveler's guide
to wonderful
Australia's largest city*

**Zena L. Polin
& Stephen G. Gatward**

MARLOR PRESS, INC.
SAINT PAUL, MINNESOTA

THE OTHER SIDE
OF SYDNEY

Published by
Marlor Press, Inc.

Copyright © 1996
Zena L. Polin and Steven G. Gatward

A Marlin Bree Book
Mary Strasma, Assistant Editor

Photos of the Sydney Opera House courtesy of the
Australian Tourist Commission

Distributed to the book trade by
Contemporary Books, Chicago

ISBN 0-943400-87-2

Printed in the U.S.A.

M A R L O R
P R E S S
I N C .

4304 Brigadoon Drive
Saint Paul, Minnesota
55126

CONTENTS

Surry Hills, Little India and Little Turkey, Newtown,
Glebe cafes, and Darlinghurst Food Row.

and pool competitions. Pubs with live bands and entertainment, American-style pubs with DJ's, Hotel bars, Irish pubs, and Aussie pubs. Author's sample Pub Crawl. RSLs history and membership details, information on two best RSLs. Regular and alternative movie theaters that focus on artsy, foreign, and bizarre films. Includes prices, addresses, and bargain nights/specials. Theaters that show "Off Broadway" style productions, including phone numbers, style, and dress codes.

137   SHOPPING

Where to get the best deals and find the unique buys, from Aussie clothes to aboriginal artifacts. Where Sydneysiders go: Paddington, Redfern, Pitt Street, Chatswood, and Kings Cross. Also: camping supply stores, closing down stores. Alternative bookstores: esoteric, feminist, Buddhist, travel, and others. Markets: a description of a dozen markets that sell antiques, handicrafts, souvenirs, and exotic and inexpensive clothes. Information and guidelines for the traveler who wants to set up his or her own stall.

150   ANIMAL & PEOPLE PARKS

Parks that have the best selection of kangaroos, koalas, wombats, devils, emus, and other native wildlife. A description of some of Australia's favorite animals. Where to go to pet a kangaroo or hug a koala. Includes animal parks within Sydney (Taronga) and up to 120 miles away (Featherdale, Nowra, the Koala Sanctuary). People Parks: A description of local parks, their history, and attractions (Centennial and Moore Park, Hyde Park and the Domain, Tumbalong and the Chinese Gardens) as well as Harbour Parks (Ashton and Nielson Park, Balls Head Reserve) and parks within a one hour drive (Lane Cove River, Davidson, Ku-ring-gai Chase).

158   SPORTS

The ABCs of Sports: Where to go to do everything from abseiling to zen tennis. Contains information on prices, times, and phone numbers. Includes descriptions on how to play Aussie national sports, such as cricket, rugby, and, of course, gambling.

167   FESTIVALS AND SPECIAL EVENTS

A calendar of events that describes the most popular and entertaining events, such as the Gay and Lesbian Mardi Gras, Festival of the Winds, Surf Carnivals, The Teddy Bear and Dinosaur picnics, parades, the Film Festival, and Music in the Zoo.

SYDNEY MAPS

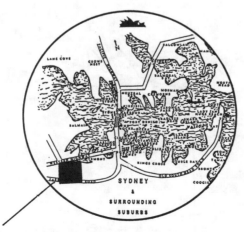

Shaded square shows area covered in larger map

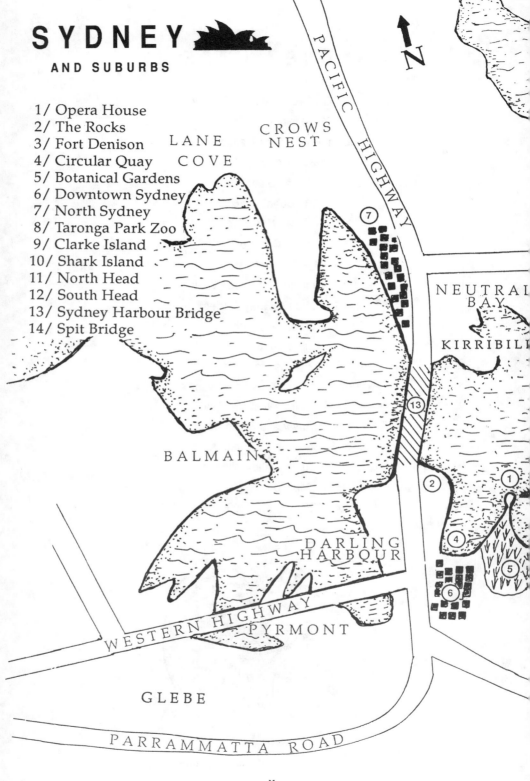

SYDNEY

AND SUBURBS

1/ Opera House
2/ The Rocks
3/ Fort Denison
4/ Circular Quay
5/ Botanical Gardens
6/ Downtown Sydney
7/ North Sydney
8/ Taronga Park Zoo
9/ Clarke Island
10/ Shark Island
11/ North Head
12/ South Head
13/ Sydney Harbour Bridge
14/ Spit Bridge

LANE COVE

CROWS NEST

PACIFIC HIGHWAY

N

NEUTRAL BAY

KIRRIBILLI

BALMAIN

DARLING HARBOUR

WESTERN HIGHWAY

PYRMONT

GLEBE

PARRAMMATTA ROAD

INTRODUCTION

What do you think about when Sydney, Australia, is mentioned? Kangaroos and koalas? Shrimp on the barbie? Foster's beer? The Opera House?

These are classic tourist ideas, but what you should really be looking forward to are: wombats and devils, Tooheys and Bundie, bugs on the barbie, underground dunnies, and even the Olympic Games!

Most travel guides on Australia concentrate on the entire country from Sydney to the Outback to Perth. A handful of these books are written strictly about Sydney, but no guide book informs travelers about *The Other Side of Sydney* — the Sydney of the Sydneysiders, the secret Sydney unfamiliar to even the most die-hard Aussie aficionado.

The *Other Side of Sydney* is a guidebook on alternative tourist sites in Australia's largest city. You will learn how to become an Aussie and speak Strine, eat dog's eyes and vegemite, order and drink beer, play rugby and cricket, buy a car, and dress and act like a local in Sydney's clubs, pubs, and neighborhoods.

The two of us have lived in Sydney, Australia for a combined total of over 20 years. We have explored almost every city street, park, beach, and neighborhood. We've discovered hidden tunnels, alternative museums, and local restaurants. We created beach and bush walks and pub crawls. There are even sections on day and weekend trips from Sydney.

Well, G'day Mates and hope to see you one arvo around the barbie, drinking a schooner and eating snags, bugs, and maybe even some dead horse!

Zena L. Polin
&
Stephen G. Gatward

CHAPTER 1:

THE STORY
OF SYDNEY

Although the British claim to have been the first to have discovered Australia, this is not altogether true. Chinese sailors of the Ming Dynasty bumped into Australia numerous times in history. They never really discovered it though, perhaps because they couldn't speak English or perhaps because Australia didn't have any really good Chinese restaurants (it still doesn't).

The Dutch explorer Van Diemen sailed along the coast of Australia until he discovered Van Diemen's Island, known today as Tasmania. A variety of other explorers seem to have sailed by Australia, including the French and the Spanish.

The Aboriginals actually came before all of these other explorers. But, according to the British, the Aboriginals never really discovered Australia. As far as historians are concerned, in order to discover a country, you have to arrive by ship. They just walked across, and that, apparently, doesn't count.

The Aboriginals had been living in Australia for over 40,000 years before English explorers "discovered" Australia. New research may prove that the Aboriginals hiked from south-east Asia across the now submerged continental shelf to Australia at least 120,000 years before Captain Cook crashed into the Aussie Coast. Over 300,000 Aboriginals lived relatively peacefully in a country the size of the United States. The Europeans quickly changed all that, as the British almost succeeded in systematically wiping out the entire population.

Aboriginals are a nomadic, tribal people who used to roam Australia's vast plains and deserts. The most important aspect of Aboriginal culture is "Dreamtime," or the very distant past when the land was formed and huge mythical beasts wandered the plains. Creatures such as "The Rainbow Serpent" slithered across the landscape creating mountains and rivers.

Aboriginal tribes have different Dreamtimes and each tribe dances its own unique dances. Even today songs and dances, such as "The Bush Onion and Bush Carrot", serve to pass on Aboriginal history to the younger generations. Dreamtime seems to have come to an end with the arrival of the Europeans in the late 1700s.

The expression "Go Walkabout" was coined by the Aboriginals and the term is still in use today. When a young boy reached puberty, he was sent off alone into the desert for about three months. He carried only his spear and boomerang. If he returned, he earned the right to hunt and fish alongside the other men in the tribe.

Very few nomadic Aboriginal tribes still exist, but those that do continue to "Go Walkabout." As recently as the 1960s an Aboriginal tribe that had never had contact with the outside world was found in South Australia.

In the late 1700s, British troops went on an "abo hunt" in Tasmania. They divided the entire island into sections, marched with little more than 100 feet or so between soldiers, drove the Aboriginals from their hiding spots, and when they ran, shot them. The few that were left were "Westernized" (i.e made into slaves).

By the early 1800s only 200 or so Aboriginals were left on Tasmania. They were deported to Flinders Island in the Bass Strait between Melbourne and Tasmania. The last of the full-blooded Tasmanian Aboriginals died in the 1800s.

In 1770, Captain Cook was on his way to Tahiti when he was sidetracked by a massive continent. He kept running his ships aground on the coast of Australia, but finally made it into Botany Bay.

He was accompanied by Joseph Banks, a botanist, who gave the area its name because he had never seen such a wide variety of trees, plants, and flowers. Today a buoy marks the spot where Captain Cook landed his ship and the crew went ashore.

Captain Cook went on to "discover" more islands, including Hawaii. Nine years after charting the east coast of Australia, he was slain and eaten (perhaps between two slices of bread) by the cannibals of the Sandwich Islands.

In 1788, 18 years after Captain Cook discovered Australia, another fleet of British ships was sent to OZ. So as not to confuse matters, this second fleet is called the First Fleet. The second fleet, or the official First Fleet, had 11 ships, 759 men and women convicts, 400 sailors, and livestock.

The British were in search of new lands to send their convicts to because the American Revolution had closed those colonies to the British. Within a few weeks of landing at Botany Bay, the crew packed up and moved north to what is now Sydney Cove.

On January 26, 1788 Captain Philip stepped ashore at the Rocks, named the area Port Jackson and the entire territory New South Wales (NSW), declared the territory a colony of the British Empire and proclaimed himself Governor. When Philip made this proclamation he did not know if the colony was an island, a continent, or a piece of land joined to China. Today, on January 26, Australians celebrate Australia Day, the anniversary of the "First" Fleet's discovery of Australia. The entire month of January is a holiday with parades, workshops, dances, parties, and races.

The Second and Third Fleets (or third and fourth if you want to be technical) landed within three years of the First Fleet. Soon the population of Sydney was more than 4,000 people. The first few years were desperate; times were tough for both the early free settlers and the convicts.

Disorder reigned, the Rocks had become a slum, prostitution and gambling were rampant, and the corrupt government had little control over the colony. Many convicts continued to work in chains, while free settlers could not figure out how to grow their British seeds in this land where even the weather was backward. The few people who were not convicts had only come to Sydney to try to get rich quick and were not at all concerned with creating a stable community. To top this off, all supplies had to come by boat from England. The only thing the settlers had in plentiful supply was rum. Although rum was illegal, many people, including government officials, used it as a form of currency.

The Rum Corps created even more chaos. The members of the Corps were officers of the New South Wales military who had been granted land and began to pay for labor and services in rum. Workers gladly accepted this form of payment, in order to block out the hellish conditions: disease, hunger, and killings.

Ex-Captain-now-Governor Bligh, of the Bounty mutiny fame, tried to suppress the use of rum, but everyone else was quite happy being drunk. This conflict culminated in the Rum

Rebellion of 1809, which brought down Bligh and sent him sailing back home to England. Governor Macquarie was sent in to restore peace and order.

In 1809 Matthew Flinders circumnavigated the entire 3,000,000 square miles of Australia, which is roughly the size of the continental U.S. Flinders renamed the country "Australia." The name comes from the Spanish word "astral" which means southern or south.

When convict transport ended in 1853, about the same time gold was discovered in New South Wales, over 100,000 convicts and 200,000 settlers had arrived in Australia. England finally realized the wealth that was hidden in New South Wales. Tunnels were built and armaments were set up around the harbor to protect Sydney from potential attack. Today these hidden tunnels and armaments can be seen as part of a tour given by the NSW Department of Parks and Recreation.

During the mid-1800s the Bushrangers began to make their appearance. They arrived on the scene at about the same time the railroad was built. The Bushrangers were the equivalent of the cowboys with black hats, the bad guys.

Ned Kelly was the most famous of all. When he robbed and murdered he wore a suit of armor, a helmet with a slit for his eyes, and a breastplate. He is famous in Australian folklore as being a Robin Hood-type character since he only robbed and murdered from those who did it to him first.

In December of 1900, Queen Victoria declared that Australia would be a self-governing nation as of January 1, 1901. Although Federation meant Australia was independent from Great Britain, many financial, military, and political ties remained. The Queen still has a representative, the Governor General, in Australia. He answers directly to the Queen and has the power to dissolve the Government.

The Governor General's power is mainly ceremonial. However, in 1974, under the orders of the Queen of England (and with possible pressure from the American CIA), Sir John Kerr, the Queen's Representative, dissolved the Australian Government of Gough Whitlam. This, of course, caused an uproar in Australia. Many older Australians still resent this American intrusion in their business.

Federation revamped the Australian political system. Women were granted the vote more than twenty years earlier than in Great Britain and the United States! Today, failure by any citizen to vote incurs a $60 fine. Many wonder if the fine should be higher if you don't vote for the proper party!

Despite heavy casualties, Australia survived World War I (WWI) and World War II (WWII) relatively intact. During WWI, the Aussies were so intent on saving democracy that conscription was not even needed. On April 25, 1915, the Australians and New Zealanders landed at Galipoli, Turkey. Thousands were killed and Turkey was eventually lost to the enemy.

Anzac Day is now a national holiday in both Australia and New Zealand. Pubs open at 6 a.m. (immediately following parades and speeches) and the gambling sport of Two-Up is played in pubs and Returned Servicemen League (RSL) clubs all day long, or until the players fall over drunk!

WWII was even harsher on Australia. Both men and women were conscripted. The harbor of Darwin in the Northern Territories was bombed by the Japanese and Sydney Harbour was attacked by Japanese midget submarines. One of the submarines was never found, one destroyed an American battleship, and the other was captured and is on display at the Australian War Museum in Canberra.

The Aussie retreat from the Indonesian side of Papua New Guinea along the Kokoda Trail was one of the saddest events in Australian history. The soldiers were forced to walk for five days over the harsh, mountain terrain with little food and water.

In the 1970s Australia was known as the "Lucky Country". Unemployment was under one percent, the economy was thriving, the standard of living was high, and immigrants were welcomed with open arms.

With the 1990 world-wide recession, Australia did not fare so well. Officially, unemployment was over 10 percent and unofficially as high as 18 percent; the housing market stagnated, immigration slowed, and Australia curbed its welcome to the many ethnic groups she once embraced.

Despite her troubles, Australia still has a successful national health program, adequate pensions, and an additional 17.25 percent vacation pay.

Sydney, lucky still, has fared better than the rest of the country. The recession succeeded in slowing growth, but as the economic and cultural center of the country, Sydney has not experienced the recession as badly as Melbourne and many bush towns. The response to the recession has been to promote tourism and other services.

The best thing about Australia is not Ayers Rock, the Opera House, the Outback, or the kangaroo, but the people. As you explore Sydney and the surrounding areas, use the information provided in this book to find out how to meet and to befriend Aussies. To take advantage of all Sydney has to offer, learn the language, the style, and the attitudes of Sydneysiders, find some of the secret city sights, and try to spend at least a month exploring this fascinating city and surrounding areas.

Although Aussie mateship has its downside, the benefit is that Aussies are always willing to make a new friend. However, keep a few things in mind. Since most Australians are somehow descended from convicts, an interesting mentality (however subconscious) remains.

In general, Aussies do not like to give service, in part because they view everybody as *equal*. The customer is not always right. However, due to recession and the growing realization that service is a given almost everywhere else in the world, this mentality is changing.

The "Tall Poppy Syndrome" (chop down those who strive to be better than the rest) still exists. Aussies are likely to ask your annual income, your Christmas bonus, and the price of your house or car. They expect, and in return give, direct answers. Some say such blunt questions are a means to keep management from controlling the workers by keeping wages private. If everyone knows what everyone else is making, then the employees have the upper hand. Also, Aussies want to pay the least for the best. They're not impressed by ostentatious wealth.

Lastly, always remember that this is a country where a woman's child was reportedly eaten by a dingo (a wild dog). The Aussies took the dingo's side, insisted that the dog was innocent, and believed that the baby was a sacrifice by a bizarre religion! When the movie version (starring Meryl Streep), which leaned heavily towards the Chamberlain family's innocence, was shown in Sydney, people marched down the streets and held banners proclaiming, "The dingo is innocent."

So, if an Aussie's action or response ever confuses you, remember the dingo!

CHAPTER 2:

LEARNING
THE ROPES

This chapter is an introduction to the basic information needed to get along in Sydney. Read this alphabetical listing to find out: what clothes to bring during which months, how to buy gas (for your car, that is), how to tune into the radio station that plays Crowded House and Midnight Oil, how to phone home, and where to get medicine if you are poisoned by kangaroo meat. For in-depth information on many of these topics, see the individual chapters.

AIRLINES

Air Canada 232-5222
Air New Zealand 957-4388
Ansett 13-1300
British Airways 258-3200
Continental 249-0111
Quantas 13-1313
United 13-1717

BANKS

There are two types of banks in Australia: building societies and national banks. Building societies are similar to American credit unions; their popularity grew from their commitment to customer service, longer opening hours, service with a smile, and better interest rates. Banks have responded by becoming more competitive and are also offering more services. The State Bank has consistently offered good interest rates, while the St George Building Society (which is actually now a bank) has the best customer service.

If you plan to open a bank account and don't want your account to be subject to taxes (10 percent), you should get a tax file number. Your account will still be subject to transaction taxes, but at a much lower rate. To get a tax file number, simply apply at the local Post Office, with passport in hand. It takes about 30 days to get the number. If you don't have a tax number, you can still open an account. You can use just your passport as an ID to open an account during your first six weeks in Australia. After this you will need to present a lot of other IDs, including a birth certificate.

Australian Banks are national. This means they have branches all over the country and in every small town. Opening a bank account in Australia is a great idea and even safer than carrying travelers checks. Also, if you have an Aussie account it makes getting money and cashing travelers checks easier and cheaper than if you don't.

Banks are generally open 9:30 a.m. to 4 p.m., Monday to Thursday; 9:30 a.m. to 5 p.m. on Friday. Certain branches are also open on Saturday mornings. ATM cards that access the Cirrus, Star or Plus systems can be used in Australia. Check with your local bank first to make sure your card is enabled for international access.

CONSULATES & IMMIGRATION

All visitors to Australia need a visitor visa and a current passport which is valid for three months longer than the visa. For a stay longer than three months, a $27 fee is required. If you need to renew your visa in Australia, make sure you have your passport, proof of funds, an onward ticket, and money to pay for a renewal. The cost to renew will depend on the length of time you plan to stay, your citizenship, and various other factors.

Once you are in Australia, the Immigration Office is usually quite helpful. Just remember that although the Australians tend to dress casually, they are very particular about looks, so dress neatly, i.e., clean jeans and shirt — not ripped shorts and a t-shirt. Call 258-4555 for the immigration office nearest you.

As of November 1, 1995, Australian embassies issue different visas for tourists and business travelers. Tourist visas (up to three months) are still free, while business visas (multi-entry, five-year) cost $27.

If you plan to travel onward, to India or Asia for example, check to see if visas are required and if they cost money. Visas can take from one day to more than a week to process. To save time, call ahead and ask what documentation (photos, proof of funds, onward tickets, fees, etc.) is required to facilitate the visa process. The following is a list of consulate phone numbers:

India 275-540
Indonesia 344-9933
Japan 231-3455
Nepal 264-5909
New Zealand 247-1999
Papua New Guinea 299-5151
Philippines 299-6633
Thailand 272-542
United States 261-9200

CREDIT CARDS

These numbers are for credit card company offices in Sydney. American Express, Visa, and other cards also have free phone numbers that connect you with a U.S. operator. Get these numbers in the U.S. before you leave. A "1 800" number in Sydney is a toll-free call.

American Express 239-0666 or 886-0666 for lost/stolen cards
Mastercard 1 800 022-017
Diners Club 236-8923
Visa International 957-6133

The American Express Office is located at 388 George St., the City.

CURRENCY

In 1992, the Australian Government (under Prime Minister Paul Keating) decided to take the $.01 and $.02 coins out of circulation. These coins are still accepted by most businesses, but are gradually being phased out of everyday use. Thus, for charges that cost between $.01 and $.02, round the cost down, and for charges that cost $.03 and $.04 round up. This means if the shopping bill comes to $10.02, you pay just $10.

Beware of the one and two dollar coins! It's easy to get a pocketful of coins worth $20 or more! The $5, $10, $20, $50 and $100 notes still exist. There are no notes larger than $100.

All prices quoted in this book are in Australian dollars, unless otherwise mentioned. The Aussie dollar does tend to fluctuate against the American dollar, so you should keep up-to-date on the exchange rate fluctuations.

DEPARTURE TAX

The current departure tax is $25 payable at a post office prior to departure or at the airport on the day of departure.

DISABLED TRAVELERS

The National Industries for Disability Services has information for disabled travelers, including travel agents, guides, wheelchair rentals, and support organizations. For more information, write to them in care of the Australian Council for the Rehabilitation of the Disabled, PO Box 60, Curtin, ACT 2065. Phone: 06 282-4333.

ELECTRICITY

Voltage is 240. A converter and a flat three-pin adapter plug are needed to convert North American plugs to Australian. These are available from hardware, department stores, and camping stores in the U.S. and Australia.

EMERGENCIES

Ambulance, Fire, Police 000
Crisis Center 358-6577
Dental Emergencies 692-0333
Poison Information 692-6111
Rape Crisis Center 819-6565
24 Hour Pharmacy 438-3333
Sydney Hospital 282-2111
Lifeline 264-2222
Emergency Prescription Service 438-3333

THE FLAG

The small Union Jack in the corner of the Aussie flag represents the link with Great Britain, the large seven-pointed star represents the six States (New South Wales, Queensland, Victoria, Western Australia, South Australia and Tasmania) and all the Territories. The small stars form the Southern Cross.

Since Prime Minister Paul Keating and other prominent officials stated their support of Australia completely separating from Great Britain in the year 2000, the fate of the flag has been hotly debated. Many expect a new flag, minus the Union Jack.

GASOLINE

If you need gasoline for your car, ask for a petrol station, not a gas station. Gas, to an Aussie, is what you cook with. Petrol is sold by the liter (five liters to the British Imperial Gallon, which is slightly larger than the American gallon), and costs about $.60 to $.70 a liter. Most cars take super, which is regular leaded petrol, although the newer cars use unleaded.

INFORMATION CENTERS

The following centers offer information on festivals, special events, and general tourist information:

- Rocks Visitors Center, 104 George St., 247-4972 (Open 9 a.m. to 5 p.m. daily)
- The NSW Government Travel Center, 19 Castlereagh St., 231- 4444 (9 a.m. to 5 p.m. weekdays)
- Sydney Information Booth, Martin Place, 235-2424 (9 a.m. to 5 p.m. weekdays)
- Tourist Information Service, 669-5111 (8 a.m. to 6 p.m. daily)
- Travellers' Information Service, 281-9366, for bus and accommodation reservations only, daily
- Travellers Information Center, Sydney Airport, 281-9366, daily
- Metrotips, 954-4422 daily (7 a.m. to 10 p.m. daily)
- YHA Membership and Travel Centre, 422 Kent St., 261-111 (9 a.m. to 5 p.m. weekdays)

STATE TOURISM OFFICES

Northern Territory 345 George St., 363-1733
South Australia 143 King St., 232-8388
Tasmania 149 King St., 202-2022
Queensland 75 Castlereigh St., 232-1788
Victoria 403 George St., 299-2088
Western Australia 92 Pitt St., 233-4400

LANGUAGE

The official language is English, not by law but by common usage. However, most locals tend to call the language "Strine," which does not differ significantly from American English except for all of the colloquialisms and slang. See page 46 for an explanation.

MAIL

Sydneysiders will tell you that their mail service is excellent, although it seems to take ten days, or more, for a letter to reach Sydney from the east coast of the U.S. Most post offices are open 9 a.m. to 4 p.m. Monday to Friday, and Saturdays from 9 a.m. to Noon.

Letters to the U.S. are expensive: $1.10 for a standard letter and $.95 for a post card. For some reason, it costs only $.90 to send a letter in a card envelope. Just write "card only"on the front of the envelope. Aerogrammes are even cheaper at $.70 for anywhere in the world. It is quite expensive to ship things home. Two to four kilos of sea mail cost about $20. There are no special rates to ship printed materials.

The General Post Office is located at 159 to 171 Pitt St.. The poste restante window (230-7033) is open from 8:15 a.m. to 5:30 p.m. Monday to Friday and Saturday from 8:30 a.m. to Noon. All local post offices also offer post restante service. Telegrams can be sent 24 hours a day from the Martin Place office, or during regular office hours at any Post Office, or by dialing 015 at any time.

MAPS

The best map available is a UBD (Urban Business Directory, but no one in their right mind would use the full name.) They are available for $4.15 at most newsagents, bookstores and petrol stations. A city map costs only $4, while a state map costs about $30. If you have become a member of the National Road and Motorists Association (260-9222), they have some great free maps which are available from their offices at 151 Clarence St., the City.

MONEY EXCHANGE

It is best to exchange your money at the banks during the week, but if you are stuck on a weekend there are a few exchange offices around. These give lower exchange rates and usually charge a higher commission than banks. It also may be possible to change money at large hotels, although some of them insist you must be a guest.

Seven Day Exchange Bureaus

Kings Cross - Thomas Cook on Darlinghurst Road
The Rocks - WestPac Bank on George St.
Circular Quay - Bureau de Change on the Wharf
International Airport - WestPac Bank
Pitt St.- Bureau de Change

NATIONAL ANTHEM

"Advance Australia Fair" was declared the national anthem of Australia in 1984. It is a revised version of a late 19th century patriotic song and replaced the former anthem, "God Save the Queen," which is now the "royal anthem."

NEWSPAPERS

The Sydney Morning Herald is the most popular morning paper, The Telegraph Mirror is the afternoon tabloid, and The Australian the national. Every town has its own local paper as well. The Thursday edition of the Mirror (Time Out section) and the Friday section of the Herald (Metro section) have the weekend entertainment listings.

It is possible to buy the Wall Street Journal, New York Times, and other international newspapers in Sydney. Try the following places: World News Centre at Darling Harbour, near the middle entrance and the Water Sculpture, or City Library, 321 Pitt St. (For reading not buying.)

OLYMPICS

Sydney is host to both the Olympic and the Paralympic Games in the year 2000. The Games will take place between September 16 and October 1, 2000. For more information see the Olympics chapter (Page 222).

POPULATION

Sydney has 3.7 million people from over 140 countries and is Australia's most populous city. About one fifth of the nation's entire population lives in this multicultural, cosmopolitan city.

PUBLIC HOLIDAYS

Australians take their holidays seriously, so when it is a public holiday almost everything closes down. Whoever coined the phrase "Land of the Long Weekend" was certainly correct. There are actually laws governing the types of stores that must close on legal holidays. Buy food, drink, and other necessities the day before a public holiday, but don't worry about beer because pubs are almost always open. Most pubs and tourist sites close Christmas Day and Good Friday.

HOLIDAYS

January 1 - New Years Day
January 26 - Australia Day
Good Friday
Easter Monday
April 25 - Anzac Day
June 13 - Queen's Birthday
August 1 - Bank Holiday
October 3 - Labor Day
December 25 - Christmas
December 26 - Boxing Day (except South Australia)

RADIO STATIONS

Australia has a wide range of AM and FM radio stations. Triple J is an alternative radio station that is funded by the Government. This gives the station a bit of artistic license, so all types of music are played.

Triple M is a Top 40 album station, and is currently the number one station in Sydney. Today FM (nicknamed G'day FM) plays rock a la Neil Young. Smaller local radio stations, such as 2SER, broadcast from the Technical College in Sydney, are supported by membership. They have a lot of talk shows on political issues and play alternative music. Aussie AM stations play exactly the same type of music as the AM stations in the US. Need we say more?

RELIGION

Almost all religions are represented in OZ. For information on services in your area, call the following places:

Anglican 269-0642
Baptist 211-1833
Interdenominational 33-4863
Jewish 267-2477
Lutheran 419-5686
Presbyterian 29-1301

Roman Catholic 232-3788
Seventh Day Adventist 858-4061

SIZE OF AUSTRALIA

Australia is the only nation to occupy an entire continent. It has a land mass of almost 50 million square miles, and is the flattest and driest (after Antarctica) of continents. Australia possesses more than 22 million miles of coastline.

TAXIS

Either hail a cab on the street, telephone, or take the first one in a taxi rank. Taxis cost $1.80 at flag fall and $.92 a kilometer thereafter, or more if there is traffic. There is a telephone charge of $1, and a charge if they are kept waiting. Taxi drivers usually don't expect tips.

Don't be surprised if the cab driver expects you to sit up front with him. This goes more if you are a single male. Women and couples sit in the back.

RSL Cabs 581-1111
Legion Cabs 289-9000
Premier Radio Cabs 897-4000

TELEPHONES

A local phone call costs $.40 from a pay phone. It is a good idea to purchase multi-use phone cards ($2, $5, $10, $20) to carry around. These are available from local newsagents. If you are calling home on a pay phone, phonecards prevent the need to drop money in every few seconds from some phones. Or, you can use a bank or credit card. The minimum charge is $1.20.

All phone numbers listed in this book are based in Sydney (area code 02), unless otherwise specified. However, Australia is running out of phone numbers. The numbering system will be changed over a five-year period beginning July, 1996. New South Wales and the ACT will have a 02 area code. 03 will cover Victoria and Tasmania; 07, Queensland; and 08, Western Australia, the Northern Territories, and South Australia. The 047 that was previously the ACT's area code will now be incorporated into the actual phone number.

The plan is to gradually switch from a six or seven digit number, to an eight digit number, plus two more for the area code. The last two digits of regional area codes will be added to the front of the local number, while the zero will be dropped. Eventually, Australia will have only four area codes, instead of 54!

In July 1996, all Sydney phone numbers beginning with 90 to 98 will get an additional 9 added to the front to become 990 to 998. For more information, call AUSTEL, 1-800-888-888. Other changes are also scheduled for the rest of the country.

To call the U.S. direct (no extra operator charge) dial 0011 1 Area Code Number. The rates are $2 per minute from 8 p.m. to 6 a.m. and $2.50 per minute outside of these hours. AT&T, MCI, and Sprint all have country direct dialing, although it is cheaper to call the U.S. direct than to use their services.

AT&T 0014-881-011
MCI 0014-881-100
Sprint 0014-881-877

The Telecom Phone Center, 100 King St., 232-2252 is open 24 hours. Direct dial calls can be made here and the call is paid for immediately afterwards.

Emergency calls 000 (free)
Collect Calls 0101
Operator 013
International Operator 0103

Free Calls begin with 1800. 0055 numbers are similar to 900 numbers in the U.S. The cost for a call is usually $.25 per 20 seconds.

TELEVISION

SBS and ABC (Channel 2) are both owned by the Federal Government. Channel 2 carries no commercials while the programs on SBS are sponsored by corporations, so there are only a few sponsorship spots at the beginning and end of each show.

As with PBS in the United States, having the Government sponsor television stations allows the stations to be more creative in their programming. SBS shows three or four foreign films every night and Channel 2 carries a lot of British comedy and Australian documentaries.

Channels 7, 9 and 10 have regular commercial television

shows. Late in 1995, Australia launched Pay TV and viewers have a choice of 17 channels.

TIME

Australia is divided into three time zones: Eastern Standard (10 hours ahead of Greenwich Mean Time), Central Australian (9.5 hours ahead) and Western Time (8 hours ahead). During the summer all states, except Queensland, go on daylight savings. Since their seasons are opposite to ours, this means that Sydney can be 14, 15, or even 16 hours ahead of New York, depending on Daylight Savings times (U.S. and Australian).

WEATHER

Sydney tends to have only two seasons, cool and hot, although the Sydneysiders insist that there is a full-blown winter season. The following guide is what the weather is really like, along with the matching season, not the official seasons.

December, January, February: **Summer**
Very Hot, unsettled, humid, 80 to 100 degrees.
March, April, May: **Mild Summer**
Very pleasant, mild temperatures, 65 to 80 degrees.
June, mid-July: **Fall**
Warm days, cool nights, 50 to 70 degrees.
Mid-July, August, mid-September: **Winter**
Cool mornings, warm days, cold nights (leather jackets needed), 35 to 65 degrees.
Mid-September, October, November: **Spring**
Warm days and nights, 50 to 75 degrees.

MEDICAL CARE

The Australian national health care system not only functions, it functions well. The federal health care organization, Medicare, is funded by a one percent tax on all earnings up to an annual income of $50,000. Pensioners, the unemployed, single mothers, and other special cases receive extra benefits in the form of low-cost prescriptions. Every Australian resident is issued a Medicare card which means that certain doctor's visits are free. The program is similar to an American HMO. Legal residents of Italy, Malta, Sweden, New Zealand, and the United Kingdom can also receive free Medicare in Australia.

For the rest whose countries do not provide Government

health care, never fear! A doctor's visit in Australia costs only $25. Certain sexual health (pregnancy, HIV), dental and eye clinics are free for travelers as well as residents. Medicare clinics are small, clean and usually open until about 8 p.m.. Prescriptions can be filled on the spot.

FREE EMERGENCY DENTAL The United Dental Hospital, Chalmers St., 282-0200, is open from 8:30 a.m. to 3 p.m. Weekdays and 1:30 p.m. to 5 p.m. weekends. The clinic is a student hospital that will even pull teeth for free. The emergency number for after hours problems is 692-0333.

FREE SEXUAL HEALTH The Sydney Sexual Health Center (SSHC), Nightingale Wing, Sydney Hospital, Macquarie St., 223-7066 is open different hours every day. The clinic provides free checkups, testing for STD's, HIV (& counseling) and pregnancy, and will give you a prescription for contraception. If you run short, the clinic will usually throw in a pack of free pills to keep you going.

VACCINATION The Traveler's Medical Center, (TMVC) 428 George St., Level 7 (above Dymocks), 221-7133 is open from 9 a.m. to 6 p.m. Monday to Friday and 9 a.m. to noon on Saturdays. For a fee, the TMVC will provide all vaccinations, antimalarial tablets, and advice on travel requirements.

A bit of advice for those who are travelling on to Asia from Australia: If you are entering an area that has malaria, check with other travelers before starting a course of tablets. A lot of malaria in Asia is now chloriquinine resistant. Before taking any drugs you may want to ask yourself, "Are the locals taking prophylactics? What are the side effects? What are my alternatives?"

PHARMACIES Two major chemists are open 24 hours: 197 Oxford St., Darlinghurst and 28 Darlinghurst Road, Kings Cross. The emergency prescription service number is 438-3333.

POISON Although you may think that you've been poisoned by kangaroo meat or beer with 9 percent alcohol, you are probably mistaken. But, just in case, call 692-6111. The line is open 24 hours.

CHAPTER 3:

GETTING
AROUND
SYDNEY

Sydney has modern and comfortable buses and taxis, and some of the trains are double-deckered and air-conditioned. It's very easy and inexpensive to get around Sydney and even to the outlying suburbs by train.

However, most of Sydney's sights are in the downtown area and are easily accessible by foot, as long as you are wearing a good pair of walking shoes. Buses are much more expensive than trains. Round-trip tickets are available on trains, but cannot be purchased for bus rides.

A couple of tips to save money while you explore Sydney:

1/ If you are traveling with four or more people, hail a taxi.

2/ Read the following information on purchasing travel passes.

AIRPORT TRANSPORT

If you arrive alone in Sydney, *do not* jump into a taxi. There are many other cheaper options. However, if you are traveling with another friend or two, the taxi can be a quick and inexpensive way to get to your hotel. A ride to town center costs between $15 and $20.

The best way to get into town is to jump on the green and yellow Airport Express Bus which leaves the City and the airport every 20 minutes seven days a week. Buses leave the airport between 5:53 a.m. and 10:55 p.m. and leave the City between 5:15 a.m. and 10:05 p.m. Tickets cost $6 one way and $8 round trip and are valid for two months. Tickets cost $2.50 to travel between terminals.

Make sure you get on the correct bus, because there are two routes. The #300 bus travels between the international and domestic terminals (for $2.50) and Circular Quay (not the best place to find inexpensive hotels) via Central Station. The #350 goes to Kings Cross (the "Backpacker Hostel" center).

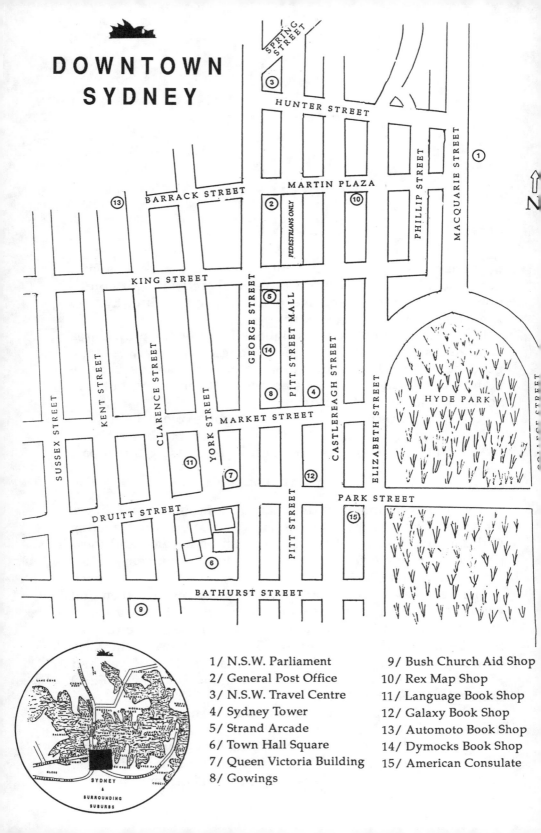

DOWNTOWN SYDNEY

1/ N.S.W. Parliament
2/ General Post Office
3/ N.S.W. Travel Centre
4/ Sydney Tower
5/ Strand Arcade
6/ Town Hall Square
7/ Queen Victoria Building
8/ Gowings
9/ Bush Church Aid Shop
10/ Rex Map Shop
11/ Language Book Shop
12/ Galaxy Book Shop
13/ Automoto Book Shop
14/ Dymocks Book Shop
15/ American Consulate

Public bus #400 goes to the beaches of Bondi/Coogee (another "Backpacker Hostel" center).

Another alternative is the Kingsford Smith Airport Bus which takes you from the airport to any hotel in the city center for $5. Buses run every half hour between 6 a.m. and 8 p.m. Call 667-0663 for more information and advance reservations when leaving Sydney.

Before you hop on the Airport Shuttle you may want to purchase a Sydney Pass (see below), if you plan to explore Sydney by public transport. The Pass includes transportation on the Shuttle. Another option is to call the Glebe Backpackers Village. This is an inexpensive, fun place to stay which offers free transportation from the airport. From the hotel it is just a short bus ride or ambitious walk into town. Many other hostels also offer this service. Read through the "Places to Stay" section for more information on free hotel/airport transport.

If your luggage is light, you already feel like beginning your exploration of Sydney, and you want to be a bit cheap, you can hike for about half an hour to Arncliffe Train station. A train to Central Station costs only $1.60 from there.

BUSES

Riding around in Sydney's air-conditioned, comfortable buses can be fun. Many of the buses are covered in advertisements. This means your bus may occasionally be transformed into a zoo, a package or a house. Unfortunately, bus rides can be quite expensive ($1.20 and $2.50 for local one-way rides and $3.30 and $4 for one-way longer distance rides). Also, Sydney traffic can be horrendous and nerve wracking, especially if you are not used to being on the "wrong" side of the road.

If you still want to travel by bus, take either the Free Buses (#777 through the city center or #666 from Hunter St. at Wynyard to the Art Gallery of NSW) or make sure you take advantage of the following multi-ticket deals. These tickets are available from State Transit bus depots and most newsagents. Also, bus drivers actually do give change, and if you're looking lost will tell you when it's your stop. When locating your bus stop to board, remember that driving on the left means that you will feel like you're waiting on the wrong side of the street for the direction in which you're traveling.

For more information, call 13-1315 or 954-4422 or visit the State Transit Booths at Circular Quay (near Jetty 4) and at Martin Place.

Buses for the north of the city (100 and 200 series) leave from Wynyard Park, while those for the east, south and west (300, 400 and 500 series) leave from Circular Quay. Reduced rate bus transfer tickets are not available.

METROTEN: Provides 10 bus rides in a single ticket. You can use them now, on your next visit to Sydney, or you can sell them to a fellow traveler. Tickets are colored according to the distance you want to travel. For most travelers, a blue metroten ticket for $7.30 is sufficient.

TRAVELPASS: This pass provides unlimited weekly, monthly or yearly travel through certain zones in Sydney. This pass offers combination Train/Bus/Ferry, Bus/Ferry or Bus only tickets. The Travelpass is a great bargain if you plan to use the ferries a lot, although trips to Manly are not included. Most people will need a weekly red pass for $17 for the city and inner suburbs. A green pass costs $24 and allows extensive bus, ferry (except the RiverCat and JetCat) and rail travel for one week. If you purchase your ticket after 3 p.m., the week begins the following day.

BUSTRIPPER: This provides unlimited bus travel during any one day for $6.80. If you are planning to do a lot of exploring in one day or if you are going on a return trip to the suburbs, this is a good pass to buy.

SYDNEY PASS: This is a three day ($50), five day ($70) or seven day ($80) ticket. You are entitled to unlimited bus and ferry rides, including the Manly Ferry and JetCat, the Zoo Ferry, the Harbour History Cruise, the Harbour Sights Cruise, the Harbour Lights Cruise, the Rocks/Darling Harbour Shuttle, the Sydney Explorer (see below) and the Airport Express (see above).

SYDNEY EXPLORER: If you don't have much time in Sydney, this is the pass for you. The $20 Explorer ticket (family discounts available) allows all day travel on a continuous circuit around 26 of Sydney's most popular tourist sites. Buses leave every 20 minutes between 9:30 a.m. and 9 p.m.

A sampling of the sites are: the Opera House, Circular Quay, the Royal Botanical Gardens, Parliament House, Mrs. Macquaries' Chair, the Art Gallery of NSW, Kings Cross,

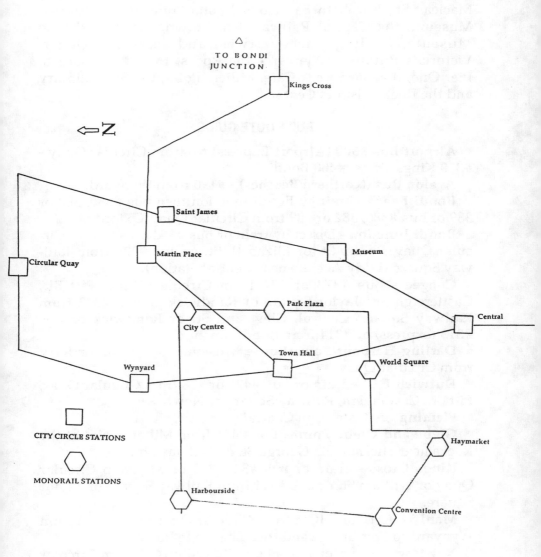

TO BONDI
JUNCTION

⟵ N

Kings Cross

Saint James

Martin Place

Museum

Circular Quay

Park Plaza

City Centre

Town Hall

Central

Wynyard

World Square

☐
CITY CIRCLE STATIONS

⬡
MONORAIL STATIONS

Haymarket

Harbourside

Convention Centre

DOWNTOWN
SYDNEY
TRANSPORT
SYSTEM

Macleay St., Elizabeth Bay House, Potts Point, the Australian Museum, the Central Railway, Chinatown, the Powerhouse Museum, Darling Harbour (west and east), the Queen Victoria's Building, Wynyard, the Rocks, the Village Green, Pier One, the Hard Rock Cafe, Millers Point, the State Library and the Rocks Visitors Center.

BUS ROUTE GUIDE

Airport Bus #300 (Airport Express) to/from Circular Quay - #350 Kings Cross, #400 Bondi.

Avalon Bus (Northern Beaches) - #190 from Wynyard.

Bondi Beach - Train to Bondi Junction then bus #380, 382 or 389 or bus #380, 382 or 389 from Circular Quay, Oxford St.

Bondi Junction - Direct by train or bus #382 or 389 from Circular Quay, Phillip St. or Elizabeth St. or bus #378 from Railway Square (Eddy Avenue near Central Station).

Coogee - Bus #373 or 374 from Circular Quay, Pitt St., Castlereigh St., Taylor Square or Randwick or bus #372 from Railway Square, Central, Cleveland St. or Randwick or bus #313 (express) or #314 from Bondi Junction.

Darling Harbour/Powerhouse Museum - Monorail or ferry from Circular Quay.

Dulwich Hill - Train or bus #426 or 428 from Circular Quay, Pitt St., Castlereigh, Railway Square or Newtown.

Flemington Train from Central.

Glebe and Glebe Point - Bus #431 from Millers Point at the Rocks near Hickson St., George St. or Railway Square.

Kings Cross - Train or bus #324, 325 or 327 from Circular Quay or William St. or bus #311 from Railway Square or Taylor Square.

Manly - Ferry or JetCat from Circular Quay or any bus from Wynyard to Spit Bridge and then change to bus #144.

Newtown - Train or bus #422, 423, 426 or 428 from Circular Quay, Pitt St., Castlereigh St., Railway Square or City Road.

Oxford St., Paddington - Bus #380 or 382 from Circular Quay, Phillip St., Elizabeth St. or Taylor Square or bus #380 or 382 from Bondi Junction or Bondi Beach.

Redfern - Train or bus #309 or 310 from Circular Quay, Pitt St., Castlereigh St. or Elizabeth St.

TRAINS

A faster and cheaper way to travel within Sydney is by train.

There are three types of trains: The modern, air-conditioned, comfy trains are called Tangara trains and they run mainly between Central Station and the outer suburbs. Silver double-decker trains that are marginally comfortable are the most numerous and travel all around Sydney. Then come the Red Rattlers, or single level trains, that are not air conditioned, are very noisy, and are a nightmare to be on during rush hours. The doors tend to be operated manually, that is by your own hand, and often remain stuck open, even when the train is filled to capacity. The last Red Rattler to go to North Sydney crossed the Harbour Bridge in 1992, and the Department of Transportation is gradually retiring them.

To get the cheapest train fares, travel off peak (after 9 a.m. weekdays and all day weekends) and purchase round-trip tickets. For a round-trip, off-peak ticket within the Inner West of Sydney, you should pay $1.80 ($1.60 one way).

The City Hopper ticket, $2.20, allows unlimited one-day travel, after 9 a.m. weekdays and all day weekends, around the City Circle. The Circle includes: North Sydney, Milsons Point, Wynyard, Town Hall, Central, Museums, St. James, Circular Quay, Martin Place and Kings Cross.

TRAMWAY

The tramway, actually a bus that has been made to look just like a tram, takes people between Circular Quay and Darling Harbour. This service is available every day between 9:30 a.m. and 6 p.m. Trains leave every 15 minutes. Tickets are $2 each way or $3 for an all-day pass. Look for the yellow and black signs which indicate tramway stops.

FERRIES AND JETCATS

A fun and relaxing way to get around Sydney is to boat around the Harbour. Unfortunately, single trips are expensive and round-trip discounts are not offered. The best deal is the Bus/Train/Ferry pass ($24) or the Ferry Ten Pass ($22.80). The one-way ferry to Manly costs $3.40 while the JetCat is $4.60. The Special Taronga Park Zoo ferry/bus/zoo admission ticket is $17 ($8.50 for kids).

MONORAIL

The monorail has been surrounded by controversy since its inception. Most Sydneysiders despise the monorail because they either feel it is out of place and does not match the architectural style of downtown Sydney, or they feel as if Mickey Mouse and Disneyland invaded Australia. Just about everyone agrees it is a waste of money.

When the monorail was completed, but had not yet been officially opened, a Buddhist monk, dressed in saffron robes, was seen walking on the tracks (which are 30 feet in the air). Whether he was exorcising demons or cursing the rails, no one seems to know because he disappeared before any officials arrived on the scene.

The controversy is not helped by the fact that the monorail doesn't really take you anywhere and overcharges to get you there. To take a $2.50 ride on the monorail, get on at Darling Harbour (where there is no other transportation except by water) and zoom past the Convention Center, The Powerhouse Museum, George St., Town Hall, and Pitt St. shopping. Whether you travel only one stop or all of them, the price is the same. For more information, call 552-2288.

TAXIS

If you are traveling around Sydney with four or more people, hop in a cab. Taxis cost $1.80 at flag fall, plus $.95 a kilometer, or more if there is traffic, $0.45 per minute waiting, and a $.50 maximum luggage charge. There are no night fees.

Do not whistle for a cab or wave frantically. Instead, point your index finger at the curb. Basically, you are saying, "Hey, taxi! Stop right here." Don't worry, it may look funny, but it works. Actually, hitchhikers do the same thing when trying to catch a ride.

The major taxi companies are: Combined (361-8222) and Legion (289-9000). Expect at least a 15-minute wait if you phone for a taxi (plus a $1 surcharge), even if the cab company says otherwise. If you're leaving early in the morning and have called for a taxi the night before, call again when you wake up.

JOYFLIGHTS

If you're in the mood for a splurge, then try a flight around Sydney. For $59 per person, you'll be whisked away for one hour in a small plane and flown over the Harbour Bridge, Opera House, Circular Quay, east to Bondi Beach, then straight up the coast to the Northern Beaches, the Central Coast and back again. The company provides free pickup and delivery from your hotel. Call 358-5811 or 016-289-411.

CARS

Driving a car in Sydney is not the smartest thing to do, especially if you have never driven on the "wrong" side of the road. Sydney drivers rank with Indy 500 race car drivers as far as speed is concerned. Parking in downtown Sydney is a joke. It costs $1 for 15 minutes, if you can find an empty meter — and most meters have a maximum time limit of one to two hours. However, if you and some mates are planning to explore the rest of Australia, buying a car, van or camper is a good idea.

It is easy to get the hang of driving on the left—if you are going in a straight line! It's the turns that are confusing, especially if there are no other cars on the street and you forget which side of the road to turn into. Remember to aim the steering wheel at the center line of the road, but try not to go too far towards the center! This method generally keeps you on the right, or rather left side, of the road. Corners in Sydney allow a left on red if signposted, but don't try a right on red!!

The hardest thing to remember is not which side of the road to be on, but which side to get in to drive and where the turn signal is. You will probably turn your windshield wipers on instead of activating your turn signals. When you finally find the turn signals you'll probably signal left when you want to turn right. Australia isn't nicknamed Downunder for nothing! Just to clarify, the windshield wipers are on the left of the steering wheel and the turn signals on the right. To make a right turn, push the signal down and to make a left turn push it up (exactly the opposite as in the United States).

Sydney drivers insist they have the right of way, whether or not they really do. This goes double for trucks, buses, taxis and couriers (beware of drivers in white vans). Just swallow your pride and let the other drivers cut in front of you.

Aussies love roundabouts (traffic circles) almost as much as the British. The circles are a bit difficult to navigate at first. Remember the person to the RIGHT has the right of way, or whoever has the guts to go first!

Seat belts are compulsory for front and back seat drivers. Drunk driving laws (or drink driving as the Aussies say) are very strict. The law assumes that women who drink more than one beer per hour and men who drink more than two will have a Blood Alcohol Level of .05, which is the maximum permitted level. Fines are hefty, and foreigners are expected to pay them.

If you will be in Australia for under three months, you can drive on your national license. However, if you are planning a long stay, you should obtain an International Drivers License before you leave home. It is a good idea to get one no matter how long you will be visiting.

Distances are measured in kilometers, "ks" or "clicks". One click is about .6 of a mile. To figure out distance, multiply the number of kilometers by "0.6." For example, 20 "ks" are 12 miles. If you are out in the Bush, the distance might be measured in cans (of beer, that is). If the distance between Town A and Town B is 12 cans, then the approximate distance is six hours (based on two cans of beer per hour). Before recycling, empty beer cans used to line the roads.

If you are planning to "Go Bush", you may want to get a "Roo Bar." This is a metal bar/contraption that is attached to the front of your vehicle. The idea is to prevent kangaroos from crushing the front of your car when you hit them. A kangaroo can cause as much damage as a cow! Or, you can get a wire mesh contraption to fit over the front windscreen to prevent rocks breaking the window as you drive over dirt roads. Some people who live in the Bush believe if you put your outstretched fingers on the front window, your fingers will absorb the shock from being hit by a rock, and the window won't break.

BEFORE BUYING A CAR

Only buy a car if it has: 1) a valid pink slip issued by a registered garage that shows that the car is roadworthy, and 2) all registration papers. Next, call the Registry of Encumbered Vehicles (600-0022) to make sure the documents are valid and that there are no outstanding tickets. Have the registration, engine, and chassis numbers on hand. It is very important that the car be registered in the state you bought it in. It is very difficult to buy and sell a car out of state.

When you purchase a car, you do not need to change the registration to the new owner, although you need to file for change of ownership with the Department of Motor Vehicles. The cost for the transfer is based on a percentage of the bill of sale (or occasionally on the blue book value). Since it costs about $200 a year to register your car, and you must have a vehicle inspection as well (which costs about $11 or more), make sure your car has a long registration before buying it.

Remember, you must register the car in the state that the car was purchased. For example, if you buy a car in Sydney with nine months registration left on the car, you can tour Australia for six months without having to worry about being back in New South Wales to re-register the car, and you can sell it to the next buyer more easily with some registration left.

INSURANCE

Australia requires that you purchase Third Party Insurance, (aka A Green Slip). Prior to July, 1991, this insurance was included in your car registration fee. However, it is now necessary to purchase this insurance separately. The NRMA and AAMI are private companies that have competitive prices on insurance, and the GIO is the government owned insurance company. Third Party Property Insurance is also available. This provides coverage if you hit another vehicle or someone's property. It is not mandatory. If you are a non-resident this insurance may be difficult to obtain. Ashcroft Insurance (018/272-912) provides coverage to nonresidents, or talk with the dealer from whom you bought your car.

NATIONAL ROADS AND MOTORIST ASSOCIATION

The NRMA is Australia's largest auto club and costs $72 for the first year to join. Members of U.S. motoring associations enjoy reciprocal rights; however, membership is $36. NRMA membership includes free roadside breakdown service throughout Australia, maps, directories, an accommodation directory with discounts at hotels, and lots of information. As a non-member you can obtain the directory for $10. NRMA is located at 151 Clarence St. (13-2132) and is open Monday to Friday 9 a.m. to 5 p.m.

CARS, VANS OR CARAVANS

There are benefits to buying all three types of vehicles. If you are travelling with more than six people, you probably want to look at purchasing a caravan/trailer. Caravans comfortably sleep six to eight people, and many caravan sales companies will include dishes, cutlery, tables, and more. You can save money by sleeping in the caravan and cooking your own meals. However, petrol (gasoline) is expensive and towing a caravan is even more difficult for those people who are not used to Aussie driving conditions.

A van is useful for two or more people, depending on whether you plan to sleep in it, or just use it to transport as many people as cheaply as possible from one place to another.

Cars are the best buy for two to four people. If there are only two of you, check backpacker hostel's notice boards to see if anyone is traveling in your direction and is willing to pay their share of gas and expenses.

BUYING PRIVATELY

Look at hostel notice boards, newspapers or go down to one of the car markets if you want to buy privately. The Kings Cross Car Market (358-5811 and 358-5800/fax) is located on level two of the Car Park, corner of Ward Avenue and Elizabeth Bay Road. The Cross Market is open 24 hours a day, seven days a week. Many travelers sell their cars here.

Prices for cars start as low as $500, many have free camping gear, plus transfer and registration forms are available for every state in Australia. You can sell your car here for $5 per day. Car insurance is also available.

The Flemington Car Market on Parramatta Road at Paddy's Market is a bit out of the way (take a train to Strathfield and then a bus to Flemington Market, take a bus the entire distance, or catch the shuttle from Kings Cross. To sell a car here, the charge is $50.) Paddy's is open Friday 11 a.m. to 4:30 p.m. and Sunday 9:30 a.m. to 4 p.m. Sydneysiders tend to sell their cars here.

The major problem with buying from other travelers is that you are probably buying a car that has already been up and down the Coast and on the harsh, dirt, Outback roads. Take the time to read the newspapers or buy from Flemington Car Market. However you buy your car, make sure to bargain for a fair price before handing over the cash. It is pretty safe to buy privately, but do not count on buy-back arrangements. These are only valid from licensed dealers who write out a formal contract.

BUYING AT AUCTION

If you are an expert at cars, it is a lot cheaper to buy at auction. This is where most of the used car dealers get their cars. The main drawback is that you cannot drive the car prior to purchasing it. Usually, the only way you can see how the car runs is when it is driven through the auction shed. In order to purchase a car through auction, you must have 10 percent of the total available immediately, and the remaining payable within 24 hours. If you are not a car expert it is probably better to buy your car elsewhere and sell it at auction at the end of your trip.

BUYING FROM A DEALER

The prices from a dealer may be a bit higher, but the cars are generally in good working order and the dealer must guarantee that the cars are registered, unencumbered, and roadworthy. Most dealers that cater to backpackers arrange written buy-back contracts. The following are generally regarded as reliable companies:

Kiwi Car Company, 774 Parramatta Road, Lewisham, 560-7000. Provides free NRMA membership, Third Party Insurance, registration, maps and touring information.

MACH 1, 495 New Canterbury Road, Dulwich Hill, 569-3374. Guaranteed Buy-Back.

Parraville Motors, 186 Parramatta Road, Granville, 637-6033. Sells caravans for 6-8 people, including cutlery, fridge/cooler, fold-up table and chairs, water containers, and guaranteed buyback.

RENTING A CAR

An alternative to buying is to rent a car with a few friends. This is not a bad idea for a weekend trip to the Blue Mountains, Hunter Valley or areas not frequented by tour buses. In addition to international companies such as Avis, Budget or Hertz, you can try the following smaller companies which cater to backpackers. Rent-a-Ruffy, 48 Pittwater Road, Manly, 977-5777 (provides NRMA and accept credit cards) and Cut Price Rent-a-Car, 242 Elizabeth St., near Central Station, 281-3003/4, $25 a day, with unlimited kilometers.

PUBLIC TRANSPORTATION

Transportation throughout Australia is not as expensive as it used to be. Bus companies offer specials between the major Aussie cities, and they usually allow stopovers in other towns along the way. Even air tickets have dramatically decreased in price, owing to the deregulation of the airline industry and the impact of discount airlines. Whatever you decide, it's wise to check all your transportation options first.

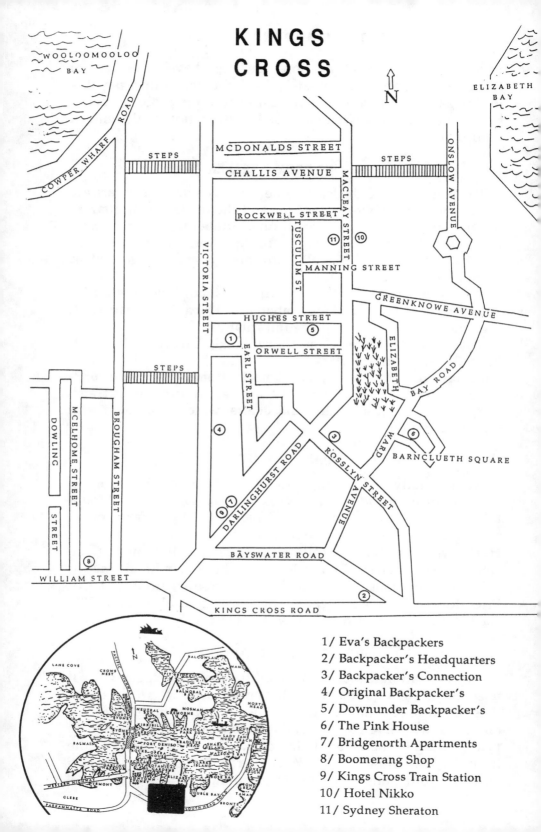

KINGS CROSS

N

1/ Eva's Backpackers
2/ Backpacker's Headquarters
3/ Backpacker's Connection
4/ Original Backpacker's
5/ Downunder Backpacker's
6/ The Pink House
7/ Bridgenorth Apartments
8/ Boomerang Shop
9/ Kings Cross Train Station
10/ Hotel Nikko
11/ Sydney Sheraton

CHAPTER 4:

PLACES
TO STAY

Sydney has dozens of affordable and comfortable "Back-packers Hostels." Most hostels have dormitory rooms as well as single and double rooms. This chapter concentrates on the better value, low-end of the market hostels.

If you want to try something different, stay in a pub. For $40 and up a night you can stay in a traditional Aussie Hotel Pub. The price includes free entry to the pub (if there is live entertainment and/or a cover charge), and a big "fry" or English breakfast of eggs, sausage, lamb chops, toast with vegemite, and coffee. It's a great idea to stay in a pub if you plan to drink schooners into the wee hours of the morning. Just check first to see if any loud bands are playing. Some pubs allow entertainment to last until at least 3 a.m.

Backpacker hostels tend to be concentrated in four or five areas of Sydney. It is very trendy at this time to cater to back-packers, so the term hostel should not bring to mind dreary, impersonal rooms with 20 beds and a single cold shower. Many hostels offer table tennis, outdoor seating areas with barbecues, notice boards, and a library with book swaps. Usually, there is a communal fridge for storing food and use of the kitchen is free. Some hostels offer tours, pub nights and pub crawls, discounts on entertainment, and more.

Kings Cross

The Cross has the largest selection of hostels in the smallest, most crowded area of downtown Sydney. The Airport Express leaves the airport for the Cross every 20 minutes, there is a train stop in the middle of Darlinghurst Road, and there are numerous bus stops in the area as well.

If you are a night owl, then the Cross is the place for you. It is the OZ version of New York's 42nd St., but a lot friendlier. Pubs, clubs, strip shows, cafés, transvestites, and working girls line Williams St. and Darlinghurst Road, the Cross' main drag.

The following is a list of hotels in the area. All of these are slightly off the main street. However, if you like noise there are plenty of hotels right in the thick of things.

EVA'S HOTEL, 6 Orwell St., 358-2185 (fax 358-3259). Just a few blocks walk to the center of the Cross, this hotel offers cooking facilities, rooftop barbecues, and private and shared rooms. Prices start at $15 per night per person for a shared room. The hostel will even refund your airport fare if you stay more than two nights.

BACKPACKER'S CONNECTION, 2 Roslyn St., 358-4844. Five-star luxury includes color tv in all the rooms, sunbathing on the roof, washers and dryers, full linen, and more. Double, twin, and dorm accommodations are available. Prices start at $14 per night for dorm rooms. It's located next to Les Girls, where female impersonators dance and strip to the latest hits.

BACKPACKER'S HEADQUARTERS, 79 Bayswater Road, 331-6181. Situated near the thick of things, this hotel has a lively atmosphere and a range of facilities, as well as work possibilities within the hotel (such as cleaning, etc.) Dormitory accommodations start at $13.

THE ORIGINAL BACKPACKER'S, 162 Victoria St., 356-3232 (fax 368-1435). This hostel offers dorms, doubles, and self-contained flats for four people. Dorms start at $10 per night. Located on a street lined with quieter cafés, this Victorian mansion is still only a stone's throw from the Cross.

DOWNUNDER BACKPACKER'S, 25 Hughes St., 358-1143 (fax 357-4675). Only a five-minute walk from the Kings Cross train station, this hostel also has an airport pick-up and delivery. The facilities include kitchen, laundry, tv, common room, and a rooftop garden with barbecue. Dorms start at $14 per night; singles and doubles are also available starting at $32.

THE PINK HOUSE, 6 to 8 Barncleuth Square, 358-1689. The Pink House is one of the least expensive hotels in the Cross. For $14 per night, the hostel offers log fires, a quiet location, 24 hour message service, safety deposit boxes, cooking facilities and a common room. For those that are really short on cash,

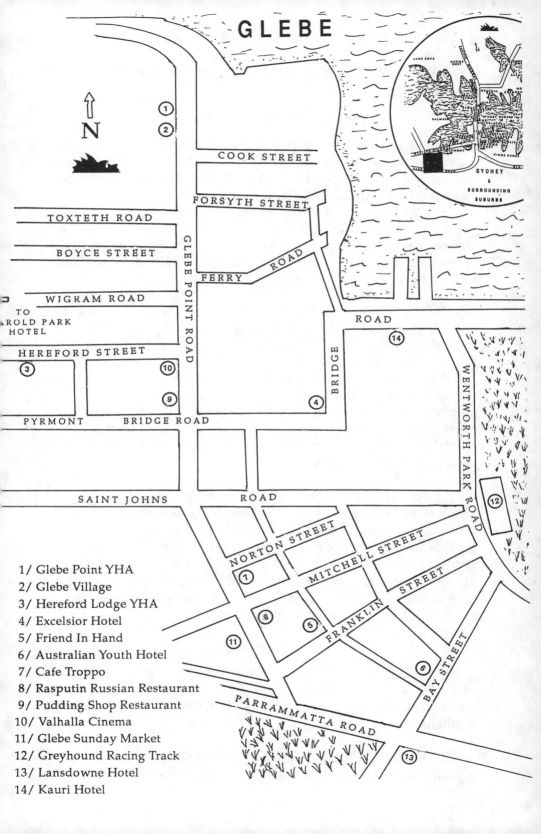

GLEBE

N

COOK STREET

FORSYTH STREET

TOXTETH ROAD

BOYCE STREET

GLEBE POINT ROAD

FERRY ROAD

WIGRAM ROAD

TO AROLD PARK HOTEL

ROAD

HEREFORD STREET

BRIDGE

WENTWORTH PARK ROAD

PYRMONT BRIDGE ROAD

SAINT JOHNS ROAD

NORTON STREET

MITCHELL STREET

FRANKLIN STREET

BAY STREET

PARRAMMATTA ROAD

SYDNEY & SURROUNDING SUBURBS

1/ Glebe Point YHA
2/ Glebe Village
3/ Hereford Lodge YHA
4/ Excelsior Hotel
5/ Friend In Hand
6/ Australian Youth Hotel
7/ Cafe Troppo
8/ Rasputin Russian Restaurant
9/ Pudding Shop Restaurant
10/ Valhalla Cinema
11/ Glebe Sunday Market
12/ Greyhound Racing Track
13/ Lansdowne Hotel
14/ Kauri Hotel

there are opportunities to work, stay for free, and make some spending money.

Glebe

Located only a short bus ride to the city, Glebe is a trendy area. The main street, Glebe Point Road, is lined with restaurants, cafés, shops, the Valhalla (an alternative cinema), weekend markets, and Glebe Park.

Many of the people living in this area are students or artsy people with an "alternative" lifestyle. To reach Glebe from the airport, take the Airport Express to Central Station and then take either bus #431 or #433 to Glebe Point Road. Also, Glebe Village Hostel offers a free pickup from the airport.

YOUTH HOSTELS (YHA): Two of the three officials YHAs in Sydney are located in Glebe: Hereford Lodge at 51 Hereford St., 660-5577 (fax 552-1771), and Glebe Point at 262 Glebe Point Road, 692-8418 (fax 660-0431).

A YHA card is required to stay, but you can purchase one on the spot. The YHAs have cooking facilities, a kitchen and common rooms. Dorms start at $15 per person per night, but you must vacate the rooms during the day. The Hereford also has furnished apartments, rooms with balconies, and a big sunroof with a pool and a sauna.

GLEBE VILLAGE, 256 Glebe Point Road, 660-8133 (fax 552-3703). This is our favorite. The hostel goes out of its way to provide as many services as possible to backpackers. The Village offers free airport pickup, tours to the mountains and around Sydney, a library, cooking facilities, a kitchen, table tennis, pub nights, mystery tours, video nights, BBQs, outdoor tables, and pool and backgammon competitions. Prices start at $15 a night for dormitory accommodations.

Apartments

Another option, for those travellers who are planning to stay in the area for a week or more, is to stay in a self-contained apartment. Although they cost a bit more, they usually have kitchens, tv's, linens, etc.

BRIDGENORTH APARTMENTS, 99 Darlinghurst Road, Apartment 1, 357-2700 (fax 02-358-4357). These apartments are

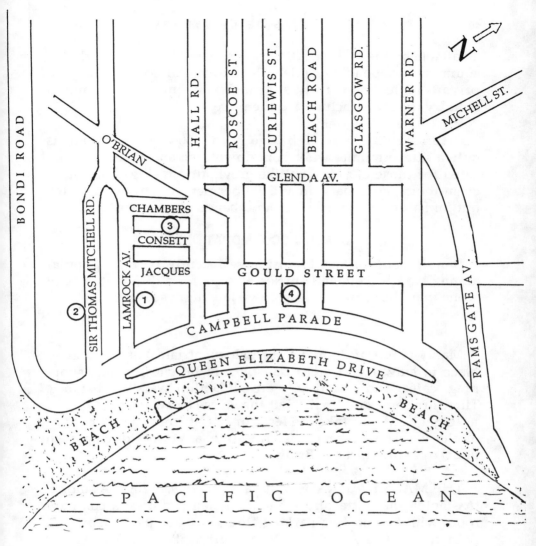

BONDI BEACH

1/ Lamrock Hostel
2/ Bondi Beach Boarding House
3/ Bondi Beach Guest House
4/ Bondi Beach Traveller's Hostel

available by the day for $20 per person, or for a week with discount rates depending on length of time. Air conditioning, tv, private bath, linen, fully supplied kitchen, and a common laundry room are included in the price.

THE KAURI HOTEL, 2 Bridge Road, 660-2350. The Kauri is only a fifteen minute walk from downtown and is centrally located for those of you who like greyhound racing! Their nice, clean rooms are a bargain at $100 per person per week. Watch out for Saturday nights when loud bands play downstairs.

BEACH ACCOMMODATIONS

Bondi, Coogee, and Manly have recently become popular among backpackers and surfies who prefer a different type of scene than the crowded downtown late night scene.

Manly

Manly is full of Pommies (British expatriates) and is a great place to stay if you are a day person. Beaches, walks, shopping, cafés, and restaurants are all within walking distance. There are some good pubs, but they close early.

To get to Manly, take the ferry or JetCat from Circular Quay, or the very long, scenic bus ride (not advisable during rush hour) over the Harbour Bridge.

THE MANLY ASTRA, 68 Pittwater Road, 977-2092. A smoke-free hotel, the Astra offers linen, kitchen facilities, a common room with tv, and free parking from only $13 per person in a twin room. The Astra is only a short walk from the Manly Wharf and the ocean beaches.

MANLY HOLIDAY FLATS, 48-50 Darley Road, 284-247. The Flats offer color tv in every room, rooftop sundeck, and kitchen. This is a bunk-free hotel room, for all of you who are tired of being above or below a total stranger. Small shared flats start from $60 per week.

Bondi Beach

Bondi Beach is a "surfer's" paradise. The surf tends to be consistent, the beach is beautiful and there are stores, restaurants, cafés, pubs, surf shops, and even bagel bakeries. Bondi also has a Pavilion that is used for art exhibits, festivals, bands, classes, and much more. The crowd ranges from 10 to 60 year old surfies, families, and groups of tourists.

The Japanese love to come down to Bondi to snap photos and take videos of Bondi's topless bathers. Most of the hostels provide discount weekly rates and/or self-contained apartments available by the week.

To get to Bondi Beach, take a train to Bondi Junction and then catch the #380 bus to Bondi Beach, or take the #400 bus from the Airport to Bondi Junction and then the #380.

LAMROCK HOSTEL, 7 Lamrock Av., 365-0221. Not only is the hostel a mere 300 feet from the beach, but it also offers free pick-up from Bondi Junction. The Lamrock provides tourist information, bus ticketing, safe deposit boxes, and fax services. The weekly special starts at $80 per person or $15 per night.

BONDI BEACH BOARDING HOUSE, 28 Sir Thomas Road, 365-2265. A hop, skip and a jump from the beach, the House provides quiet accommodations (no bunks!) from only $14 per person. A shared kitchen is available for the guest's use and all cutlery and linen is supplied. This is a non-smoking hotel.

BONDI BEACH GUEST HOUSE, 11 Consett St. (off Hall St.), 389-8309. The Guest House is only a two-minute walk to Bondi's shops and beaches. From only $15 per person, cozy rooms for a maximum of four people are available. Each room comes with a tv, fridge, linen, towels, and tea-making facilities.

BONDI BEACH TRAVELLERS HOSTEL, 124 Curlewis St., 358-1433. For only $13 per night, in bunk-bed dormitory accommodations, you will be a mere 300 feet from the beach. The hostel is centrally located, and is within crawling distance of the Bondi Hotel, restaurants and shops.

Coogee

The infamous Coogee Bay Hotel/Selinas has made Coogee the latest haunt for backpackers. The beach is smaller than Bondi, the cafés a bit more expensive, and the bus ride to town longer, but the live entertainment and cheap food at the Hotel makes the hassles worthwhile.

MANLY

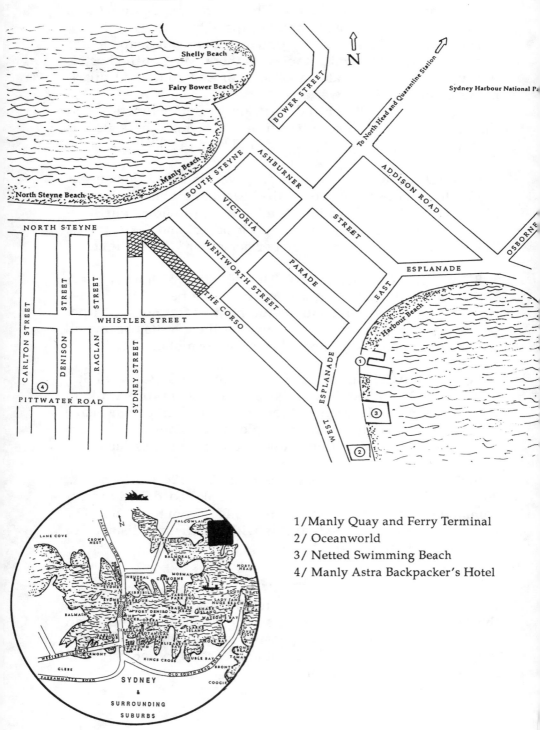

1/ Manly Quay and Ferry Terminal
2/ Oceanworld
3/ Netted Swimming Beach
4/ Manly Astra Backpacker's Hotel

AARONBROOK LODGE, 116 Brook St., 315-8222. The Lodge provides free airport and city terminal pick up (a big plus!). Located only 300 feet from the beach, this hotel offers cooking facilities, two common rooms with tv, laundry, and sunbathing areas. Downstairs the restaurant and pub serve up food and drink. Dorm prices start at $12 per night; singles and doubles are also available.

THE AEGEAN, 40 Coogee Bay Road, 398-4999. Color television, a gym, barbecue facilities, kitchen, laundry, free long-term storage, smoke-free rooms, free airport pickup, and adventure trips and mystery tours are samples of what the Aegean offers its guests. Prices start at $12 per night for dorm rooms; twins are slightly more expensive. Fully furnished, self-contained apartments are available by the week or longer.

GRAND PACIFIC, Corner of Carr & Beach Sts., 665-6301. For only $13 per night you can practically jump onto the beach from your hotel window! The Pacific provides fridge, color tv's and tea-making facilities in all 11 rooms, plus a shared kitchen and laundry room, making this hostel the best deal in Coogee.

COOGEE BEACH BACKPACKERS, 94 Beach St., 665-7735. Hostel dormitories are available for $15 per person. The hostel also has a common kitchen complete with cooking supplies and a common room with tv. It is only a short walk to the beach.

Other Areas

If you have decided to explore Sydney off the beaten track, then never fear, because low-priced hostels outside the typical backpacker's areas are scattered all around Sydney.

SYDNEY HOLIDAY HOSTEL, 94 City Road, Chippendale, 698-1195. Single, twin, and triple rooms are available from $70 per person per week. All rooms have tv, fridge, stove, plus there are common laundry facilities and storage rooms. The hostel is only a 10-minute walk from Central Station and the University of Sydney's swimming pool.

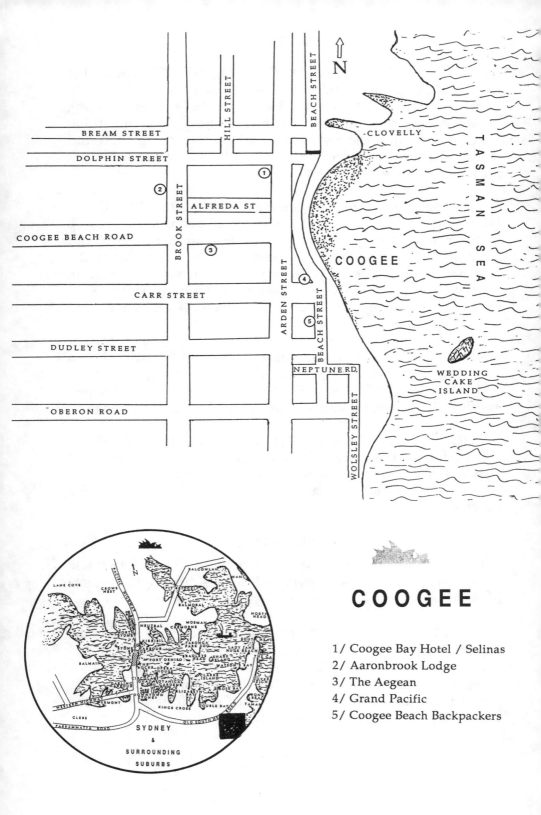

COOGEE

1/ Coogee Bay Hotel / Selinas
2/ Aaronbrook Lodge
3/ The Aegean
4/ Grand Pacific
5/ Coogee Beach Backpackers

LANDSDOWNE HOTEL, 2 to 6 City Road, Chippendale, 211-2325. If you don't mind loud bands playing until 3 a.m., then the Landsdowne is an ideal backpackers hotel that is usually full of young travelers. The hotel has a big-screen tv, a lounge, dining room, and a rooftop for sunbathing and barbecues. The hotel is located across the street from the University pool and is only a ten-minute walk to Central Station. Mixed (WOW!) dormitories start at $13 per night.

EXCELSIOR HOTEL, 64 Foveaux St., 211-4945. This hotel is located close to the Trade Union Club, which attracts a funky, inner-city crowd. For only $13 per night, including linen, you can stay in a beautifully restored National Trust hotel. Live entertainment lasts until the wee hours on the weekends.

KINGSGATE, 495 Bourke St., Taylor Square, Darlinghurst, 380-5983. For those of you who plan to spend your nights in Darlinghurst, the center of the club scene, Kingsgate is the ideal, albeit pricey, hotel. For $45 per night for a double room, Kingsgate is a quiet hotel that is just down the street from Restaurant Row and the clubs.

University Accommodations

During schoolbreaks, many of the colleges of Sydney University and the University of NSW open their doors to travelers. It's possible to get a bed and breakfast deal, or just a bed. If you plan to stay longer than a couple of nights, most colleges will offer cheaper rates.

DARLINGTON HOUSE (692-3322). Houses with room to sleep from four to eight cost between $350 to $400 per week.

WOMEN'S COLLEGE (516-1642). Students and YHA members pay from $32 for B&B to $42 for full board. All others pay between $40 and $50.

INTERNATIONAL HOUSE (663-0418). Rooms with full board are $35 for students, $45 for everyone else.

CHAPTER 5:

LANGUAGE: SPEAKING STRINE

Crocodile Dundee introduced U.S. audiences to Australian slang with the phrase, "Throw another shrimp on the barbie!" But to an Aussie that sounds like a perversion of the American sport of Midget Bowling. You would be more likely to hear someone calling in a pub, "G'day, Mate! I'll shout for a schooner of New and a middy of Blue if your Sheila gets me a dog's eye with some dead horse." The Aussie is only offering to buy a round of beer, if his friend's girlfriend buys the meat pie and ketchup! Clear enough if you know the language and customs. Contrary to popular belief, Australians do not speak English. They speak Strine, the language of OZ. The language doesn't sound remotely like English, while the customs are unique to OZ. To get you started, the following is a short list of do's and don't's.

DO bring wine (not French) when you are invited to someone's house or a BYO restaurant, order bugs, rockies and caps to eat, have a cuppa during smoko in the arvo with your mates, and shout a round of Tooheys in the pub!

DON'T order Foster's beer, wear a tuxedo to a "Fancy Dress" Party, order an entree for the main course, disappear to the bathroom after you've received five free beers, or look at someone strangely when they say, "Don't come the raw prawn!"

Strine, the official Aussie language, can be divided into three major classifications. First, there is the infamous Aussie slang. This includes words like, "Blue, sheila, fair dinkum." Second are the non-slang terms that are actual Aussie words. Some of these words would never be used in America or Great Britain and the ones that are have a totally different meaning than they do in OZ. These include, "smoke-o, entree, crook, bugs."

Last comes our favorite, rhyming slang. This slang

originated in the markets in England. Speaking rhyming slang allowed the salespeople to talk among themselves in a way so that customers could not understand. Phrases such as, "Trouble and strife" and "current bun" were brought over by boat with the convicts, while "Baked beans and dead horse" were coined in Australia. Unfortunately, rhyming slang seems to be dying out in the cities, although it remains in use among the Ocker Aussies.

AUSSIE SLANG

The following is a list of commonly used Aussie slang. Most slang is formed by dropping off the last syllable of a word and adding "ie" or "o", for example Paddington (a Sydney suburb) becomes Paddo. Unfortunately, the words that get shortened may also be hard to understand. A "bickie" is slang for biscuit, but a biscuit is really a cookie! Aussies also shorten numbers by saying double or triple, for example 500333 is five double-oh, triple three.

OZ - Australia
Bloke - Guy
Slab - Case (of Beer)
Chock-a-block - Full
Bickie - Cookie
Lollie - Hard candy
Cozzie/Bathers - Bathing costume/Swim suit
Chrissie - Christmas
Ta - Thank you
Sheila - Girl
Cuppa - Cup of tea
Smoke-o - Coffee break (taken often)
Arvo - Afternoon (barbie time)
Yobbo - Lazy, shady character
Dag - Nerd
Eskie - Cooler (to hold the beer)
Dunny - Outside toilet
Agro - Aggravation
Sussed - Suspicious/Suspect
Rego - Car registration
Whinge - Whine
Breckie - Breakfast
Prezzie - Present
Mozzies - Mosquitos
Surfies - Surfers
Bikies - Motorcycle Riders

Postie - Mail Carrier
Pokies - Slot machines
Sickie - A sick day from work
Uni - University
Ute - utility/pickup truck
Garbos - Garbage collectors
Cabsav - Cabernet Sauvignon (a wine varietal)
BYO - Bring your own

NON-SLANG TERMS

Non-slang terms are a must to learn if you are traveling in OZ, otherwise you won't be able to get any food or refreshments! The following are every day terms — don't be afraid to use them. If you don't, everyone will know you're a "Septic tank!"

Middy/Pot - 10 ounces of Beer
Schooner - 15 ounces of Beer
Queue - Line
Can of Drink - Can of soda
Pissed - Drunk
Carton - Case of beer
Booking - Reservation
Fancy Dress - Costume
Soft Toys - Stuffed animals
Jumpers - Sweaters
Tucker - Food
Entree - Appetizer (Don't confuse this with Main)
Main - Entree (Or main dish)
Mushies - Mushrooms
Bugs - Type of crayfish which taste like lobsters
Brown bread - Whole wheat bread
Yum cha - dim sum
Flat-white - American-style coffee
Boutique beer - microbrewed beer
Rockmelon/Rockies - Cantaloupe
Capsicum/Caps - Bell peppers
Prawns - Shrimps
Chook - Chicken
Hot Chips - French fries
Chips - Potato chips
Snags - Sausages
Take-Away - Take-Out
Offsider - Assistant
Bludger - A lazy person
Sticky Beak - A nosy person

Pushbike - Bicycle
Petrol - Gasoline
Duco - Paint job on a car
Good Nick - Good condition (Used mainly for cars)
Bonnet - Hood of car
Boot - Trunk
Wing - Fender
Gaol - Jail

NON-SLANG AND SLANG PHRASES

The next section is a bit trickier and we don't recommend using most of the following slang. "G'day, No Worries, and Good On Ya" are OK, but in order not to sound silly while saying "Don't Come the Raw Prawn" or "Fair Dinkum," you must be a true blue, Ocker Aussie.

However, play it by ear and if you feel comfortable, go ahead and have some fun with Strine. Remember, most phrases are followed by, "Mate."

G'day (pronounced G'die), Mate - Used any time
of day to say, "Hello."
No Worries (Mate) - No Problem, Sure (Said all the time)
Good On Ya - Used when somebody has done something well
Usually accompanied by a pat on the back
She'll Be Right - It'll be o.k., No worries
Fair Dinkum! - No Kidding! Really! Also used to describe someone as
being honest and fair
Too Right - Definitely. (Example: Are you having a beer, mate? Too
Right I am.)
Spot On - Exactly. Right on the nose
Ocker Aussie - A good old boy, such as Crocodile Dundee
Don't Come the Raw Prawn - Don't try to trick or tease me
Beyond the Black Stump - A long way inland
Back of Bourke (pronounced berk) - A long way inland
Not Within Coo-ee - Nowhere close to wherever you are. (Cup your
hands around your mouth and shout Coooo-eeeee. If no one
answers, then you are "Not Within Coo-ee" of anyone else.)
Stands Out Like Dog's Balls - Very obvious
Give It a Miss - Skip it
Gone Troppo - Gone crazy
Gizza ... thanks - Give me a ...., thank you
Stunned Mullet - Surprised
Dob in - To tell on someone
Call by - Come over
Ring me - Call me on the telephone

RHYMING SLANG

The last section is the most colorful one. Ocker Aussies and older Aussies still tend to use a bit of rhyming slang on a daily basis. Almost everyone knows "Dead Horse, Dog's Eye, and Septic Tank". Have some fun and use these! Remember that Aussies tend to shorten rhyming slang even further, so "Septic Tank" becomes "Sepo!" If you can make sense out of this slang, you're on your way to becoming a Fair Dinkum Aussie!

Steak & Kidney - Sydney
Pig's Ear - Beer
Dog's Eye - Meat pie
Dead Horse - Tomato sauce (ketchup)
Septic Tank -Yank (any American from the Yankee North or the Confederate South!)
Baked Beans -Jeans
Cheese & Kisses - Misses (wife)
Tin Lids/Billy Lids - Kids
Trouble and Strife - Wife
Brown Bread - Dead
Joe Blake - Snake
Noah's Ark - Shark
Current Bun - Sun
2KYs - Eyes (2KY is a Sydney radio station)
I Suppose - Nose
North & South - Mouth
Billy Goat - Throat
Shark Fin - Chin
Rocky Boulders - Shoulders
Warwick Farms - Arms
Fruit Flans - Hands
Ham - n - Eggs - Legs
Bobby McGees - Knees

Don't be alarmed at being called a Septic Tank. Aussies have nicknames for all nationalities. The Greeks are occasionally called "Bubble and squeak" in rhyming slang. New Zealanders are called "Kiwis" after the fruit. The British are stuck with "Pommies." Some say they got the nickname in the 1700s because the British turned the color of a pomegranate when they came to Australia and exposed their skin to the bright sun. Others say the name comes from "Prisoners of Mother England." Last, but not least, don't forget the letter "Z" is pronounced zed. If you feel like taking a nap, make sure you say, "I'm going to catch a few zeds!"

CHAPTER 6:

FOOD & DRINK: DOG'S EYE AND PIG'S EAR

Beer and pubs play an important part in the social lives of Australians. In addition, over the past 10 to 15 years, more and more Aussies have begun drinking wine. The Aussie wine industry, centered in the Hunter Valley (New South Wales) and the Barossa Valley (South Australia) has matured into a thriving multi-million dollar industry. Hard liquor is still not very popular mainly because it is very expensive and also because pubs measure out exactly their tiny shots of alcohol. Or else, it could be that Aussies like to stay standing as long as possible, while barbecuing in the hot summer sun!

Alcohol is purchased at bottle shops. These are located next to hotels and pubs, in large shopping centers or supermarkets, and as stand alone stores on the street. Bottle shops tend to be near a large congregation of Bring-Your-Own (BYO) restaurants. These shops carry only liquor and some munchies, and usually do not have soda.

BEER

When it comes to beer there are certain customs that should be followed. If you are out drinking with Aussies, you have to make sure that you "shout a round." This means you must buy at least a round, or two, for your mates and your mates' mates. Australians will immediately accept you as a life-long friend if you walk into a pub and announce, "It's my shout!" Be careful, "shouting" can get expensive. If you don't drink as much as your mates (a strong possibility) you can ask to be left out of the shout. But, still offer to buy at least one round.

It's considered bad manners not to buy drinks for the whole crowd, worse manners to drink beer when you're paying and Jack Daniels when anyone else is, and the epitome of awful manners to disappear to the toilet when it's your turn to shout. If after you shout a round someone says, "Cheers", this is just another way of saying, "Thank you." The correct response is "Cheers" and a slight lifting of the glass. There is no need to clink glasses.

When you are buying beer, do not act like a "Sepo" (American) and order Foster's. An Ocker Aussie like Crocodile Dundee can order Foster's without looking silly, but travelers usually can't. Stick with a Toohey's brand: Red (natural brew), Blue (low alcohol), Old (dark), or New (regular). Some people order the stronger beers: Powers, Victoria Bitter (VB), Coopers Ale or Guinness. Order your beer in a schooner, which is a three-quarter pint glass or a middy, a half pint glass.

If you want to be daring, try one of the "boutique beers" available in select pubs. These are specialty beers that are generally brewed at the back of the pub. Be careful! Some beers, such as Dogsbolter, are 9 percent alcohol! A lot of the high alcohol beers have a malty taste similar to Colt 45. The Lord Nelson and other pubs have windows so you can watch the beer being brewed as you drink it.

Bartenders don't get tipped in Australia. There are a few reasons for this. First, most bartenders make a base salary of $10 to $15 per hour and up, so they do not have to rely on tips in the same way American bartenders do. Secondly, very few people drink mixed drinks, and if they do it is usually just a measured shot of some type of hard liquor. Bundaberg rum and coke (bundee and coke) is a favorite. Lastly, being a bartender in Australia is as far removed from Tom Cruise and Bryan Brown in the movie Cocktails as you can get. Unless you go to one of the clubs that hire American bartenders to put on a bit of a show and mix up complicated cocktails, all a bartender has to worry about is serving beer and wine on tap.

For a review of Pubs, see page 121.

WINE

Australians usually drink wine with dinner regardless of whether they eat at home or go to a restaurant. Luckily, many restaurants are Bring Your Own (BYO) wine (and occasionally beer and liquor). Although some restaurants charge a corkage charge by the bottle ($1) or by the person ($.50), this includes chilling, opening, and serving the wine and the use of wine glasses. If there is no mention of a corkage charge, ask. Restaurants are permitted to charge a fee, without mentioning it anywhere on the menu. The restaurants that don't post prices often charge $3 and up per bottle!

If you are going over to someone's house for dinner, never arrive empty handed! The custom is for each guest to bring a bottle of wine or two.

With the expansion of the Aussie wine industry, there are many different types of wines to choose from. Red wine, in the $5 to $15 range, is on a par with French wine. Aussie wines have beaten French wines in some recent competitions. For an inexpensive but satisfactory table wine ($3.50 to $5), Jacob's Creek, Tyrell's, and Matthew Lang are perfectly acceptable. If you want to splurge, try Wolf Blass (Yellow, Red or Grey label) which costs around $10. Australian Beaujolais (fruity), Pinot Noir (fruity, but drier), Cabernet Sauvignon (dry), Shiraz (drier), and Cabernet Merlot (very dry / claret style) are good red wines to try. If you prefer white wine, try Aussie Chablis (fruity) or Chardonnay (dry).

The Aussie development of the century is the cardboard cask with a plastic insert that holds two to four liters of wine. These are fine for your house or a casual party, but not really acceptable to bring to a formal dinner. Casks serve many useful purposes. After the wine is finished, fill the bag with water and freeze it. Use the bag in your eskie (cooler). Once the ice melts, drink the water, and then when you're done blow up the bag and use it as a pillow!

CHEESE

Why not enjoy some Australian cheese with your Aussie wine? Even most Australians do not realize the wide variety available to them. The following is a small sample of some tasty cheeses.

Seal Bay Creme-de-la-Creme is a triple cream cheese, with a rich golden center. It has a slightly nutty taste and goes well with a Chardonnay or a light and fruity wine such as a dessert Riesling. Milawa Blue is a soft, light, creamy, blue cheese which is delicious when served with fruit.

Jendi Supreme is similar to the creamy French Brie.

Kervella Chevre Affine is a mature goat cheese that tastes best when served with a dry, red wine, such as a Cabernet Sauvignon or Merlot.

A couple of bottles of Aussie wine and a selection of Aussie cheeses make for a great sunset picnic at Lady Macquaries' Chair, overlooking Sydney Harbour in the Royal Botanical

Gardens. If you are not so daring, try one of the "imitation" European cheeses, such as Feta (not as tangy as Greek), Edam, Jarlsberg, and Swiss.

There is also a popular cheese called Coon cheese, which is just a brand name for a locally-made cheese. Australia has very strict import controls on cheese, so the Australians created their own brands. Don't get a craving for real European cheeses because their prices are exorbitant.

COFFEE

The beverage section wouldn't be complete without a section on coffee. The large influx of Europeans, especially Italians in the 1950s, has made coffee drinking very trendy. Since the price for either plain or exotic coffee is about the same, most people tend to drink capuccino or cafe latte.

To order an American-style coffee, ask for a flat white. A regular is served with milk, no sugar. A cafe latte or long white is similar to the French cafe au lait, and is half coffee/half milk with fresh cream. If you like capuccinos, but not the caffeine, order an eccochino. Ecco is a mixture of roasted barley herbs, but it still tastes a lot like coffee. For something stronger, order a short black (espresso).

For a leisurely place to sip your coffee or capuccinno, to read the newspaper, and to eat an almond croissant or focaccio sandwich, head over to Leichhardt, the Little Italy of Sydney, or Darlinghurst, a trendy neighborhood. In Leichhardt, try Cafe Sport or Via Veneto on Norton St. In Darlinghurst the Bar Coluzzi or Tropicana are the places to go. Usually Darlinghurst is a third more expensive than Little Italy.

Coffee bars in Sydney are not known for their speedy service, but there is never any rush for you to leave either. Just sit back, relax, and sip your coffee. But remember, refills are not free!

FOOD

There are only two Aussie national dishes: meat pies and vegemite. A meat pie (dog's eye) is similar to the American version of a pot pie. A light, crusty pastry surrounds a substance (hamburger, perhaps) that is submerged in lumpy gravy.

There are many variations on the basic meat pies: mushroom, curry, chicken, steak and kidney, and cheese and bacon.

All are served hot and should be eaten in the following manner: turn the pie upside-down, smear a packet or two of $.20 tomato sauce (dead horse) all over the pie and dig in. Make sure you have plenty of napkins!

Pies are accompanied by hot chips (thick french fries sprinkled generously with salt) and a schooner or two of beer. Meat pies cost between $1.50 and $2.20 and are served at all pubs across Australia.

Vegemite, the second Aussie wonder, is a concentrated yeast extract loaded with salt, mineral salt, and malt extract. Kraft, an American company, makes it, but it is rarely found in America. Unless you were fed Vegemite from the day you were born, it is almost impossible to acquire a taste for it. If you are daring and would like to try some, spread the Vegemite THIN-LY on toast. Don't worry if you make a face or gag when you taste it—most non-Aussies do!

MIXED BUSINESS/MILK BAR

Every street corner in Sydney has a milk bar/mixed business. At the front of the store is a hot counter filled with assorted Aussie delights: meat pies, sausage rolls, battered savs (smoked sausages dipped in batter and fried), fried fish, hot chips, and other fried foods. Prices are usually low, so a cheap meal can be put together if you don't mind the calories and cholesterol!

Toward the back of the store is a sandwich bar, where thin little Australian sandwiches are served. In most cases mayonnaise, mustard, tomato, lettuce, and toasting or jaffling (a popular way to eat Aussie sandwiches) cost extra. A ham sandwich includes two buttered slices of bread with one slice of ham. Everything else is extra. Sandwiches are always buttered. You must specifically say, "NO BUTTER, THANKS." Even if you order mustard and mayonnaise, the sandwich maker will normally add butter. What a mixture! White bread is used, unless you ask for brown (whole wheat) bread, which does not cost extra.

Aussie sandwiches can be unique, such as our favorite, salad sandwiches. These usually cost under $2 and include lettuce, tomato, onion, beets, sprouts, carrots, and any other salad vegetable available (except for avocados, which cost extra). Other Aussie favorites are: baked bean, banana, hot chip (as in french fries), and vegemite-with-anything sandwiches.

Jaffles are toasted sandwiches that are sealed at the edges.

Served piping hot, they are delicious! An Aussie hamburger with the works includes a thin hamburger, plus Canadian bacon, all the salad ingredients, and a fried egg on top!

Moving to the back of the store, you come across the drink section. Cans of drink (sodas) cost between $1 to $1.20. Or, you can sample one of the many types of flavored milk or soy drinks. Mooove, Soo Good, and Sustagen are popular brand names.

BARBECUED CHICKEN

If you feel like something hot but not fried for lunch, stop in for Portuguese or barbecued chicken. A whole chicken costs about $7 and can serve four or five people. Don't forget an order of hot chips!

DESSERT

For dessert, sample a typical Aussie cake from one of Sydney's hundreds of hot bread shops, which are similar to an American bakery. Pavlovas (meringues), custard pies (custard in a pie shell), lamingtons (light sponge cakes coated in chocolate and sprinkled with coconut), and vanilla slices (napoleons or mille feuilles with a rich, stick-to-the-roof-of-your-mouth icing) are true Aussie desserts.

ICE CREAM

Sydney is not a place to crave ice cream. Most ice cream is pre-packaged. New Zealand and Danish ice creams have gotten popular, but they are very expensive. Be careful when passing one of these shops! The cones are made in the windows and the smell can lure you in.

ETHNIC FOODS

Sydney is a city chock-a-block full of ethnic influences. Perhaps this is why restaurant food is so delicious and why Sydneysiders spend almost one third of their income eating at restaurants. Aussies love to linger over dinner the same as Parisians and other Europeans. This means that a dinner starting at 8:30 p.m. usually lasts until at least 11 p.m. Some restaurants have special priced 'Early Bird' dinners for people who like to eat between 6 p.m. and 8 p.m.

Don't forget to bring along a bottle of wine or two and get

settled comfortably for a night of good food and conversation. Restaurants are usually Bring-Your-Own (see page 52). These restaurants are a much better value than licensed restaurants that force you to purchase their wine at a high mark up. Occasionally, some licensed restaurants offer you the option of either BYO or buying on the premises.

When preparing to leave the restaurant, remember the Aussie rule of tipping: Tip As Little As Possible! A $25 meal may require a $2 to $3 tip. Tipping is usually around 5 percent, at most 10 percent, if the service was exceptional and/or you are at an expensive hotel restaurant. Don't worry about the waiters; they usually make $8 to $10 per hour, and do not rely on tips to survive. It is not customary to tip in small, family-owned restaurants.

Below is a list of some inexpensive, but interesting restaurants. Except for the first two restaurants (among the most popular in Sydney), we have divided this chapter into areas to eat in, rather than specific restaurants to visit. Sydney has a Chinatown, Little Italy, and Turkish, Lebanese, and Spanish sections of town. It is hard to go wrong if you stop in any of Sydney's restaurants for a meal.

HARRY'S CAFE DE WHEELS, 1 Cowper Wharf Road, Woolloomooloo, 264-1843. Located directly across from the Aussie Navy Base, Harry's is not a cafe, but a trailer that serves meat pies to the crowds of night owls that flock here, seven days a week. It is open until 3 a.m. so the crowd is usually quite interesting. Our suggestion: an Adelaide Floater, which is a meat pie floating in green, mashed pea soup.

NO NAMES ITALIAN RESTAURANT, 81 Stanley St., East Sydney (360-4711) or 58 Cowper St., Glebe (660-2326). The original No Names is located in an alley. The entrance on Chapel St. is so narrow that when trucks drove through they knocked down the restaurant's sign, which was hanging above the door. No one remembers what the original name was and No Names seems to have stuck since the owners gave up replacing the sign.

One of the other more popular No Names restaurants is in Glebe, located in the back of the Friend in Hand Pub, only a five-minute walk from the Glebe YHA. Both No Names tend to get very busy after 8 p.m., especially on weekends. Don't be shy about sharing a table with total strangers.

The East Sydney No Names restaurant is very sparse and still looks like an economy diner for young, Italian immigrants, to whom it catered to when it first was created. Most diners order a huge portion of spaghetti ($6), which includes salad, thick, crusty Italian bread, and a watery orange drink. Beef, veal, and meatballs are also available for $7 all inclusive.

When you are finished go downstairs to the Arch coffee lounge for a capuccino, or better yet, walk around to the corner of Crown and Chapel St. for coffee and a pinball game.

CHINATOWN

Sydney's Chinatown is divided into two parts: the flashy tourist section and the authentic Chinese Chinatown.

The real Chinatown is in the area of Sussex, George and Pitt Sts., between Goulburn and Hay Sts. This area is filled with dozens of Chinese restaurants, each as good as the other. For a real taste of Chinatown, try one of the grocery shops on Sussex St. and buy Royal Jelly, Deer's Horn extract, and Durian Cakes (which according to the Chinese "Smell like Hell and taste like Heaven").

The small shopping arcade, also on Sussex St., has a Chinese video store and a bakery where fresh pastries and pork rolls are available. While you are in the area, catch a Chinese movie ($11) on Goulburn St. All movies are in Chinese, with English subtitles, and are guaranteed to be full of action.

The Sussex Center on Sussex St. is the entrance to the touristy Chinatown. But first, sample some Chinese delicacies: dried cuttlefish, spiced whole and sliced fruit (including love prunes), and dried shellfish. All these are available from the Chinese food store across the street.

The Sussex Center Food Court is the best place in Chinatown to eat cheaply and to sample a large variety of Chinese and Vietnamese food. All-you-can-get-on-one-plate-bars charge $5 for a heaping plate of food. Huge bowls of Vietnamese soup with egg noddles or rice and your choice of meat or fish are great bargains at $4 to $5. Downstairs is a Chinese pharmacy which has a wide range of unique, bizarre, and sometimes scary ancient remedies.

Outside the Sussex Center on Dixon St. is the center of tourist Chinatown. The Marigold, the Regal, and the New Marigold are all owned by the same people and provide good food at tourist prices.

The New Marigold serves the best yum cha (dim sum) in

town. Any of the restaurants on Dixon street are adequate for a traditional Chinese meal. Expect to spend about $15 per person plus wine.

LITTLE ITALY

Leichhardt is the Little Italy of Sydney. The majority of restaurants are on Norton St., near Parrammatta Road. Sydneysiders go to Leichhardt to drink capuccinos and read the paper or to eat Italian food and to drink lots of BYO red wine.

As you walk through Leichhardt you can almost imagine being on the Via Veneto in Rome, especially since a restaurant on the corner of Norton St. and Parramatta Road is called "Via Veneto." Italian is the predominant spoken language and people are always standing around gossiping. Although the pasta is of the same high quality in most restaurants, we have listed a few favorites.

BAR VIA VENETO. A real "working man's" restaurant, open from 4 a.m. to 6 p.m., seven days a week. A popular place for early morning breakfast or weekend capuccino. Lots of tables are available.

CAFFE SPORT. Next door to Via Veneto is the much smaller Caffe Sport. Although this cafe used to have a similar working clientele to the Veneto, it now attracts young families and couples for weekend cafe lattes, almond croissants, focaccias and aranchinis (breaded, fried rice balls with filling). Not many tables are available, so come early, especially on weekends.

EL TITIANA. Across the road from Caffe Sport, this restaurant serves filling but not memorable food. Everything in Titiana is covered in graffiti: tables, walls, chairs, pictures, ceilings, floors, and even some of the help! Bring along lots of red wine and a pen. The service is slow, allowing time to create your own graffiti.

LA RUSTICA. Just around the corner from the above restaurants, La Rustica at 435 Parramatta Road is one of the best restaurants in Little Italy. Restaurant owners eat here on their days off from working in their own places. The house specialties, roast suckling pig and baby goat, are only available on Saturdays. A good buy is the mixed pasta plate, for two or more people, at only $9 per person. La Rustica is noisy and friendly and worth a visit.

Don't be afraid to sample any of the restaurants at the top of Norton St. or on Marion St. up to the Leichhardt Plaza. People are friendly and allow you to enjoy your dinner Italian Style, relaxed and slowly. If you are in Sydney at the end of March, make sure you visit the Leichhardt festival. Food, fun, and games will keep the whole family busy for an entire afternoon.

THE SPANISH SECTION

The Spanish have not yet taken over whole parts of Sydney as have the Chinese and Italians. Instead, they have been relegated to a small section of Liverpool St., between George and Sussex Sts., near Chinatown. You can get a good paella or a piping hot chocolate with some fresh churros in the small restaurants.

THE SPANISH CLUB. This is similar to a very small RSL club, with pokies (slot machines), a cheap bar, and a Spanish twist to the counter food. Upstairs is a restaurant and there's also an area where live Latino bands come to play. If you are a member you can take Spanish lessons for free. Ask at the door how to become a member. It's pretty cheap and they'll be happy to take your money and make you an official member.

CAPTAIN TORRES. This restaurant has delicious Spanish sea food dishes, especially paella. A bit pricey, but good food and atmosphere.

LA VINA. A great Spanish restaurant/wine bar that is not located on Liverpool St., but on Parramatta Road, Leichhardt near Little Italy. The Spanish food is reasonably priced and very filling. The place gets packed on weekends (cover charge varies) when Latin American bands get the crowd dancing.

SURRY HILLS/REDFERN

The intersection of Cleveland and Elizabeth St. is home to some of the best Lebanese and Turkish restaurants in Sydney. Recently, some Indian restaurants have opened their doors in the same area.

ERCIYES. On Cleveland St. near Crown St., this is only one of the four family restaurants that serve Turkish Pide Pizza, which is served flat with toppings or folded with fillings. One pide is plenty for two people, especially if baba ganoush (egg plant dip) or humus (chick pea dip) are eaten as appetizers. If the pide is too spicy, as is the case with sausage pide, order cecik, which is a yogurt dish similar to Greek tzatziki. For dessert have a special dessert pizza and a thick, rich Turkish coffee, guaranteed to keep you awake all night.

NADAS, 270 Cleveland St., and ABDUL'S, on the corner of Elizabeth and Cleveland Sts., have food available for take-out. In order to sample all the dishes, order a set banquet at $13 per person. The banquet includes all the trimmings. While Abdul's has been a Sydneysider favorite for years, Nadas deserves a mention for its delicious vegetarian Lebanese Food.

INDIAN SWEETS. On Cleveland St., around the corner from Crown St., is the original Indian sweet store. As the popularity of Indian food grows, more sweet shops are popping up all over Sydney. Most of the desserts are made with ghee (clarified butter) and cardamon. Although the sweets are not very sweet at all, they are interesting to sample.

INDIAN FOOD. Also on Cleveland St., to the west of Crown St., is a new Indian restaurant. The decor is simple, tables with red checkered cloths, and the menu small, but you must try the delicious tandoori chicken and nan. This small but good value restaurant has become a favorite among backpackers.

NEWTOWN

If you don't like to eat ethnic food and to wear black, then you may as well give Newtown a miss. Dozens of Indian, Thai, Indonesian, Mexican, Italian, Greek, and vegetarian restaurants line King St. Narrow smoke-filled cafés that serve light meals and provide live entertainment are alternatives to the restaurants. Newtown restaurants are small and tend to get very crowded, especially on weekends, so make a reservation.

SAFARI. 26 King St., 514-458. This Indonesian restaurant gets an A+ for value, variety, decor and service. All appetizers are under $6. The sates ($5) and spring rolls ($2) are delicious. All entrees cost less than $10, even the barbecued king prawns.

The Cumi Cumi (stuffed squid) is the most popular dish, and its reputation is well deserved. Go with a group of people and sample as many dishes as possible. The manager may even suggest a special buffet. For five to seven people this is not a bad bargain, but if you are in a larger group, suggest creating your own mix of foods.

HARD NOX CAFE. 45 King St., 550-1106. The place to go for creative vegetarian food, Aussie-style. Aussie bagels (not water boiled) can be a sandwich base. Soya and tofu are popular; the specials are always changing. For a light meal, drink a fruit smoothie and read the "Green Left" newspaper.

ALEX CORDOBES PIZZA. 67 King St., 516-1310. As far removed from New York pizzas as possible, at least Alex Cordobes' pizzas are stacked with lots of toppings. The supreme is a monument: ham, salami, cabanossi sausage, mushrooms, peppers, shrimp, onion, anchovy, olives, and pineapple. Take-out is also available.

THAI TANIC. 127 King St., 517-1350. Sydney's has dozens of Thai restaurants with original names like Thai One On, Thai Me Up, and Thai Foon. The Thai Tanic is a huge restaurant that serves delicious and authentic Thai food at a bargain price. In fact, the Thai food here is better than in Thailand! Make sure you come with a group of people in order to be able to sample the wide varieties of soups (under $4), spicy curries ($7), and vegetarian ($5.50), meat and poultry ($7.50) and seafood dishes ($9.90). Rice costs extra, but you can choose between boiled, fried or rice cooked in milk, tumeric, and saffron.

GLEBE

Once a popular neighborhood for workers commuting to downtown Sydney, Glebe has become a place for people who like an alternative lifestyle. The main drag, Glebe Point Road, is full of restaurants, cafés, hot bread shops, and mixed businesses.

CAFE TROPPO, 175 Glebe Point Road, 552-1233. Troppo is slang for Tropical, as in "Gone Troppo" or in American English "I've Gone Crazy." Open until 1 a.m., Cafe Troppo is a late night spot that is usually filled with people who have just come from the late night show at the Valhalla or from a local pub. The main courses are a bit pricey ($9 to $16), so I suggest sticking with the savory appetizers or delicious desserts. A basket of fresh veggies ($7) and then a slice of cake makes a satisfying late nite snack for one or two people. Sit outside in the courtyard in the summertime.

CAFE OTTO, Glebe Point Road. Otto's is another late night trendy spot. The fare is similar to Troppo's but the prices are cheaper, the courtyard is out front, and the tables are plentiful. Nachos with everything ($10) makes a meal for two or appetizers for four. Focaccio, salads, and vegetarian dishes all are good bargains.

HAROLD'S BAR & GRILL, 115 Wigram Road, 552-2999. The Grill is connected to the pub, which has nights for amateur writers, comedians, and political raconteurs. The best deal in The Grill is to order pasta ($8), with a choice of sauce. On Sundays, head over for a brunch of bagels and lox or eggs benedict and a bottomless cup of coffee ($2). If you have a sweet tooth, try one of their cakes, which are baked fresh daily.

DARLINGHURST

Food Row on Oxford St. is for those Charlie Browns that can't make up their minds what they want to eat. African, American, Balkan, Cambodian, Chinese, Greek, Italian, Indian, Indonesian, Thai, and Vietnamese restaurants line Oxford St. Prices in Darlinghurst are one third and more higher than elsewhere, but the service and variety make the neighborhood a good place to go to if you feel like a splurge.

ROCKEFELLER'S EASTSIDE, 225 Oxford St., 361-6968. For an All-American night out complete with red, white, and blue and Mickey & Minnie Mouse decor, stop by Rockefeller's. Burgers (try the New York Giant), ribs, and barbecued chicken (served with coleslaw, french fries, and barbecue sauce) are just some of their specialties. For a lighter meal, try the Superbowl Salad. If you are feeling homesick, head over here.

ANGKOR WAT, 227 Oxford St., 360-5500. This Cambodian restaurant is the best value on Oxford St. The food is similar to Thai, but is not as spicy. Appetizers are only around $5, and main meals are under $9 (except for seafood).

BALKAN & BALKAN SEAFOOD, 209 & 215 Oxford St., 357-4970, 331-7670. For a hearty Yugoslavian meal try one of the Balkan restaurants. Peer through the window to see what is being grilled. Barbecued bugs are an exotic (but not quite Yugoslavian) dish served at the Balkan Seafood, while goulash and other Eastern European fare are the Balkan's specialties.

GOVINDA'S, 112 Darlinghurst St. A Hare Krishna vegetarian restaurant featuring an all-you-can-eat buffet between 6 p.m. and 10 p.m.

PUB & RETURNED SERVICEMEN LEAGUE CLUB (RSL) FOOD

Most pubs serve counter lunches between 12 p.m. and 2 p.m. and dinner from 6:30 p.m. and 9 p.m. Meals cost between $4 and $10. Don't expect anything fancy: a counter meal means fried chicken, lamb, or beef, with chips and salad.

If you feel like a meal just like Mom makes, head over to the local RSL. Hearty, filling meals at bargain prices are available to all members and guests (you can be made a guest on the spot). Lamb with gravy, carrots, string beans, potatoes, and bread and butter costs only $6 to $7. Complement your meal with a subsidized beer ($1.50 to $2). When you've finished eating, head over to the poker machines to win some money!

FAST FOODS

Of course, Sydney has its fill of McDonald's, Kentucky Fried Chicken, Hungry Jack's (Burger King), and other burger joints. Try McDonald's McFeast, which is only available in Australia. It's a hamburger with lettuce, tomato, and beetroot. Or try the Hungry Jack equivalent which is a hamburger with an egg and beetroot.

Sizzlers is very popular in the northern and western suburbs of Sydney. All-you-can-eat appetizer, salad, and dessert bar is $10. If you don't mind eating in a brightly lit, freezing cold cafeteria, then Sizzlers is a good bargain for the hungry traveler. You can even get wine with your meal.

The Pizza Huts at 630 George St. and 238 Pitt St. have all you can eat pizza and salad dinners on Tuesdays or Wednesdays for only $4.99. On other days, in our opinion, Pizza Huts are not good bargains. Have a meat pie instead!

CHAPTER 7:

SYDNEY'S NEIGHBORHOODS

W hen people think of New York City, Washington D.C., San Francisco, and many of the other major cities in the United States, they think of the city in terms of uptown, midtown and downtown. Sydney is actually more similar to Los Angeles in that the surrounding areas provide most of the entertainment. From Balmain to Woolloomooloo, all of Sydney's neighborhoods have their own style and attitude.

INNER WEST

Stretching from Chippendale to Leichhardt, the Inner West is comprised of a mix of trendy students, the twenty-something "alternative crowd," and because of the old Victorian townhouses, the thirty-something "renovation crowd."

Glebe

Most of the activity in this neighborhood takes place on Glebe Point Road, which has the largest density of cafés and restaurants in Australia. The University of Sydney (Uni) students and the alternative crowd live here. The Valhalla movie theater, colorful weekend markets, and vegetarian cafés help create a Bohemian atmosphere.

The Church of England was the original owner of 160 hectares of the property that now makes up Glebe. In the mid-1820s, this land was sold to upper-middle class settlers. To see the huge mansions built by these residents, walk down Pyrmont Bridge Road. In the 1850s, the rich began to move into the suburbs and the area was leased to build cheap housing. Soon Glebe became a slum.

In the 1970s the Federal Government stepped in and began renovating the area. Today, the neighborhood is filled with tree-lined streets and restored terrace homes. A youth hostel and Glebe Village Hotel are located towards the end of Glebe Point Road, near the park.

Newtown

Black is an integral part of the Newtown scene. This means black shirts, jeans, shoes, hats, and don't forget the eyeliner! The action centers on King St. Newtown is "the flavor of the month" among the gay crowd, which is good news because original and exciting clubs, restaurants, and cafés are opening continuously to cater to this crowd. Most of the other people who live here are students or inner city trendy twenty-some-things. Don't ever drive to Newtown: the streets are narrow, twisty, and only wide enough for one car, although signs assure you they are two-way streets!

Leichhardt

This is the Little Italy of Sydney. Until the 1950s, there were very few Italians in Sydney. The influx of immigrants changed Leichhardt from a boring suburb to a bustling town. The cafés open at 6 a.m., just like in Rome. The residents are either young families who work in downtown, or older, retired Italians.

On weekends, Leichhardt caters to the yuppy crowd and young couples who come for capuccinno, focaccio, and croissants. Most of the excitement is on Norton St., north of Parrammatta Road. Marion St., which intersects with Norton, also has some good restaurants such as La Botte D'Or which has seafood specials on Thursdays.

Balmain

This suburb was named after its founder, William Balmain, who was a surgeon in the First Fleet. Most of the homes here were built between 1855 and 1890. Balmain is a very artsy neighborhood.

A walk along Darling St. takes you past bookstores, antique shops, earthy-crunchy New Age crystal shops, and cafés. The Saturday markets in Saint Andrew's Church on Darling St., across from the London Tavern, have a mixture of unique handmade items and recycled trash.

To get the feel of the neighborhood and view some of Balmain's old, waterfront homes, make a right onto Round Tree Road from Darling St. Another right into Ballast Point

Road, and a left onto Lemm St. to Wharf Road takes you into a part of Balmain that has some of the most beautiful old homes in the Inner West. Follow Wharf Road down to Birch Grove Park, make a left onto Grove St., and cut through Grove Park to Louisa Road. Follow this road all the way to Long Nose Point Wharf and Reserve. From here, you can take a ferry to Circular Quay ($2.50 one way). Ferries only operate during peak commuting hours in the morning and evening.

Surry Hills & East Sydney

The suburbs nearest Central Railway Station, just south of the City, are known as Surry Hills/East Sydney. This neighborhood is for night owls. The Journalist, Taxi and Trade Union Clubs operate 24 hours a day and attract a bizarre mix of characters. A few years ago, the club crowd was mainly Punk, complete with ripped leather and spiky hair. Since then, the crowd has mellowed a bit, but the Hopetoun Hotel still gets a punk crowd.

Elizabeth and Cleveland streets incorporate the ethnic Indian, Turkish, and Lebanese restaurants, while Reilly and Foveaux Streets have the Trade Union and other clubs and pubs. On the corner of Reilly and Foveux is the infamous Touch Of Class—a house of ill repute.

Redfern

Unfortunately, Redfern has gotten a bad reputation as being a rundown, dangerous "Abo" town. Only one block from Redfern Station and around the corner from some of Sydney's elegant townhomes, Sydney's Aboriginals (or Koories as they prefer to be called) live in appalling conditions, among dilapidated homes, broken glass, and the burnt-out cars that litter the pot-holed streets.

The worst street is Everleigh which can compete with anything New York's Harlem has to offer. Do not visit this area—it is not safe.

The rest of Redfern is beginning to pick up. Regent St. is lined with clothing stores that sell irregulars and overstocked brand name clothes at inexpensive prices. New pubs, restaurants and cafés are beginning to open.

To get to Redfern, just walk across the park from Central Station. All trains that travel west from Central Station also stop at Redfern.

Darlinghurst

Once the heart of the gay scene, this neighborhood now has a Crossover Club scene. When people refer to Darlinghurst, they usually mean the strip of clubs on Oxford St. from College St., immediately past Taylor Square to Restaurant Row. (See page 120 for a review of the numerous pubs along Oxford St.)

PADDINGTON

Like Glebe, Paddo was another Inner City slum until the 1970s. From WWII until the mid-1960s, Paddington was a run-down, working-class suburb. The houses were crumbling and the roads and footpaths were in ruins. The Local Council did not want to spend any money to renovate the town, so they contemplated buying large tracts of Paddington land, razing the buildings, and beautifying the neighborhood by building modern townhouses.

In the mid-1960s, an architectural lecturer from the University of Sydney bought a terrace home in Paddo. He did such a beautiful job of renovating his terrace home, that the Council used it as a model for the future development of Paddo.

Today, people wander through the quiet streets of Paddington, just to admire the old, Victorian homes. If you want to tour the neighborhood, go on a Saturday and shop in the Paddington Village Bazaar in the grounds of the Uniting Church on Oxford St.

KINGS CROSS

More commonly referred to as "The Cross", this neighborhood *is a cross between* an adult-only night spot and the center of the backpacker hostels. The Telecom 24-hour phone center, tourist shops, and cheap hostels and take-out shops run up and down Darlinghurst Road. The Cross rivals New York's 42nd St. for glitz, atmosphere, and noise.

Most of the action is on the three blocks or so of Darlinghurst Road from El Alamein Fountain to the huge, neon Coca-Cola sign. Porky's Adult Toy Shop, The Pink Pussycat Strip Joint, The Pink Panther, and The Wolf's Den Adult Book Store are favorite hang outs among locals and tourists alike. Tony Roma Ribs and The Bourbon & Beefsteak are popular restaurants, Studebakers a fashionable club, and OZ Rock a mellow pub with entertainment.

Most of the "Working Girls" walk up and down Darlinghurst Road, while the transvestites tend to hang around in a little square near the car dealerships on Williams St. Perpendicular to Williams St. is Victoria St., a quieter area, filled with little cafés.

WOOLLOOMOOLOO

Formerly a run-down neighborhood, Woolloomooloo is now very up-market and home to the Royal Australian Navy. An interesting way to get to this area is to walk through King Cross' Darlinghurst Road, to El Alamein Fountain, make a left onto Macleay St., walk down to Orwell St. and make a left.

At the end of Orwell St. make a right onto Victoria St., and walk toward the Harbour until you get to McElhone Stairs. Walk down the stairs to Cowper Wharf Road.

The Royal Australian Navy Base is on this road. Once a year the base opens its doors to the public. Hundreds of people play sailor for a day and visit the navy's submarines and warships. Walk past the base and stop in at one of Sydney's favorite restaurants, Harry's Cafe de Wheels (page 57).

CHAPTER 8:

BEACHES:
SOUTHERN, NORTHERN,
& HARBOUR

The beach is a major part of the life of a Sydneysider. Surfies can be as young as eight and as old as eighty. Those who can't surf, usually swim, body surf or worship the sun. However, the latest skin cancer threats and the increasing holes in the ozone have frightened Australians into taking a bit more care in the sun. The national "Slip, Slop, Slap" campaign is a big success. It stands for, "Slip on a t-shirt, Slop on some sunscreen, and Slap on a hat." These items plus sunglasses are an absolute necessity during the summer months of December, January, and February.

But what about *JAWS* and other assorted creatures with fins and sharp teeth? Never fear, the Shark Patrol helicopters fly over Sydney's major beaches on a regular basis. Occasionally, sharks do come awfully close to the beaches while feeding. Luckily, sharks tend to feed on other fish and not on swimmers. Even when there is a shark warning, surfies still stay out in the surf!

The last time a person got eaten by a shark was in 1964 in the shallow waters off Balmoral Beach, a Harbour beach. Most of the people who get attacked by sharks (and one or two people a year do get nibbled on) are surfies or other fools who are out splashing about in deep water. Some of the beaches have shark netting which provides a bit of extra protection. The best advice is to forget about the above and just go out to the beach and have some fun!

THE DRESS CODE. Aussie men love to wear the skimpiest swimmers (bathing suits) available. Anything the size of a speedo or smaller is perfect. Women wear bikinis and usually sunbathe with just the bottom half of their "cozzie" (bathing suit) on. It's rare to see a woman swimming topless. For some reason, although women sunbathe topless, they put their top back on to swim in the water. Most beaches allow topless bathing, although it is not recommended in Maroubra and Bronte and some of the Northern Beaches. These are family beaches and aren't much fun for the topless crowd anyhow. The best rule of thumb is to look around and see what everyone else is doing.

Lady Bay (also known as Lady Jane) and Wreck Beaches are the two semi-official nude beaches. However, even Australia is experiencing the tide of conservatism and people in nude beaches may be forced to cover up. This topic is being debated constantly. The two nude beaches tend to attract an older, gay crowd.

SURF LIFESAVERS CLUBS. All the beaches in Sydney are protected (from October to Easter) by the volunteer members of the Surf Lifesavers Clubs. The clubs were started in 1907 and since then have saved hundreds of thousands of lives. The Lifesavers are in constant communication with the shark patrols, who are in helicopters above the beaches. If a school of sharks is heading toward a beach, the Lifesavers are immediately informed and they sound the shark siren which warns people to get out of the water. The Lifesavers main purpose is to prevent people from drowning. In the early days, a canvas belt was worn around a Lifesaver's waist and the belt in turn was attached by rope to a giant spool. The Lifesaver would swim out in the ocean to rescue a drowning person, while the other Lifesavers would stand on shore, let the rope out, and then pull the two of them in. In cases where there were multiple people a few Lifesavers would jump in a wooden boat and row out to the rescue.

Today, more modern equipment is used. Lifesavers need only jump into a motorized rubber dinghy. The wooden rowboats are still preserved: the Lifesavers use them every year in Surf Carnival competitions. The Australian Maritime Museum has an excellent permanent exhibition on the history of the Surf Lifesavers Clubs.

SOUTHERN BEACHES

The closest ocean beach to the city is Bondi. To get there take bus Number 380, 382 or 389 from Circular Quay or take a train to Bondi Junction and change to Number 380, 382 or 389.

Sydney's infamous Bondi Beach is the center for surfies and tourists who come out to watch the surfies manipulate waves that normally reach six feet. When people say Bondi, they mean the Beach, not Bondi Junction which is the shopping area and as far as the train goes east.

Campbell Parade is chock-a-block full of restaurants, cafés, beach shops, pubs, hotels, and surfie shops. Both the day and night life are excellent. The Bondi Hotel deserves a mention here for acting as a cafe, restaurant, pub, pool hall, disco, and live entertainment center.

Surfboards, boogie boards ($5/hour), chairs, umbrellas, and wind tents are all available for rent on or near the beach. If you want protection from the sun and you have forgotten your lotion, you can either buy it at the beachside shop or you can get an oil spray—$1.50 for a spray with #4 SPF.

The two skateboard ramps at the south end of Bondi are beginning to attract roller bladers as well as the usual crowd of skateboarders.

At the back of the beach is the Bondi Pavilion, which has art exhibits, classes, a restaurant, and a bar. On Sundays, street musicians and buskers gather around the Pavilion and entertain the passersby. The annual South American Festival, live bands, and other activities are all held in and around the Pavilion.

Bondi Beach seems to attract a varied crowd: the young, beach-loving, party crowd, Kiwis (New Zealanders), and a large Jewish community. Curlewis St. has a variety of butchers selling kosher meats and bakeries that specialize in bagels and authentic Jewish pastries.

From Bondi to Tamarama beach it's only a short clifftop walk. Follow the path that starts at the south end of Bondi, near the swimming pool, and then follow the crowd toward the water. The path angles around the cliff top for about two miles.

Tamarama is a trendy, somewhat gay beach. The surf tends to get rough because it is a narrow cove beach. You should be able to be there and back from Bondi in an hour, in time for a happy hour schooner at the Bondi Hotel or cake and coffee at the Gelato Bar. From Tamarama, you can continue to walk to Bronte Beach/Park. This is the first of three family beaches that are good places for Aussie barbies.

Clovelly Beach has a deep, ocean-water swimming pool where a lot of scuba schools do their training. The beach itself is small and sandy; one of the quieter southern beaches.

The next beach, Coogee, is a bit too far to walk from Clovelly. The main reason to go to Coogee is to visit Selinas Nightclub/Coogee Bay Hotel. This huge hotel has a restaurant, outdoor seating, a pub, dance area, and live entertainment. Popular bands, such as the Hunters & Collectors, Crowded House, and even America's George Thorogood have played here.

Maroubra, the next beach in line, is one of the most popular family beaches. There is not much to do at Maroubra, except surf and swim. The surf here is very consistent and when there is a good southerly wind, the surf is exceptional. On weekends, it gets very crowded with younger families.

The Maroubra Bay Hotel and the Seals Club provide the only night-time entertainment in the form of live bands and/or wet t-shirt contests (definitely not family material!).

Last of the good, southerly beaches is Cronulla, the beach for the hippies of the 1990s and young surfies. Watch out for the stinging blue bottle jellyfish that occasionally congregate near the beach. If you do get stung, see a lifeguard or do as some others do: urinate on the sting!

NORTHERN BEACHES

To get to the first northern ocean beach take a ferry to Manly. Most of the northern beaches attract people who live in expensive homes in the wealthy, northern suburbs. However, the beaches also draw a young, party, surfie scene, because the surf tends to be more consistent than that of the Southern beaches. These beaches tend to be very long and sweeping, with fine sand and peaceful views.

"Seven Miles from Sydney, A Thousand Miles From Care," was the slogan used for Manly before the Harbour Bridge was completed. Manly used to be a family seaside resort for Sydneysiders and it is still used as a weekend getaway. Manly also attracts a young, British crowd as well as a few Aussies who live in flats near the beach.

The first Governor of New South Wales, Captain Philip, named this area Manly after the Aboriginals who greeted him when the British first stepped ashore. Although most Aboriginals tended to run from foreigners, these held their ground, with spears in hand, and stood tall and "manly".

To get to the beach, take a half hour $3.40 (one way) ferry ride or a 15 minute $4.60 (one way) JetCat ride from Circular

Quay. As you alight from the ferry, the first stop is the Fun Pier, which has a ferris wheel ($3 for one ride) and some kiddy rides. The new Manly Wharf ferry terminal is filled with stores and fast food restaurants. As you leave the terminal, you are faced with a choice: to your left is the Harbour beach, waterslide, and other attractions, while straight ahead is the ocean beach and promenade.

If you choose the Harbour beach, you also get lots of excitement. The Waterworks has four giant water slides. You are entitled to soar down giant water slides lying flat on a mat for only $9.95 for one hour or $14.95 all day.

Manly Oceanarium (949-2644) has become almost as popular as the Sydney Aquarium. Sharks, stingrays, marine mammals and fish are all on display. Visitors travel along a 110-yard moving walkway surrounded by sharks, which are, lucky for us, behind plexiglass. If you have a scuba certificate (and are slightly crazy) you can arrange a special dive with the sharks! The dives cost $55, plus an additional charge for equipment, if necessary. You can bring along a non-diving friend at night for $5. If they come with you during the day, they have to pay full price. The Oceanarium costs $11/$5 children and is open 9 a.m. to 5:30 p.m., seven days a week.

The Manly Museum and Art Gallery (949-1776) has Australian paintings and other exhibits on display. The museum is free and is open Tuesday to Friday from 10 a.m. to 4 p.m., and noon to 5 p.m. on Saturday and Sunday.

To reach the ocean beach walk down the Corso, which is the pedestrian mall. Clothes stores, surf shops, restaurants, take-away shops, bakeries, ice cream parlors, sidewalk cafés and boutiques line the mall. Surfboards, boogie boards, and rollerblades can be hired on the beach or across from the Manly Wharf at 48 East Esplanade.

The beach can get pretty crowded on weekends. The swim areas vary day to day, so keep an eye out for the flags and only swim in between them, under the watchful eye of the lifeguards. Manly, as with many other beaches in Sydney, is susceptible to heavy riptides. The surfing area is usually to the right, or south, of the Corso, in front of the Surf Club.

For a smaller beach, walk toward the Surf Club and follow the path to Fairy Bower beach, an ocean beach with a lawn and barbecues at the back.

The six-mile Manly Scenic Walk begins at Manly on the Harbour side and continues to the Spit Bridge. Either pick up a map from the Manly information center on the beach or look in the Walks Section of this book (page 91).

The Quarantine Station (977-6229) is a two-mile hike from Manly or a short bus ride on the #135. Both ghost tours and regular guided tours are available from the National Parks and Wildlife Service. Tours cost from $6 to $12 depending on the type of tour.

There is not much to say about the individual beaches north of Manly, since they have most of the same features: good surf with some take-out shops at the back. The major beaches after Manly start with Curl Curl, then Dee Why (ocean rock pool), Long Reef (wind surfing), Collaroy (ocean pool carved from the cliff face), and North Narrabeen (great surf and a good windsurfing lake at the back of the beach).

Mona Vale (ocean rock pool at the north), Newport (reef at the southern end, windsurfing), Avalon, Whale (a bit of a hike from the bus stop), and Palm beaches (Sydney's most northern beach) are located on a peninsula and are sometimes referred to as "The Insular Peninsula", because the people who live there never seem to leave their neighborhoods!

HARBOUR BEACHES

Sydney's Harbour beaches are not as exciting as the ocean beaches. The water isn't very clear, there is no surf at all, and the beaches are small. Plus, you know that nurse sharks are swimming about not very far from where you are! Good thing they don't like the taste of people.

Besides the two nude beaches mentioned above, Lady Bay and Wreck, there are only about four harbour beaches worth visiting. The most popular is Watson's Bay at Camp Cove, because the Watson's Bay Hotel and Doyles restaurant serve up ice cold schooners and the best fish in Sydney. Lady Bay is reached along a rocky path (or the newer, dirt path) that starts out at the back of Watson's Bay Hotel.

Balmoral Beach is a popular beach that attracts people from the surrounding wealthy suburbs. Nielson Beach is located within Nielsen Park, Vaucluse. The beach is shark netted and is quite peaceful and lovely. Besides the ocean beach at Manly, there is a Harbour beach (also netted), that attracts many local windsurfers.

CHAPTER 9:

SIGHTS
AND
ATTRACTIONS

What do people think about when Sydney, Australia, is mentioned? The Opera House? The Harbour Bridge? The Zoo and Aquarium? These are classic tourist ideas, but what you should really be looking forward to are the Quarantine Station, hidden tunnels, underground dunnies, and free tours, museums and concerts.

QUARANTINE STATION. The Quarantine Station was officially opened in 1832 in Spring Cove on North Head. When immigrants first arrived in Sydney they were checked for communicable diseases. If people were unlucky enough to have a contagious disease, they were sent to the grim Quarantine Station. There they stayed until they were healthy, by Australian standards.

In 1974, the Station was used for a different, not so grim, purpose. Cyclone Tracy succeeded in nearly destroying the town of Darwin in the Northern Territories. The victims of the cyclone stayed at the Station until the damage was assessed and Darwin was virtually rebuilt. In 1984, the Station ceased operation and opened as a tourist site.

Today the National Parks and Wildlife Service (NPWS) offers a variety of guided tours. The tours walk you through the residents' quarters, burial grounds, disinfecting chambers, and isolation hospital. Tour guides also point out the rock engravings and graffiti that were left by residents.

Public tours are available on Saturdays, Sundays and Wednesday afternoons, and private tours can be arranged.

The special Ghost and Ghouls Tour is offered on Friday and Saturday nights. The cost is $12 for the tour, ghost stories, and Billy Tea and Damper bread.

To arrange any of the above tours, call 977-6229.

TUNNELS. During the 1800s, gun emplacements were erected on the Sydney headlands to protect Australia from the greedy European empires.

Tours of the network of tunnels at Middle and Georges Head are available from the NPWS, or you can tour the tunnels alone. The guided tour costs $6. For more information, call 977-6522.

Middle Head tunnels offer a bit more to see than Georges Head, but both are worth a visit. The best plan is to visit Middle Head with a guide and then go on to explore Georges Head on your own. Bring flashlights and sturdy walking shoes.

MORTUARY STATION. Officially known as Regent Street Station, this terminal was nicknamed Mortuary Station because it was the departure point for funeral trains from Sydney to Rockwood and Woronora cemeteries. In the mid-1980s, the station was converted into a restaurant and became a popular late night spot for Sydneysiders.

Unfortunately, the inside of the station is now closed. To see the outside, walk along the west side (toward Railway Square) of Central Station to Regent St. Continue down the street until you come to Mortuary Station on the left.

CEMETERY TOUR. Speaking of mortuaries, if it's Halloween time and you feel like doing something suitable, take a tour of Gore Hill Cemetery. Call the Friends of the Cemetery (only in OZ would cemeteries have friends!) at 349-2631 and talk to them about arranging a tour. The cemetery is located at Pacific Highway and Westbourne Streets.

UNDERGROUND DUNNIES. Believe it or not, a walk through Sydney's underground toilets is a tour of Sydney's architectural achievements.

A 19th century cast-iron urinal is located on George St. at the Rocks. These urinals were once very common, but sadly, this is the only one left in Sydney. A Gent's lavatory, located in Wynyard Park, was built by the City Council around 1900.

The Hyde Park toilets, built in the early 1900s, have two stairwells bounded by a cast iron fence decorated with art nouveau designs on the handrail. The dunnies in Taylor Square and Macquarie Place also have art nouveau decorations.

The one at Macquarie Place is built from stuccoed brickwork, and includes a curved staircase that leads to a circular keeper's office where a glazed dome allows in natural light.

Unfortunately, a lot of dunnies are now closed and in heavy need of repair. If only the toilets of today were built with such tender loving care!

WOOLLOOMOOLOO FINGER WHARF. The Wharf, built in 1913, is a classic example of Federation architecture. At first, it was used for wool and cargo transportation. During World Wars I and II, the Wharf was used for the embarkation and arrival of Australian troops. During the 1950s and 1960s, the Wharf was the first arrival point for many immigrants. By the mid-1980s, the Wharf was closed down and was in a complete shambles.

Today it is surrounded by controversy. This major industrial structure, supported by 4,000 timber piles with a 400-yard-long by 50-yard-wide wharf deck has a 16-yard-wide sunken roadway down the center. Some Sydneysiders still view the Wharf as a "Tin Shed With A Rusty Roof." The State Government still hopes that a private company will come forward to redevelop this historic landmark, before they are forced to destroy it.

GRAFFITI HALL OF FAME. Graffiti art is located all over Sydney: in Newtown at Bondi Beach, across from the Redfern train station, and elsewhere. None of this compares to the work done in a driveway of a building in an industrial part of Sydney. If you have a car, drive over to Botany Road, Alexandria, near the corner of McEvoy St. and take a look at the masterpieces. Directly behind the Hall of Fame is a Buddhist Temple that is closed to the public.

FISH MARKET. Although the market is not really a hidden spot in Sydney, it is a place few tourists visit. Sydneysiders go to the Fish Market on Gibbes St., Pyrmont, to purchase all types of seafood from the 3000 different species available: Balmain bugs (similar in taste to lobsters), barramundi (expensive, but delicious), orange roughy, tiger, king and banana prawns, and Australian lobsters (crayfish). After a tour around the market, purchase some ready-to-eat fish from Doyles, a picnic at Blackwattle Deli, or sushi from the Sushi Bar, grab a bottle of wine and sit outside at the cafe tables along the waterfront.

The seafood auction held in the early hours of the morning is quite a production. The day's catch is displayed by batch.

The buyers sit like spectators around the catch. The batch number and price are announced. The price goes down until a buyer is interested and pushes a button which signifies his purchase of the batch. This is known as the Dutch System.

The Fish Market gives free tours for groups of ten or more by prior arrangement only. For more information see Free Events (later in this chapter).

PYLON LOOKOUT AND THE HARBOUR BRIDGE. The Bridge contains 6,000,000 rivets, 485,000 square meters of steelwork and was painted with 30,000 liters of grey paint. Crocodile Dundee (Paul Hogan) himself helped paint on a few liters of paint when he was just a lowly bridge painter! The Bridge was designed with the assumption that 40,000 people and 6,000 cars per day would cross from downtown Sydney to North Sydney. In 1992, 200,000 cars crossed over every day. These are only some of the many facts that you can learn about the Bridge from a visit to the Lookout.

The entrance to the Bridge is on Cumberland St. at the Rocks. Walk partially across the Bridge to the first lookout and begin the climb of 200 steps. On the way up the stairs is a history of the Bridge, along with fabulous old photos showing the workers building the Bridge from start to finish, which is well worth the $2 admission charge. The view from the top is breathtaking and much more affordable than the touristy Sydney Tower ($8). Once you've reached the bridge again, you can continue your walk across the bridge to Milsons Point and catch a train back to the City.

HARBOUR ISLANDS. The Harbour is filled with dozens of small islands which are used for research, pleasure, and other activities.

Many people are familiar with Pinchgut Island where Fort Denison is located. The island, which is situated right off the Opera House, was nicknamed Pinchgut because it was here that convicts who committed minor crimes were quartered and starved. During the Crimean War, the Australian Government fortified the island because they feared an attack by the Russians.

Hegarty's Ferries (241-2733 weekdays and 247-6606 weekends) arranges tours to Pinchgut every day except Mondays. Ferries leave Jetty 6 at Circular Quay at 10 a.m., 12:15 p.m. and 2 p.m. The tour costs $8.50 and takes an hour and a half. It is rumored that a small restaurant will be built on the island, which should increase the number of tours going there.

The most visited "island" is Bennelong. After Captain Philip landed in Sydney Harbour, he captured an aboriginal, named him Bennelong, and built him a hut on a small island to have him handy for observation. Later, when Bennelong was sent to visit the King of England, the Government of Sydney decided to fill in the channel between the island and the town. Today, the Opera House sits on Bennelong Point!

Shark, Clark and Rodd Islands are three little, lesser known Harbour islands that allow small groups of tourists to visit. The only drawback is that there isn't any public transportation to the islands. In order to get to any of the three islands, you need to hire a water taxi. Try calling Water Taxis at 955-3222 and booking a reservation a day or so in advance: Shark Island costs $25 for the first two people and $5 per person thereafter, Clark Island costs $35 and $5, and Rodd Island is $30 and $5.

Clark Island, located out from Double Bay, is the smallest of the three islands. There is no fee to visit, but the NPWS does not permit more than 15 people to visit the island at any one time. By contrast, Shark Island, in the middle of the entrance to Rose Bay, is the largest island and is therefore a bit more touristy. Entry is $2 per person. Rodd Island, situated across from Birkenhead Point, has very few visitors. It is the best island of the three to explore, if you are looking to get away from it all. Entry is $2 per person.

BOOMERANG SCHOOL. What better way to learn the oldest sport in OZ than for free! The proprietor of the store on 138 Williams St. has his own factory, which makes the best value, easiest-to-throw boomerangs in Sydney. Different versions, painted with Aussie Bush paintings, sell at $6 each or a pack of six for $25 to $30. The more intricate, expensive, and long-range 'rangs can cost over $100.

If you purchase a boomerang from the Boomerang Shop, or if you bring your own, you can show up at Centennial Park every Sunday at 2 p.m. There you will learn the finer points of boomerang throwing, and also learn which boomerangs return, which were used for hunting, and which for competitions.

If you feel like an American lost in OZ, just picture yourself trying to hit one bird in a flock of 20 or so. It may help you understand the purpose of 'rang throwing a bit better. Also, remember The Boomerang World Championship is usually won by an American.

FREE EVENTS

There is nothing better than getting to visit a museum or see a concert for free! Sydney is chock-a-block full of opportunities to experience culture without having to pay.

THE DOMAIN. As close to Speaker's Corner in Hyde Park, London as you can get in Sydney, Australia. From 10 a.m. Sundays, speakers gather to give speeches on any subject that interests them. From politics to social issues, all topics are permitted to be discussed in this corner of the park, near the Art Gallery of New South Wales. In recent years, both the crowds and the orators have thinned out, but the Domain is still a worthwhile place for all lovers of free speech.

FREE MUSIC AT MARTIN PLACE. Lunch time concerts are held every Monday to Friday, during warm weather, in downtown Sydney at Martin Place. The entertainment constantly varies, but it has a tendency to range from ethnic folk song and dance to Australian Bush music. This means that one day there may be a Greek group belly dancing, while the next day may bring an Aboriginal using his didjeridoo.

FREE MUSIC AT THE OPERA HOUSE. Every Sunday during warm weather, between 2 p.m. and 5 p.m., the Sydney Opera House presents free entertainment on the steps of the Opera House. Once again the lineup varies, but brass, jazz bands and ethnic music are usually featured. While the bands perform, people stroll around the Craft Market, tour the Opera House, or stand along the steps to admire the view of the Harbour and Circular Quay. Call 250-1777 for more information.

FREE MUSIC AT THE CONSERVATORIUM. Every Wednesday at 10 a.m., from mid-February to mid-December, the students of the Sydney Conservatorium of Music hold free concerts. Tickets are available in advance from 230-1222.

FREE TOURS OF PLACES OF WORSHIP. Although Sydneysiders are not generally very religious, they have built a handful of beautiful old churches and a magnificent Synagogue. Tours of Saint Phillips, Saint Mary's, Saint

Andrew's, the Garrison Church, and the Great Synagogue are offered free of charge. See page 104 for more details about the history of the churches and the numbers to call for information on the tours.

FREE FISH MARKET TOURS. The tour starts at 8 a.m. at the fish auction, and continues through the smokehouse and oyster shelling section. If you are interested, call 660-1611 at least one week ahead of the prospective tour date.

FREE MUSEUMS. Most museums in Sydney charge a fee to enter. However, some have special free or half-price days and/or special free hours. The Australian Museum and the Art Gallery of New South Wales are free to the public after 4 p.m. Unfortunately, most of the museums close at 5 p.m.

FREE TOURS OF ROYAL BOTANICAL GARDENS. Every Wednesday and Sunday at 10 a.m. the Botanical Gardens offer free, comprehensive walks. Meet the rangers at the Visitor's Center near the Art Gallery shortly before 10 a.m.

FREE TOURS OF KU-RING-GAI WILDFLOWER GARDEN. These gardens are located about a half hour drive from Sydney. Tours must be booked in advance and are offered Tuesdays at 10:30 a.m. and Sundays at 1:30 p.m. To make a reservation and for more information, call 457-9322.

CHAPTER 10 :

CITY, BEACH, & BUSH WALKS

You can walk for a month straight in Sydney and still not see all there is to see or have the time to explore all of Sydney's hidden secrets. But here is a list of some of our favorite walks, complete with a mini-history lesson on the places that you will visit. The tours explore the oldest part of Sydney, the Rocks, and the Harbour Parks. They take from a minimum of 15 minutes to a maximum of four hours to complete. Find one or two that suit your schedule, put on some comfortable shoes, and get ready to explore!

THE ROCKS

Since the first settlers landed at the Rocks, this is the perfect place to start your walking tour of Sydney. The following is our self-guided tour of this historic area. If you feel like an audio tour, rent a tape from the "Switch on Sydney" booth by the wharfs at Circular Quay. Both tours take approximately two and a half hours.

Start at the Rocks Visitor's Center, 104 George St. Stop in at the Center and watch the free film on the history of the area and pick up the "What's On" pamphlet. Turn right from the Center and travel down to 100 George St. This building was built between 1856 and 1859, and contains the Old Mariner's Church.

The Story of Sydney, an audiovisual production that tells the story of Sydney's early history, is housed in the Church.

Further down at 5-7 Hickson Road is the Australasian Steam Navigation Company Building. Built in 1884 and designed by W. M. Wardell, this building sits at the sight of Wharf House, home of Robert Campbell, Sydney's first merchant and shipowner. To the right are the Custom Officer's Stairs. Take these down to Campbell's Storehouse, located at 9 to 27 Circular Quay West, which was operated by Robert Campbell.

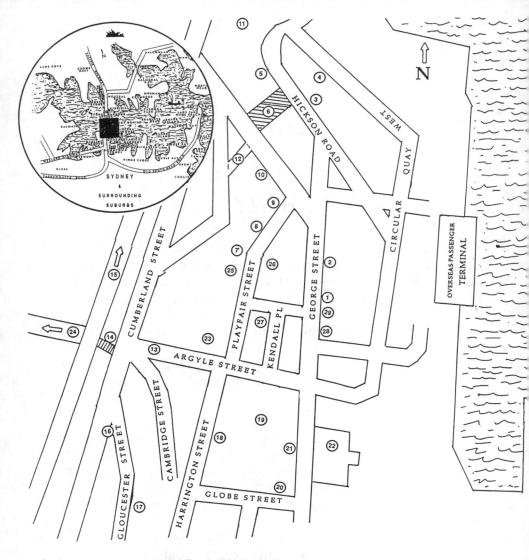

THE ROCKS WALK

1/ Rocks Visitors Centre
2/ Old Mariners Church
3/ Steam Navigation Building
4/ Campbells Storehouse
5/ Earth Exchange
6/ Metcalf Stores
7/ Atherden Street
8/ Westpac Banking Museum
9/ Counting House
10/ Mercantile Hotel
11/ Dawes Point Park
12/ Gloucester Walk
13/ Argyle Cut
14/ Harbour Bridge Stairs
15/ To Pylon Lookout

16/ Australian Hotel
17/ Susannah Place
18/ Harbour Rocks Hotel
19/ Suez Canal and Nurses Wa
20/ N.S.W. State Archives
21/ Old Police Station
22/ Museum of Contemporary
23/ Argyle Centre
24/ To the Lord Nelson Hotel
25/ Argyle Terrace
26/ Rocks Square
27/ Coach House
28/ Cadman's Cottage
29/ The Sailors Home

The Storehouse is inside the present-day Waterfront Restaurant which is in the long building behind the tall ship replicas. The first two floors of this house were built between 1839 and 1861, but the top story was not added until 1890. Take a look inside the restaurant or in the wine store and look up to see original, wide, wooden beams.

Continue on past the Storehouse, go up the ramp and turn left onto Hickson Road. The Old Geological and Miner's Museum, 18 Hickson Road, has been converted into The Earth Exchange (251-2422). The building was constructed in 1902 and was supposed to be an electric power station, but it was never used for this purpose. The museum has a $7/$5 entry fee and is open 10 a.m. to 5 p.m. You can easily spend all day watching the simulated volcano and earthquake, and wandering through the three floors of the museum.

When you're finished here, turn right and stroll down Hickson Road, and when you see the sign for "Pancakes on the Rocks" turn into the Metcalfe Stores. These were built from 1912 to 1916. Located on a sandstone quarry, the stores are now a modern shopping complex.

Go through the stores, stopping to shop in the Aboriginal shops, leather stores, and candle, poster and t-shirt stores, to George St. Turn left on George St., cross the road, turn right into Playfair St. and keep to the right. Atherden St. is a small dead-end street, Sydney's shortest street, and the home of some tiny terraced houses.

Turn back towards George St. On your left is the WestPac Museum and a little further down on the corner is the Bank. WestPac is Sydney's first bank, originally known as the "Bank of New South Wales", and dates back to 1817. The sandstone building originally belonged to the Union Bond (built in 1841).

Make a left onto George St. Shortly after the bank is the Counting House (1844) at 43 George St., and the Regency Townhouse, built in 1848 for a Sydney shipping merchant. From 41 to 43 George St. is Sergeant Major's Row, a block of terrace houses named after one of the early names for George St. The Mercantile Hotel, built between 1914 and 1915, is next. This lively Irish pub (page 129), has art nouveau tiles and good beer and ale.

Cross George St., walk under the Harbour Bridge, make a right and walk through Dawes Point Park. This was the first fortified position in Australia. The guns of the Dawes Point Battery are still here. Walk back to George St., behind the Mercantile and up Gloucester Walk, a narrow, brick, pedestrian walkway.

The first stop, about halfway up on the left, is a plaque honoring Captain Eber Bunker, an American who lived on Cumberland St. and captained the first whaling expedition from Sydney. Further down on your left is Foundation Park. Several homes used to cling to the hillside, but now all that remains are crumbling fireplaces and steps.

Climb up the stairs to Cumberland St. and cross to the other side of the street. Look below and you will be able to see Argyle Cut, a road that connects Darling Harbour and Miller's Point with Sydney Cove. The chain gangs began work on this mammoth project in 1843. Convict transportation ended in 1853 and the throughway was finally completed by hired workers in 1859.

Pass the Cut, and a little further down Cumberland St. on your right, are the Harbour Bridge stairs. Walk up the stairs and head towards the walkway that goes over the Harbour Bridge to Milsons Point. The Pylon Lookout (page 79) is in the southeast pylon. The charge is $2 to climb up 200 stairs and get a bird's eye view of the Harbour.

Coming back from the Pylon, go down the stairs, make a right and cross the road to Gloucester St., which is the "No Through Road" in front of the Australian Hotel. Stop in for a drink and a pie in one of Sydney's oldest pubs.

Continue down Gloucester to Susannah Place, which was built in 1844 and is undergoing major renovations to transform the building into a House Museum. Walk down the steps to the right of Susannah's and turn left on Harrington St. The Harbour Rocks Hotel was created from a former warehouse and workers' cottages, which were built in 1890.

The Suez Canal is the narrow street next to the hotel. Turn right and explore the infamous alley where ruthless thugs used to hide in the shadows. Especially feared were the Orange and Green gangs. They were two opposing gangs who ruled the back streets of the Rocks during the 1870s and 1880s. The street never had an official name, but the locals nicknamed the alleyway the Suez, no doubt because of the torrents of water that flooded the streets after a heavy rain.

In the Suez Canal on the left is the Well Courtyard, which is at the back of Reynold's Cottage (1830). The original occupant, William Reynolds, was an Irish blacksmith. Recently during renovations the well was rediscovered. The inside was filled with pipes, cooking utensils, bottles, and old coins.

Leaving the Suez, turn right into Nurses Walk, which is dedicated to the convict women who served as Australia's first nurses. This is also the site of Australia's first hospital. All along the Walk are interesting old terrace homes whose walls have historical plaques attached to them which give information about the previous owners. Surgeon's Court, now filled with tourist shops, runs off Nurses Walk.

The New South Wales State Archives, 2 Globe St., is on your right as you emerge from Nurses Walk. If you want to trace your family tree (for people with relatives in Australia), you can read the documents contained in their thousands of files.

From the Archives make a left and then another left and return to George St. for the last part of the tour. At 135 George St. is a Gothic Revival sandstone building (1886) which was originally a bank. The Craft Gallery is the current occupant of 127 George St., however the Police Station was located here in 1882. Look at the top of the door to see the lion's head holding a police truncheon between its teeth. Across George St. is the Museum of Contemporary Art, which is dedicated to contemporary visual art exhibits (page 114).

Make a left onto Argyle St., pass Playfair St. and enter the Argyle Center, which incorporated the Argyle Stores (1826 to 1881) and the Cleland Stores (1914). Another option is to stroll straight up Argyle St. to Argyle Place, the oldest village square in Australia. The quaint cottages date back to 1830 and 1890.

After all this walking you may want a lemon squash and porkpie in Sydney's oldest pub, The Lord Nelson (page 126), at the corner of Argyle and Kent Streets. Otherwise, from the Argyle Center, turn left onto Playfair St. and look up to admire the Argyle Terrace (dated 1875 to 1877) at 13 to 31 Playfair St. These former workers' cottages now house shops and restaurants. Across from the Terrace is the Rocks Square which contains First Impressions, a sandstone sculpture dedicated to the settlers of Australia. Follow the stairs down to Mill Lane and make a right into the old cobblestoned Kendall Lane. The Coach House (1853 to 1854) on 2 to 4 Kendall Lane, is a sandstone building that was originally constructed to be used as a storehouse and stables. Look up to see the pulley that was used to pull supplies up from the street below.

At the end of Kendall Lane, turn left into Argyle St. and left once again to George St. At 77 to 85 George St. are five sandstone buildings known as the Unwin Stores (1843 to 1846).

This area was Sydney's original Chinatown.

Cadman's Cottage at 110 George St. was built for the crew of the Governor's boats. John Cadman later lived here, between 1827 and 1846. The Cottage is the oldest surviving house in Sydney and strangely enough, the house once fronted the beach! Everything to the east of the cottage, including all of Circular Quay West, where the passenger terminal for cruise ships now stands, was underwater.

The alternative to the whorehouse, the Sailor's Home (1864 to 1926), was located at 108 George St. and provided board and lodging for the many sailors staying in Sydney.

WATSON'S BAY WALKS

Both the walk to the South Head and Hornby Lighthouse and the Gap Bluff Walking Track start at Watson's Bay. Before starting out, you should grab some sustenance at either Doyles Restaurant/take-out or at Watson's Bay Hotel. Both places have outdoor cafe tables that line the beach and both get very crowded on summer weekends. A ferry service operates between Circular Quay and Watson's Bay on summer weekends (page 93). Otherwise, to reach Watson's Bay take Bus #324, #325 or #327 from Pitt and Alfred Streets, Circular Quay.

SOUTH HEAD. Start your walk at the eastern end of Camp Cove Beach, by making a right from the beach entrance of Watson's Bay Hotel. From this point, there are two options: either follow the rocky cliff walk or take the newer paved path. Both take you past Lady Bay (nude) beach. Climb down the steep stairs and take a look at one of Sydney's most controversial beaches. The beach itself is quite small and boring.

After Lady Bay, continue along the trail to the Hornby Lighthouse and the two keepers' cottages. The Lighthouse was built in 1853 to prevent any more ships from crashing into the Heads. At night with no lights, it was easy to mistake the rocky outcrops of both the North and South Heads for the entrance to Sydney Harbour. The Dunbar and Catherine Adamson ships misjudged the entrance in the early 1800s and were totally destroyed when they crashed onto the rocks.

If you are in Sydney on Boxing Day, December 26, make sure you head down to the South Head. This is a great vantage point to picnic and watch the start of the annual Sydney to Hobart (Tasmania) yacht race.

GAP BLUFF. Enter Gap Park through Dunbar Road, Vaucluse and follow the marked, sandstone Gap Bluff Walking Track. The short path leads directly to Gap Bluff on South Head. This is the exact point where the Dunbar crashed into the rocks. The path continues a bit further down to the Navy base, where you can stop in the Officer's Mess and have a drink.

PAINTERS' WALK

This is an easy two-hour walk through the Northern Harbour suburbs of Sydney. The walk was named after the painters, specifically Australian impressionists Tom Roberts and Arthur Streeton, who were inspired by the beautiful landscape along Sydney Harbour.

To start the walk, take a ferry or #247 bus to Taronga Park Zoo, then walk to the ferry wharf. Walk west, which is back toward the Harbour Bridge, along the track that meanders through Little Sirius Cove. From the Cove, make a left onto Curlew Camp Road, climb the steps to McLeod St. and turn right at the top of the steps.

Walk along Mosman Bay, through one of Sydney's wealthiest harbour suburbs, to the end of Cremorne Point and return to Circular Quay by ferry.

If you follow these directions in reverse order, the walk makes an interesting alternative way to reach the Taronga Park Zoo.

HERMITAGE WALK

This walk passes through the beaches of Hermitage, Foreshore, and Nielson's Park. Catch a #325 bus to Bay View Road and start your walk from the bottom of the road, near the Harbour. Walk past Hermit Point which was named after a hermit who, many years ago, lived on this spot. The Point is a prime location to drop a line and catch some fish.

Next walk to the end of the Point, through tiny Milk Beach, and into Nielson's Park. Shark nets are located off the park, so it is an ideal spot for safe swimming. Nielson's Park originally belonged to William Wentworth, the Aussie explorer, politician, and publisher. His gothic mansion, called both Greycliffe or Vaucluse House, was built in the mid-1800s and is still partially furnished. Currently the house is occupied by the NPWS, who use it as their headquarters.

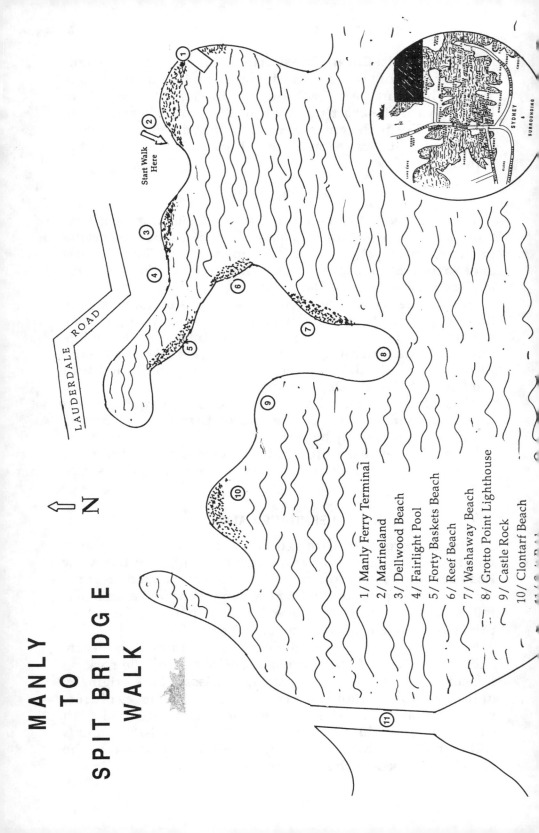

MANLY
TO
SPIT BRIDGE
WALK

N ⇐

LAUDERDALE ROAD

Start Walk Here

SYDNEY
& SURROUNDING

1/ Manly Ferry Terminal
2/ Marineland
3/ Dellwood Beach
4/ Fairlight Pool
5/ Forty Baskets Beach
6/ Reef Beach
7/ Washaway Beach
8/ Grotto Point Lighthouse
9/ Castle Rock
10/ Clontarf Beach

ASHTON PARK ON BRADLEY'S HEAD

This three-to-four-hour walk is also an alternative route to or from Taronga Park Zoo. Take a ferry or bus #247 to Taronga Park Zoo and walk east, or away from the Harbour Bridge, until you enter into Ashton Park. This is a beautiful little park, loaded with trails that can be used for running, biking, walking or even roller-blading. Along the way are little enclaves that contain forts, gun pits, cannons, tunnels and trenches that are relics from WWII.

At Bradley's Head, to the east of Ashton Park, throw out a line to catch some fish, sunbathe on a secluded beach or walk about 100 yards out to a midget lighthouse surrounded on all sides by the Harbour. The lighthouse is a good spot from which to photograph the city and Harbour Bridge, especially at sunset. Follow the trail from Bradley's Head along Taylor's Bay to Chowder Head and end your walk at the Clifton Gardens. This walk is peaceful and makes you feel as if you were miles from the city.

MANLY TO THE SPIT

A three-to-four-hour jaunt that covers almost five miles, this walk can be done all in one day or on different days, since the path is broken up into six major sections. Take a ferry or bus #182 or #184 from Wynyard to Manly. Buses stop in front of the ferry terminal. After you alight from the bus, face the Harbour and walk to your right. There is a small path that leads behind the oceanarium and has a sign indicating the start of the walk.

Along the walk you will pass Fairlight, Forty Baskets and Reef Beaches. The Reef is an unspoiled, nude beach that you can explore by taking a detour from the walkway. Back on the main road, continue your walk along Cutler Road Lookout. Between the lookout and Grotto Point are Aboriginal rock carvings that were drawn on sandstone rocks.

The next stop is Washaway Beach, which true to its name is sometimes there and sometimes not. Grotto Point, a little further, has beautiful views of the Harbour and Middle Head. The path continues to wind along the Harbour to Spit Bridge. From here you can catch bus #182 to Wynyard to get back to the city center.

CHAPTER 11:

HARBOUR, LUNCH, AND MINI-CRUISES

A visit to Sydney is not complete without a trip or two around Sydney Harbour. The traveler has a choice of touring the harbour on expensive cruises, which cost between $20 to $40, or taking advantage of the new State Transit lunch and mini-cruises. These only cost between $2.50 and $5 round trip or $12 for specials, and some of these cruises have the same itinerary as the glitzy, more expensive cruises.

Another idea is to purchase a ferry 10 Pass for $22.80 or a week-long Green Travel pass for $24 which allows unlimited bus, train and ferry rides for one week. If you purchase your ticket after 3 p.m. the week begins the next day.

LUNCH CRUISES

Bring your own lunch for a 30 to 45-minute tour of the Harbour. The $2.60 tickets can be purchased at Circular Quay and are valid for return travel on the same ferry, between 11:30 a.m. and 2:30 p.m., Monday to Friday. The lunch cruises begin at different terminals at Circular Quay and end at Darling Harbour, Mosman, and Neutral Bay returning to Circular Quay.

Tickets are sold on a round-trip only basis. You can get off and look around, but if you choose to do this your ticket is not valid for a return trip! The main purpose of these tickets is to allow tourists a cheap tour of the Harbour. If you plan to get off, buy one-way tickets. Otherwise, return trip tickets can be purchased for an additional $2.60 or so, depending on the destination.

Darling Harbour (Wharf 5). Since there is virtually no land transportation to Darling Harbour, a harbour cruise is the most enjoyable way to get there. This 45-minute cruise passes many of Sydney's historic landmarks. The cruise heads west from the

Quay, goes under the Harbour Bridge, past Pier One, the Finger Wharves of Walsh Bay, the Observatory, East Balmain, and the Aquarium before arriving at Darling Harbour.

Mosman (Wharf 4). On this 45-minute cruise, you sail past Admiralty House, Fort Denison (Pinchgut, the former prisoner island), and Old Cremorne. The cruise offers picture perfect views of the Heads out to Bradley's Head Lighthouse.

Neutral Bay (Wharf 4). On this quick ride to another wealthy area of Sydney, you pass both the Admiralty and Kirribilli Houses before arriving in Neutral Bay, the home of the Aussie Naval Submarine Fleet and the Royal Sydney Yacht Squadron.

MINI-CRUISES AND COMMUTER SERVICE

Instead of taking the train or bus, hop on a ferry for a mini-cruise to one of the seven destinations of your choice. Most trips take between 15 and 20 minutes and cost about $2.50 ($3.40 for Manly). Ferries leave Circular Quay (from different wharfs) for the various locations about every 30 minutes, with more ferries available during morning and evening rush hours (6:30 a.m. to 9 a.m. and 4:30 p.m. to 6:30 p.m.). Call 131-315 for more information on State Transit cruises.

Watson's Bay (Wharf 4). A 38-minute trip that is only available on weekends and public holidays. The ferry takes you to the famous Watson's Bay Hotel, a great place to spend the day eating seafood and sipping the occasional beer while watching the boats on the Harbour.

Manly (Wharfs 2 & 3). The Manly Jetcat and ferry both travel between Circular Quay and Manly. The ferry takes 35 minutes and costs $3.40, while the speedy, modern JetCat takes only 15 minutes and costs $4.60. Take the ferry one way (stand outside on the decks) and the JetCat the other (indoor seating only). See the description of Manly (page 73) to find out what entertainment is available. If you leave Manly after 7 p.m., only JetCats are available, but ferry prices ($3.40) are charged.

Taronga Park Zoo (Wharf 5). This cruise sails by the Royal Botanical Gardens, Fort Denison on Pinchgut Island, Farm Cove, Mrs. Macquaries Chair, and Garden Island before reaching the Zoo. If you plan to visit the Zoo, and not just take one of the local walks, then buy a Zoo Pass prior to the ferry trip. The $17 ($8.50 kids) pass includes return ferry transport, Zoo entry, bus between the zoo and ferry wharf, and unlimited aerial safari cabin rides. The pass is available at any train station or Circular Quay.

CIRCULAR QUAY FERRIES

1/ Special Excursions
2/ Hydrofoils to Manly
3/ Ferry to Manly
4/ Neutral Bay, Cremorne and Mosman
5/ Taronga Park Zoo, Balmain and Hunters Hill
6/ North Sydney and Fort Denison

WALKWAY TO OPERA HOUSE

OVERSEAS PASSENGER TERMINAL

CIRCULAR QUAY WEST

GEORGE STREET

N

Darling Harbour (Wharf 5). This is the easiest way to get directly from Circular Quay to Darling Harbour. The 15-minute trip sails under the Harbour Bridge and past the Aquarium. Get off at Darling Harbour to shop, eat or visit the Powerhouse Museum, Chinese Gardens, Aquarium or Maritime Museum.

Valencia St., Hunters Hill (Wharf 5). A 22-minute ride to one of Sydney's oldest and most elegant suburbs. If you are a lover of beautiful, old, terrace homes, don't miss this chance to explore Hunters Hill.

Elliot St., Balmain (Wharf 5). A commuter service offered during peak hours only, this 28-minute trip takes you directly to trendy Balmain. From here you can follow the walk described on page 66 which takes you past Balmain's Victorian homes, as well as the artsy sections of town.

Meadowbank (Wharf 5). At 50 minutes, this is the longest ferry ride of the lot. Ferries leave every two hours from Circular Quay, travel west under the Harbour Bridge, past Cockatoo Island Dockyard and the suburbs of Greenwich, Hunters Hill, and Drummoyne.

CRUISES

For something a bit fancier and longer, the State Transit Ferry System offers three cruises that last between one and a half to two and a half hours and cost only $14 and under. The transit ferries are basic, but comfortable.

In our opinion, these cruises are one of the best bargain deals in Sydney. Private companies offer slightly glitzier Super Cruises, but the Transit ferries are great value for money. Call Metrotips at 954-4422 or visit the Harbour booth at Jetty 4.

Harbour Cruise. A two-and-a-half hour cruise which costs only $17 (family ticket $44). This tour gives you a closeup view of the Harbour-side suburbs with their beautiful homes and the North and South Heads, which are the entrances to Sydney Harbour. Ferries leave Wharf 4 at 1 p.m. Monday to Friday and 1:30 p.m. on weekends and Public Holidays.

Harbour Lights Cruise. This is a romantic evening cruise around Sydney Harbour. Bring a light jacket, even in summer, and enjoy the night lights of downtown Sydney and her suburbs. Ferries depart Wharf 5 at 8 p.m. Monday to Saturday. The trip lasts one and a half hours and costs only $14.

River Cruise. An unusual cruise that explores an area of Sydney that few people think of visiting. Sailing westward from Circular Quay, you gradually emerge onto the Lane Cove River amid lush scenery and stately homes. The two-and-a-half hour ride is only $14 and departs from Wharf 4 at 10 a.m. daily.

SHUTTLES

A relatively new service offered by Sydney Transit and a few private companies, these shuttles travel between the tourist areas.

The privately run Darling Harbour shuttle is an O.K. bargain, although we would recommend the State Transit Darling Harbour BYO lunch cruise instead. It is cheaper and gives you a better view of the harbour.

Rocks to Circular Quay to Darling Harbour. This shuttle is offered by private companies and offers the same service as the State Transit for slightly more. The shuttles leave every 15 minutes or so and travel between the above locations. Hop on and off anywhere along the way. Tickets are $3 for the time you get on until you get off.

Jolly Boat. A pointless way to get from the Aquarium to Darling Harbour. This shuttle should be used only by people who are dying to spend their money doing silly things. The cost is $2 for the eight-minute ride that leaves whenever the ferry is full.

DARLING HARBOUR SUPER TICKET

This bargain ticket is perfect for the ultimate tourist. For $35.50 the ticket includes a two-hour Sydney cruise on a luxury catamaran, a free ride on the monorail, entry into the Sydney Aquarium and the Chinese Gardens, a 10 percent off shopping voucher valid at any Darling Harbour shop, and an Aussie BBQ at the Craig Brewery at Darling Harbour.

If you plan to visit all these places, then purchasing the ticket is a must. At the minimum, you will be saving $10 off the cost of doing these things separately. The ticket is valid for three months.

SUPER CRUISES AND PACKAGES

If you have the money to spare and want a bit more luxury or feel like riding on a tall ship or a giant catamaran, then a Super Cruise is not such a bad idea. Here is a list of some of the more interesting and better value cruises:

Captain Cook Cruises (206-1111). Coffee, lunch and dinner cruises, and a Harbour Lights and Sundowner Cruise are some of the options available with Captain Cook. The two best value cruises are: **1/** The Budget cruise which tours the Harbour for an hour and a half for only $13, and **2/** The hop on/hop off ticket for $16/$12 students/$10 children.

Matilda Cruises at Pier 26 (264-7377). A luxurious catamaran takes you on a leisurely two-hour Harbour Cruise. You can embark or disembark at three locations: the Aquarium Wharf, Campbell's Cove or the Taronga Park Zoo. This $22 cruise takes you all over the Harbour, from east to west, and includes a talk on two dozen places of interest.

Hegarty Ferries (247-2733). Tours to Fort Denison leave from Jetty 6 every day except Monday at 10 a.m., 12:15 p.m. and 2 p.m. Tickets for the one-and-a-half hour cruise are $8.50/$6.50 children. Space is limited to 50 people so call and reserve in advance.

The Richmond Riverboat (247-2979). The lunchtime jazz cruises on a harbour cruiser start at $20 for four hours of jazz, dancing, and dining on the Harbour. For those who want to explore New Orleans in Sydney, here's your chance! Cruises leave Pier 4, Walsh Bay, the Rocks at 7:30 p.m. on Fridays and 12 p.m. and 6 p.m. on Sundays. Food and drink are extra.

TALL SHIPS

For a different type of tour around Sydney Harbour, set sail on one of the tall ships, modeled after the vessels used in Captain Cook's day.

The Bounty (247-5151). An exact replica of Captain Bligh's eighteenth century sailing ship. If you are not too shy, you can even volunteer to lend the sailors a hand as they set sail down the Harbour. Cruises embark at Campbell Cove, the Rocks from Wednesdays to Sundays. Prices range from $25 for a three-hour coffee cruise, to $48 for a three-hour dinner cruise. Reservations are essential for all cruises.

Solway Lass (264-7377). Matilda Cruises also offer a tour on a 125-foot rigged topsail schooner, which was built in 1902. Four years were required to restore the yacht to its present immaculate condition, complete with 10 working sails. The Lass is luxurious and comfortable. Prices range from $22 for a two-hour afternoon sail, to $45 for a three-hour dinner cruise. Board at the Aquarium for a longer ride.

CHAPTER 12:

ART, ARCHITECTURE
AND
HISTORIC SITES

A walk through any part of Sydney is a walk back through time. Colonial sandstone and Federation-style brick buildings stand next to modern statues and fountains. Certain areas of Sydney, such as Paddington and Centennial Park, are known for their classic terrace homes, and people visit these areas just to walk around and admire the renovations. Other areas of Sydney which are less architecturally renowned also contain some remarkable buildings, fountains, and gardens.

Victorian terrace homes were the style during the earliest years of settlement. Sandstone buildings were erected around the mid-1800s. These houses are unique to Sydney. Federation buildings are easily identified by their dark bricks and were built in the early 1900's.

THE ROCKS

Start your exploration of Sydney down at the Rocks, the first permanent European settlement in Australia. You can follow the two-hour, in-depth walk as described on page 83, or you can review the history below and just visit a handful of some of the Rock's historical sights.

The Rocks were named after the rocky outcrop to the northwest of central Sydney. In the 1820s and 1830s the area was taken over by wealthy free settlers who came over from Great Britain to make their fortune. They built three-story ter- race homes along the present day Fort St.

Below the mansions of the wealthy were the slums, which soon took over all of the area that made up the lower Rocks. By the 1870s and 1880s, the neighborhood was filled with roving bands of thieves, prostitutes, drunken sailors on leave, and convicts. The bubonic plague added to the chaos. The Rocks were almost destroyed in 1900 when many streets were razed to control the Plague. It is little wonder that Queen Victoria, tired of the mess, declared Australia a self-governing nation of the Commonwealth in 1901.

Between 1920 and the early 1930s, more buildings and streets were razed in the Rocks to make room for the Harbour Bridge. The Rocks remained a poor neighborhood throughout the 1960s. At one point, in the 1960s, the entire area was almost handed over to developers, but luckily in 1970, the Government of New South Wales established an authority to conserve the historic area. Today the Rocks have been renovated, and the historical buildings have been restored.

Start the tour at the Astronomical Observatory, (241-2478) which towers above the Harbour and the Rocks. Observatory Hill is actually the highest natural point in Sydney. It is the site of the colony's first windmill, which was built in 1796. The Observatory was built in 1858 and was in active use for many years. Today, the Observatory is a museum that is open to the public daily (except Wednesday evenings). The museum houses computer games, exhibits, a telescope, and fun and educational games to play. Admission is $5/$2 children to view the night sky on Wednesday evenings. Reservations are essential.

The next stop is the Old Customs House, which was built in the 1840s. At the side of the building in Loftus St. is the area where Governor Phillip first raised the British flag, up a gum tree!

The Dutch Gable House, otherwise known as the Australasian Steam Navigation Company Headquarters, was built in 1883 on the waterfront of Circular Quay West. The central tower with its observation platform was used to sight incoming ships. The tower allowed the importers to be at the dockside in time for the ship's arrival.

The recommended Rocks tour on page 83 takes you down the tiny side streets, up the Harbour Bridge and all around the Rocks. If you have the time, the walk and historical tour is well worth following.

MACQUARIE STREET

The Main State Government buildings are located along Macquarie St. The first stop along this street is the Hyde Park Barracks (phone 223-8922). In 1810, Macquarie became the Territories' Governor after Captain Bligh was sent home during the Rum Rebellion. Governor Macquarie came in to save the day by re-establishing peace and order. He became known as the "maker of modern Sydney."

In 1817, he decided it was time that Sydney had a real prison. Until this date, convicts were turned loose at night after a day of hard labor. The Government figured the hard labor, often done in chains, would exhaust them! The resulting Hyde Park Barracks were built of red sandstone and local timber. The clock at the top of the entrance still has to be wound once a week by hand. Inside the barracks, 1,000 prisoners slept in hammocks.

Today, the Barracks are a museum which accurately depicts convict life in Sydney during the 1800s. The museum is open daily from 10 a.m. to 5 p.m., except Tuesdays when the hours are 12 p.m. to 5 p.m. Entry is $6/$4 children. During the Festival of Sydney, held every January, the Barracks are transformed into an outdoor dance club where people disco and salsa under the stars.

At the south end of Macquarie St. in Queen's Square is a Statue of Queen Victoria. Across the street is a Statue of Prince Albert, her husband. In the 1890s, Queen's Square was a gathering point for Republicans, people who wanted to split from the monarchy. They would stand on the Queen's pedestal and talk to the rowdy crowds of people. Today, Australians are actively debating Republicanism and Queen Victoria's statue may once again become a gathering point for crowds of people.

Further down Macquarie St. is the New South Wales State Parliament House. This is the oldest continuously used Parliament House in the world! The central area was built by convicts in the 1810s and at the time was the part of the Sydney Hospital that was known as the Rum Hospital. The first Parliamentary session was held in 1829. Free guided tours are available at 10 a.m., 11 a.m. and 2 p.m. weekdays when Parliament is not in session. You must reserve ahead at 230-2111.

When Parliament is in session, visitors are admitted to the Galleries during Question Time, which is Tuesdays and Wednesdays at 1:30 p.m. and Thursdays at 9:30 a.m. Aussie politicians are only slightly more polite to each other than British and are much worse than American politicians. However, most of the really nasty action takes place in sessions of the national Parliament in Canberra, the capital of Australia.

Behind the original building is a modern 14-story building

that is used by politicians and their staff. The inside of the Legislative Council, or the Upper House, is decorated in red, while the Legislative Assembly is green. Visiting hours are Monday to Friday from 10 a.m. to 3:30 p.m.

Across the street is a statue that was constructed in honor of Governor Macquarie, the creator of the Parliament Building.

Outside Sydney Hospital is the Little Boar with the shiny nose. This statue is a replica of the one in the Florence Haymarket in Italy. His nose is shiny because there is a popular myth in Sydney that if you rub the Boar's nose, your wish will come true. It's worth a try!

Behind the boar stands Sydney Hospital, which was originally a convict hospital. The patients cooked their own meals, the storerooms were morgues, cripples acted as nurses, and doctors operated in spare corners! In 1879, the original center building was destroyed and the present one was erected. The southern wing of the hospital is now the Mint Museum (217-0111). See page 114.

Stroll down Macquarie St. to the State Library of New South Wales (230-1414), which houses an amazing collection of Australian artifacts, a rare book reading room, exhibition galleries, and video links with libraries across New South Wales. In 1879, an Act of Parliament decreed that a copy of every book published and printed in New South Wales must be placed in the Library. This decree means that today there are 140 kilometers of shelves! Included in the collection are the original journals of Captain Cook and Captain Bligh's Bounty log book.

The Dixson Room contains maps, coins, and items from early life in Australia. The Mitchell Wing boasts eleven stories of information, seven stories of which are underground! The library is open from 10 a.m. to 5 p.m. Monday to Saturday, and 2 p.m. to 6 p.m. Sunday.

Outside the library is a statue of Robert Bourke, who was Governor of New South Wales from 1831 to 1847. The statue was erected in 1842 and is the oldest statue in Australia. On the Macquarie St. side of the library is a Statue of Matthew Flinders, an explorer and the first person to circumnavigate Australia.

Across from the library is a statue of Shakespeare (the library has a Shakespeare Wing). The statue was sculpted by Bertram McKennal in 1926. Surrounding Shakespeare are Falstaff, Hamlet, Portia, and Romeo and Juliet.

ROYAL BOTANICAL GARDENS

Down the road from the library is the southeast section of the Royal Botanical Gardens, which is the area known as The Domain. Sundays in the Domain are like Sundays at Speakers Corner, Hyde Park, London. In this little corner of the Gardens, people gather to lecture, listen, demonstrate, and protest. Anyone with a soapbox is welcome to speak.

A statue of Henry Lawson stands along Art Gallery Road. Erected in 1930, the statue was constructed in memory of one of Australia's greatest poet/writers. His works, written in the depression, were based on the experiences of the unemployed, homeless, and exploited.

Inside the Gardens is Governor House, built in 1838 for the Queen's Representative in New South Wales. The house is still used by the Representative and is not open to the public. In 1912, the Government of New South Wales locked out all the Queen's Representatives and opened the house as a museum. This lasted only a short time, and the house was soon returned to the State Governor.

On Bridge St. lies the Conservatorium of Music (230-1222). This is an imposing sandstone building that looks very much like a castle. The designer, Francis Greenway, modelled the building after Inverary Castle in Scotland. He wanted to impress Governor Macquarie, a Scottish expatriate. The building was used for almost a century, 1816-1913, as the Governor's stables! Tours are not allowed, but free concerts are presented every Wednesday at 1:15 p.m. from mid-February to mid-December.

To the west of the Gardens, near Macquarie St., is a statue of Governor Phillip. Surrounding Phillip are the figures of Neptune, a one-eyed cyclops, and sculptures of cereal, timber, gold, and metals. These four represent items that were important to the development of Sydney. Governor Phillips was the first Governor of Sydney (1788-1793). It was due to his strong rule that Sydney was able to survive the difficult years and start to grow.

Mrs. Macquaries' Chair is at the end of Mrs. Macquaries' Road, on the peninsula that sits to the east of the Opera House. The peninsula is surrounded by Farm Cove to the west and Woolloomooloo Bay to the east. Governor Macquaries' wife used to come down to this point to relax and watch the activity on the harbour.

The "Chair" is not really a chair, per se, but the nickname for the entire area. Today it gives an excellent view from the Harbour Bridge to Manly Beach on the North Shore. People line the shores of Mrs. Macquaries' Chair to watch Harbour activities, especially the Australia Day Ferry-a-thon.

HYDE PARK

The impressive park that is bordered by Liverpool, Elizabeth, College and James Streets is Hyde Park. A statue, a fountain, and a memorial are all located within the park. Because of the proximity to many downtown offices and apartments, the Park is a very popular spot to have lunch and enjoy the quiet in the midst of a busy city.

The impressive Anzac War Memorial (267-7668) is in the southern end of Hyde Park, at the merge of Oxford, Liverpool and College Sts., about a ten-minute walk from the statue of Queen Victoria. Built in 1934, the memorial is a continuous reminder of the sacrifices that Australian and New Zealand troops have made. The building was constructed in pink granite and stands nearly 100 feet high.

As you enter the Hall of Memory, you are confronted by the somber statue named Sacrifice. Above are more than 120,000 stars, one for every Aussie that was enlisted in World War I. On the ground floor is a permanent photo exhibit which commemorates battles, from the Sudan in 1885 to Vietnam in 1972. Every Thursday, at exactly 12:30 p.m., the army mounts a Guard of Honor, which marches from the Anzac Memorial to the Cenotaph, the memorial for the war dead, in Martin Place. The Anzac Memorial is open from 10 a.m. to 4 p.m., Monday to Saturday, and 1 p.m. to 4 p.m. Sunday.

The Archibald Fountain is in a large square in the center of Hyde Park. Built in 1933, the fountain features Apollo reigning above the mythological figures of Diana, Pan, Theseus, and the Minotaur.

To the north of Hyde Park, but still within the Park's boundaries near Park and College Streets are the small, well-kept Sandringham Gardens. These were built in memory of Kings George V and VI. Lover's Walk is located near here and the area is now lined with 200-year-old Moreton Bay Fig trees. During the early 1900's, this was a popular area for chaperoned young couples to have picnics and flirt, at arm's length of course!

A Statue of Captain James Cook stands in Hyde Park across from the Australian Museum. Captain Cook landed in Botany

Bay in 1770. He is reportedly the first white man to land on the shores of Sydney, although this claim is disputed.

DARLINGHURST

Oxford St., in Darlinghurst and Paddington, has three historic buildings: The Old Darlinghurst Prison, The Criminal Court, and The Victoria Army barracks. All three imposing structures were constructed from solid, sandstone blocks.

The Criminal Courthouse on Oxford St. at Taylor Square, Darlinghurst, was built in 1842 and is still in active use today. It is especially busy on Monday mornings, when weekend drunks have their cases heard.

If you have nothing to do on a Monday morning, head to the Public Gallery of the Courthouse for some entertainment. The stories that the lawyers or police tell are very amusing, especially when related in the cold sober light of daytime. The building was designed by Mortimer Lewis, in the Classical Greek style.

Behind the court is the Darlinghurst Prison (or as the Australians say, the "gaol," pronounced jail). It is no longer used as a prison. Instead the National Art School has made the prison its home. The walls are about 23 feet high, and they surround a five-and-a-half acre area. Over 1,000 prisoners at a time lived in this harsh prison. Blood stains can still be seen on the floors of many of the rooms, presumably from the whippings that were freely and frequently handed out to the prisoners.

Further down Oxford St. are the Victoria Army Barracks (339-3455). The Australian Armed Forces currently use the Barracks. At the stone archway entrance the guards are still changed at 10 a.m. every Tuesday from mid-February to mid-December. After the changing of the guard, the Barracks and Military Museum are open to the public.

PLACES OF WORSHIP

Sydney has a number of impressive old churches, as well as the famous Great Synagogue. Most of the places offer guided tours and services are open to all who wish to attend.

Two of the most impressive places of worship, Saint Mary's Cathedral and the Great Synagogue, line Hyde Park. Saint Mary's Cathedral (232-3788) is along College St. across from the east side of Hyde Park. The Protestant rulers actually banned Catholicism in Sydney until 1820. The cathedral was built between 1868 and 1928, and is the sixth largest cathedral in the world.

The western face of the church was modelled after Notre Dame in Paris. The central tower stretches almost 100 feet from floor to ceiling, while the two towers at the southern entrance rise 150 feet from the ground. The stained glass windows are works of art. They portray various religious scenes, except for one series of windows which depicts the history of the Church's inception. Free tours are available at 12 noon on Sundays.

The Great Synagogue towers over Elizabeth St., between Park and Market Streets, on the west side of Hyde Park. It was designed by Thomas Rowe, who used both Byzantine and Gothic styles, and was erected in 1873. The Ark, which is located at the end of the building so it can be as near as possible to Jerusalem, contains ancient, handwritten Torahs. The stars covering the ceiling symbolize the creation of the world. Free tours are available at 12 noon on Tuesdays and 1 p.m. on Thursdays.

Saint James' Church is located at the upper end, or east end, of Kings St. It was built between 1819 and 1822 and was originally intended to be a court house. The spire was added in 1824, the porches in 1834, and the semi-circular sanctuary in 1894. Beneath the Church is a crypt that was used to hold prisoners who were awaiting their trial.

Work on the oldest Church in Sydney, Saint Andrew's Cathedral, located on Sydney Square, the northwest corner of Bathurst and George Sts. (269-0642), was begun in 1819, when the foundation stone was laid. But it wasn't until 1860 that the real work began. There are 26 magnificent stained glass windows that represent religious events. On the north side is the Union Jack flag that was flown on V.J. Day in 1945 in Japan. The Church is also the home of the bodies of Edmund Blackett and his wife. Blackett, the final architect, modelled the two front towers after Saint Mary's Church in Oxford, England.

Garrison Church, Lower Fort St., the Rocks, (242-2664) was a soldier's Church at first. Work on the Church was begun in the 1840s. It wasn't completed until Edmund Blackett, architect of Saint Andrew's, came along to finish the task. The Church got its name from the Red Coat soldiers of the nearby garrison. Free tours are given daily at 8:30 a.m. and 5:30 p.m.

OTHER HISTORIC BUILDINGS

Sydney has many other historic buildings sprinkled all over the city. The following are just a sample of some of these:

The University of Sydney is Australia's oldest University. The campus incorporates both new and old buildings, but it is the Central"Uni" Building that dominates the campus. This building was another of Edmund Blackett's masterpieces. He designed Uni in a mixture of early Gothic and Tudor styles.

The Great Hall inside the main building is over 130 feet long and 45 feet wide. This is where graduations and other special events take place. It is an imposing area with rows of stained glass windows lining the Hall. The Nicholson Museum, at the southern end of the Main Square, holds a collection of ancient artifacts. The modern library and other buildings cover a huge expanse of land. The best way to see the University is just to wander around the campus, have lunch in one of the Canteens, which are open to the public, and then stop off for a swim in the pool, located in the park to the east of the Central Building.

After years of renovation, the Town Hall in George St. was officially opened by Queen Elizabeth in 1992. The foundation stone was laid by Queen Victoria's son, The Duke of Edinburgh, who was the first Royal to visit Australia. The Clock Tower, once one of the highest points in Sydney, was built in 1881. It is almost 180 feet high. The Main Hall was built in 1888 and today has seating for almost 2,300 people. The Grand Organ is one of the largest in the world. It has six keyboards and 8,672 pipes.

The Opera House is located on Bennelong Point, a former island that was situated in the Harbour and was home to an Aboriginal named Bennelong. When Bennelong was off visiting the King and being presented to the Royal Court in England, the Governor ordered the strait between the island and the mainland filled in.

The Danish architect Joern Utzon won a $10,000 prize for his design of the Opera House, which depicts Sails-Along-the-Harbour. The estimated budget in 1957 to build the Opera House was $7.2 million. In 1966, Utzon got fed up with the red tape and went back home.

The Government took over, the budget increased to $50 million (one of the ideas was to paint gold leaf on the ceilings) and by the time the Opera House was officially opened by

Queen Elizabeth in 1973, the entire cost was $102 million. The Government could ill afford the cost and held a lottery to finance the construction. Aussie gambling fever set in and the lottery was closed in 1975 when the building was paid off.

Before the Opera House began to bring in truckloads of tourist dollars, it was nicknamed the Hunchback of Bennelong Point and compared to a pack of French nuns playing football. However, everyone grew to love it. Sydneysiders, as well as tourists, pack the four performing halls and the cinema, and they even stand around the steps on weekends to watch the outdoor performances.

Tours are given daily between 9 a.m. and 4 p.m. and are expensive, about $9/$5.50 students and children. Earlier tours are the best bets because later in the day certain halls may close for performances. Call 250-1777 for information.

If you can't afford the tour, save your money for a show. The performances are mostly classical, ballet, opera, and recitals, but dramatic plays, classical guitarists, and popular folksingers can also be on the list of events. The seats are made of Australian wool, and they are designed to put you in the best acoustical position. All the performance halls were devised so that the sound does not bounce around too much, right down to the imported wood in the chairs.

The Queen Victoria Building (QVB) is located on George and Park streets, next to Town Hall, the City. The QVB took five years to build. When the mayor officially opened the Queen Victoria Market on July 21, 1898, Sydneysiders welcomed the imposing, multi-domed, baroque-style building. Unfortunately, it was downhill from there as the markets lost money year after year. The building was almost demolished. But in 1971, Mr. Barry Humphries (aka the comedienne Dame Edna) came to the rescue and wrote his "Ode to the Queen Victoria Building". The poem stirred the spirit of Sydneysiders and eventually restoration began.

The original outside facade was left intact, while inside stained glass windows, a dome, a winding staircase with wrought iron handrails, timber shop fronts, and an 18-foot-tall Royal clock were all renovated. The clock itself weighs more than one ton. The top structure features a replica of Scotland's Balmoral Castle, complete with two ramparts and two drawbridges. Beneath the castle is a copy of the four dials of Big Ben. At one minute to every hour, four heralds raise their banners and blow a fanfare of music. This is followed by a parade of six incidents in the lives of the Kings and Queens of England. Make sure you catch this incredible spectacle!

In 1986, when the building was officially reopened, it was clear that the restoration was a complete success.

HISTORIC HOUSES

The National Trust maintains more than 20 properties throughout New South Wales, which include houses, villas, bush retreats, and art galleries. The entry fee is usually about $5, which is not a bad price considering the cost to maintain these historic buildings. Many organizations in the United States offer reciprocal rights in Australia, so if you are a "Friend" to any museum or association, then find out if you can receive discount entry fees in Australia. All Trust Properties are closed on Good Friday, Christmas Day, and Mondays unless otherwise mentioned.

Elizabeth Bay House (7 Onslaw Avenue, 358-2344) was inhabited by the Colonial Secretary, Alexander Macleay, his wife Eliza, and their family. The House was designed by John Verge and is furnished in the Early Colonial Period, 1839 to 1845. It was described as one of the finest homes in the Colony. The main attraction is the sweeping staircase and oval salon with a domed ceiling. Visiting hours are 10 a.m. to 4:30 p.m., Tuesday to Sunday, closed Monday except for public holidays.

Vaucluse House (337-1957) is the home of William Wentworth, Father of the Australian Constitution. Situated on Sydney Harbour in Nielsen Park and surrounded by 27 acres of land, this was home to the Wentworth family from 1829 to 1853. The British, Gothic-style home has floor tiles from Pompeii and furniture from the Doge's Palace in Vienna. Stop in for a Devonshire tea. Free tours are also available or buy the little 50 cent booklet on your way in. The House is open from 10 a.m. to 4:30 p.m., Tuesday to Sunday and admission is $5. Bus #325 will get you there.

Elizabeth Farm (635-9488) is located on the outskirts of Sydney. To get there take a 45 minute train ride to Granville and then the Delwood Coach Bus #96 to 70 Alice St., Granville. The construction of the farm was begun in 1793, and is a fine example of Colonial architecture. Some of the first experiments in merino wool production took place here. John and Elizabeth MacArthur were the original owners and the farmhouse still contains their beds and paintings. A well-kept garden dating from the 1830s surrounds the house, which is open 10 a.m. to 4:30 p.m., Tuesday to Sunday. If you plan to visit both Elizabeth Farm and Old Government House, you can purchase a combination entrance ticket.

Old Government House (635-8149) is just a short walk from Parramatta train station. The House was originally used as the country home by the Governors of New South Wales. Now, it is a museum that is furnished in pre-1850 Australian style. The collection includes original, colonial furniture and Governor Macquaries' bedroom, dressing room, and breakfast room furniture. The House is open only from 10 a.m. to 4:30 p.m. Tuesday to Thursday, and 11 a.m. to 4 p.m. on Sundays and Public Holidays.

Experiment Farm was built on the first land grant in Australia. In 1789, the land was offered by Governor Phillip as a reward to convict James Ruse. The Colonial, Georgian style house is a museum that depicts the colony's early farming days. The farm is located at 70 Alice St., Granville only a ten minute walk from Parramatta Station. Visiting hours are from 10 a.m. to 4 p.m. Tuesday to Thursday and 11 a.m. to 4 p.m. Sundays and Public Holidays.

Rose Seidler House is one of the National Trust's more modern buildings. It was built between 1948 and 1950, by Harry Seidler. A modernist style house, with glass walls, minimalist color schemes and postwar furniture, it has a beautiful view of Ku-ring-gai Chase National Park. The House, which is located at 70 Clissold Road, is open only on Sundays from 10 a.m. to 4:30 p.m. or by special appointment by calling 989-8020. The best way to get to the House is to go by car.

The National Trust Center and S.H. Ervin Gallery is located on Observatory Hill (near Watson Road). The buildings were constructed during Governor Macquaries' term of office. Dating back to 1815, they were originally a military hospital. From 1850 to 1974, the buildings were converted to the Fort Street School, which was a government institution.

The S.H. Ervin Gallery has a permanent art exhibit on Australia and Australian themes. The shops are open 9:30 a.m. to 4:30 p.m. Tuesday to Friday, and the Gallery opens from 11 a.m. to 5 p.m. On Saturday, Sunday, and Public Holidays the shop and Gallery are open from 2 p.m. to 5 p.m.

DARLING HARBOUR

1/ Powerhouse Museum
2/ Car Park
3/ Entertainment Centre
4/ Monorail Station
5/ Exhibition Centre
6/ Tumbalong Park
7/ Chinese Gardens
8/ Monorail Station

9/ Aquarium and Ferry Wharf
10/ Maritime Museum
11/ Market Place Shopping
12/ Convention Centre
13/ Water Canal
14/ T Shirt Shops
15/ James Craig Museum

COCKLE BAY

MONORAIL ROUTE

MONORAIL

SUSSEX STREET

PYRMONT STREET

HARBOUR STREET

DIXON ROAD

N

CHAPTER 13:

MUSEUMS

From the Aquarium to the WestPac Museum, Sydney is chock-a-block full of museums, galleries, and historical buildings. Almost all tourist brochures direct you to the popular and tourist-infested Powerhouse Museum, but very few people are familiar with the smaller, almost hidden museums.

Sydney's museums range from the old (the Australia Museum built in 1827) to the new (the Museum of Contemporary Art built in 1991), from the hands on (Earth Exchange) to the eyes-only (the Art Gallery of NSW), and from the museum for train lovers (Toy & Railway Museum), to the ones for car fanatics (Australian Motor Museum) and tennis fans (the Australian Tennis Museum).

With so many to choose from, one, two or ten are bound to suit your fancy. It's best to just pick out a handful and spend at least two hours or more exploring each of the large museums and an hour or so in each of the smaller ones.

Many museums offer discounts on certain days of the week or in the evenings. Student identification, such as an International Student Identity card or a University ID card, gets you in at the concession rate (usually half price) in most museums. If a discount isn't posted, make sure you ask anyway.

DARLING HARBOUR

Home of the tourist museums. The largest concentration of museums in Sydney is in the vicinity of Darling Harbour. A train ride to Town Hall and a short walk or a ferry ride from Circular Quay will bring you to four major museums:

THE SYDNEY AQUARIUM, Pier 26, Darling Harbour, 262-2300. The Aquarium has two oceanariums with plexiglass windows and an automatic walkway. Above your head, tiger, nurse and hammerhead sharks and manta rays circle menacingly. Most of the fish believe the plexiglass is the bottom of the sea, so if you look up you may see a ray or shark lying on what they believe is the ocean bottom. What a sight! This is the place to go to conquer your fear of sharks, but not immediately before a visit to the beach!

Different exhibits feature a touching pool, saltwater crocodiles, reef fish, harbour seals, and lots of other water creatures. Open from 9:30 a.m. to 9 p.m. daily, admission is $13.50 per person/$6.50 children.

SYDNEY MARITIME MUSEUM, Darling Harbour, 552-7777. From Aboriginal canoes to beach life in the 1950s to the America's Cup exhibit, the Maritime Museum presents a comprehensive tour of Sydney's maritime past. On the water is a fleet of historic vessels, warships, yachts and more. Go on a free "Vampire Tour" offered between 11 a.m. and 3 p.m. daily or just take a picture next to the warship.

The inside of the museum is packed with audiovisual displays, free computer games (Can you get from Australia to America by ship, loaded down with merchandise, and make a profit?), wandering minstrels, tours, and exhibitions. During school holidays special classes and tours are featured, and they are open to everyone. Pick up a program guide to find out what's on. Admission is $7 /$4.50 students /$3.50 children and the museum is open 10 a.m. to 5 p.m., daily except Christmas Day.

If you'll be in town for a while, you can volunteer to work in the museum (552-7777). Another option is to become a member and enjoy discounts and special privileges.

POWERHOUSE MUSEUM, 500 Harris St., Ultimo, 217-0111. A short walk from Darling Harbour, or from the Haymarket monorail, the Powerhouse is one of the most entertaining museums in Sydney. Until 1963 the building was the Ultimo Power Station. The building was closed for a while, then restored and opened to the public as a museum in 1988. To see all the exhibits make sure you have plenty of time, and pick up a guide. Without this you may get lost in the maze!

The museum is divided into sections: Creativity & Australian Achievement, Technology & People, Everyday Life in Australia, Decorative Arts, and Bringing People Together. Exhibits have games to play, things to touch, and tests to take. Talks, films, performances and demos are also featured. The museum is open 10 a.m. to 5 p.m. daily, except Christmas Day and Good Friday. Admission is $5/$2 concessions and free on the first Saturday of every month. A free tour of the museum is offered every day at 1:30 p.m. or for $3 you can rent a taped tour.

AUSTRALIA MOTOR MUSEUM, 320 Harris St., Pyrmont, 552-3375. The newest addition to the Darling Harbour group, the Motor Museum opened in March, 1992. Located on three levels of a car park, the museum has over 120 exotic and rare cars, as well as lots of memorabilia.

The oldest car is a Garner Serporlet, which is steampowered and was built in 1900. The youngest is a 1988 Mercedes Benz 190 race car. The rarest car, only five were built, is a Haines and Grut built in 1901. The most expensive is a Mercedes Benz Super Charged 38 250 Super Special, built in 1920 and valued at $3 million.

The funniest exhibit has chickens and ducks walking around an old Hudson, because the car was parked in a chicken coop for many years! If you are a car lover, you will spend hours here. Admission is $7 and the museum is open daily from 10 a.m. to 5 p.m.

THE ROCKS

Sydney's oldest and youngest museums are in this historical area. Most of these are featured in the Rock's self-guided walk. Many of the museums are also popular stops on the tourist circuit; however, if you are a history buff, it is worth wading through tourists to visit the museums.

WESTPAC MUSEUM, 6 to 8 Playfair St., 251-1419. The Bank of New South Wales, now known as WestPac, was the first bank in Australia. It was founded in 1817. The museum is a tour through the history of Sydney's banking community.

COLONIAL HOUSE MUSEUM, 53 Lower Fort St., 247-6008. Call for an appointment before you visit. Colonial House is actually a period museum furnished in the 19th century style. The photo exhibit of the Rocks dates back to 1880. Entry is $1/$.50 children.

CADMAN'S COTTAGE, 110 George St. Built in 1816, this is the oldest house in Sydney. Before Circular Quay West was created by filling in the Harbour, the cottage was prime beachfront property and the arches to the south housed boats. The National Parks and Wildlife Service now uses the cottage as a bookshop and information center. The downstairs historical display center is open from 9 a.m. to 4 p.m. daily.

THE EARTH EXCHANGE, 18 Hickson Road, 251-2422. The Exchange was formerly the Geological and Mining Museum. There is so much to do here: track minerals through to final products, be shaken by an earthquake, experience Aboriginal Dreamtime, discover gold, pick up a fossicker's license, and take a journey though the formation of the earth's crust. Until recently admission was free, but now it costs $7/$5 concession. Open from 10 a.m. to 5 p.m., daily except Christmas Day and Good Friday.

MUSEUM OF CONTEMPORARY ARTS, 132 George St., 252-4033. Set in an art deco style building, Australia's first major museum for international contemporary visual art was opened in 1991. Hours are 11 a.m. to 6 p.m. and entry is $6/$4 concession.

OTHER MUSEUMS IN TOWN

The rest of Sydney's museums are sprinkled all around the city and the suburbs.

THE MINT MUSEUM, Macquarie St., the City, 217-0333. The walls of the museum are three feet thick. Originally, coins were minted here, but now it is a museum with exhibits on the history of Australian money. Open to the public daily (except Wednesdays), from 10 a.m. to 5 p.m. Entry is $4/$2 children.

THE AUSTRALIAN MUSEUM, 6 College St., opposite Hyde Park, in the City, 339-8111. The original, smaller museum, which was founded in 1827, is located within the present day, much larger museum. The earliest works were kept in Parliament House and transferred to the present museum in 1849.

The museum is divided into three levels: Aboriginal Australia, Papua New Guinea and Australian Mammals. The funkiest exhibit, the "skeletons", is a room full of human and animal skeletons. These include a 55-foot-long sperm whale and a human skeleton sitting on a rocking chair with his pet dog Fido's skeleton at his "feet." Very spooky, especially with the audio effects. Talks, videos, performances, special events and guided tours are all available. An Indonesian gamelan orchestra plays twice a week.

Admission is $5/$1.50 concession, half-price every Saturday and after 4 p.m. free. Opening Hours are from 10 a.m. to 5 p.m., Tuesday through Sunday and 12 noon to 5 p.m. on Monday. Closed Christmas Day and Good Friday.

ART GALLERY OF NEW SOUTH WALES, Art Gallery Road, the Domain, 225-1700. The building was begun in 1885, but the facade was not completed until the 1900's. Sixty years later the gallery was extended to incorporate the Australian and international exhibits.

The museum is divided into: English Art, Old Masters, Australian Art, Second Hall with Australian Modern Art, Tribal Galleries, European 20th Century Art, and Australian 20th Century Art. There is no admission fee, except to major international exhibits. Free tours are also offered at 1, 2 and 3 p.m. on weekends, 1 p.m. and 2 p.m. on Monday, and 11 a.m., 12 noon, 1 p.m. and 2 p.m. on Tuesdays through Fridays. Open Monday to Saturday from 10 a.m. to 5 p.m. and Sunday 12 noon to 5 p.m.

MACLEAY MUSEUM, University of Sydney, Parramatta Road, top floor of the Macleay Building, 692-2274. The museum has a 40,000-strong, historic photo exhibit, which has pictures of Sydney and New South Wales dating back to 1850; a large selection of natural history artifacts; and an anthropological display of mammals, reptiles and marsupials. Don't forget to see the exotic insect collection which has some insects from the voyages of Captain Cook and Charles Darwin! The hands-on section has quizzes, slide shows, and displays. Open weekdays from 8 a.m. to 4:30 p.m., with free admission. To get there take bus #438 from the city or take a train to Central Station and walk for about a mile.

SYDNEY TEXTILE MUSEUM, 172 St. John's Road, Glebe, 692-0723. The museum was renovated and recently re-opened. It houses a large selection of textiles from all around the world. Open Wednesday to Friday, 1 p.m. to 6 p.m. and Saturday Noon to 4 p.m. Closed Christmas Day and public holidays. Admission is free.

CHILDREN'S TREASURE HOUSE MUSEUM, 19 to 25 Beeson St., Leichhardt, 560-2044. From Lewisham train station the museum is only a 15-minute walk away. It was developed as an offshoot to a toy manufacturing company. The dolls and toys date to the 1800s.

The museum has a theater and ship, bear and doll rooms. Children of all ages love the hands-on setup, the dressing-up area full of old costumes and clothes, and the reading area filled with favorite childhood storybooks. Open 10 a.m. to 4 p.m., Monday to Friday. Closed the last week in December and all of January. There is a minimal entrance fee.

AUSTRALIAN MUSEUM OF CHILDHOOD, Juniper Hall, 248 Oxford St., Paddington. The National Trust owns this building that was originally built in 1824 from the profits of gin.

Robert Cooper lived and fathered 24 children in this house! During the 1800s the building was used as a child welfare institution. Today the house is filled with childhood exhibits that date back to the early 1800s. It is open daily from 10 a.m. to 4 p.m. Admission is $4.

THE AUSTRALIAN TENNIS MUSEUM, 30 Alma St., Paddington, 360-9290. Professional tennis is a very popular sport in Australia and many international professional tennis stars come from Australia. A large collection of tennis memorabilia, especially Australian Tennis items, are housed here. Tennis films are shown. Open daily 11 a.m. to 4 p.m.

JEWISH MUSEUM, Corner Darlinghurst Road and Burton St., 360-7999. This small museum covers Jewish history. It is open from 10 a.m. to 4 p.m. Monday to Thursday, 10 a.m. to 2 p.m. Friday, and 12 noon to 5 p.m. Sunday. Admission is $5/$2 children.

JUSTICE AND POLICE MUSEUM, 2 to 8 Phillip St., The City, 252-1144. The building, built in 1856, was formerly the Water Police Station and Court House. It has been restored and opened to the public. The museum houses an impressive display of the history of the police force in New South Wales, complete with uniforms, truncheons, and other artifacts.

OUT-OF-TOWN MUSEUMS

TRAMWAY MUSEUM, Corner of Pitt St. and Princes Hwy., Loftus, 542-3646. Take a train to Loftus station. The museum is only a short walk away, near the Royal National Park. The museum was created after 1961, when the trams stopped operating in Sydney. The original trams and a collection of old government buses are located here.

You can even catch a ride on the Sydney Electric Tram. The ride takes 15 minutes down a half-mile track. The museum is open Wednesdays, Sundays and Public Holidays and costs $6/$3 for concessions.

NEW SOUTH WALES TRANSPORT MUSEUM, Barbour Road, Thirlmere, 046-81-8001. The museum has five acres of covered exhibits, 50 locomotives, 100 carriages, and a small exhibits museum. You can ride on a steam train or charter one (744-9999) for special occasions. The museum is open 10 a.m. to 3 p.m. Monday to Friday and 9 a.m. to 5 p.m. weekends. Admission costs $5.

TOY AND RAILWAY MUSEUM, 36 Olympic Park, Leura, 047-84-1169. The museum is located in Leuralia, an art-deco mansion which is a memorial museum to Doc Evatt the former Australian Labor Party leader in the 1940s. The museum is open 10 a.m. to 5 p.m. Wednesday to Sunday. Gordon Falls Reserve, part of the Blue Mountains National Park, is nearby.

LA PEROUSE MUSEUM, Anzac Parade, La Perouse, Botany Bay. Take Bus #394 from Circular Quay or #393 from Central Station to get to LaPerouse. The museum commemorates the voyage of La Perouse, the French explorer who arrived in 1788 in Botany Bay with two ships, both of which were later wrecked in the Solomon Islands.

The museum has relics, rare maps, drawings, and navigational instruments. The rooms are divided into different portions of the trip, from the planning of the expedition to the search for the ships until the remains were discovered. The museum is open 10 a.m. to 4 p.m. daily. Admission is only $2/$1 children.

AUSSIE YOUTH PUB CRAWL

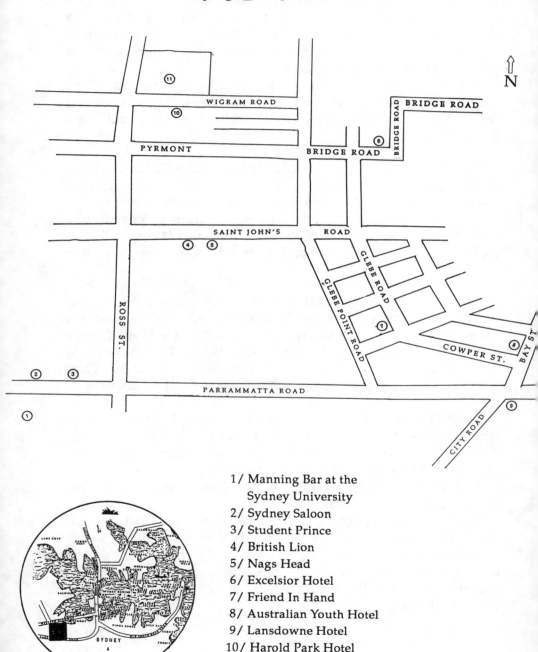

1/ Manning Bar at the
   Sydney University
2/ Sydney Saloon
3/ Student Prince
4/ British Lion
5/ Nags Head
6/ Excelsior Hotel
7/ Friend In Hand
8/ Australian Youth Hotel
9/ Lansdowne Hotel
10/ Harold Park Hotel
11/ Harold Park
    Trotting Track

CHAPTER 14:

NIGHTLIFE:
CLUBS, PUBS,
RSLs, MOVIES,
THEATERS

CLUBS

Sydney's nightclub scene is fast, funky and hot! Each club has its own style, dress, and attitude, so if you want to fit in, you need to follow certain rules. Different clubs have different nights to promote certain groups or music. Each night has its own dress code. For example, "Ragamuffin Hip-Hop" nights require comfortable, hang-loose clothes to match the reggae-style music, whereas "Soul-Funk" nights necessitate designer clothes (Gaultier is a safe bet), but jeans (Levi's or a Thai imitation Levi) and a white t-shirt can also pass—depending on your tan and muscles.

Most clubs don't get moving until midnight or 1 a.m., some don't even open until 11 p.m. If you arrive early, you let everyone know that you are not a club regular, but you do avoid lines.

To prepare yourself for a night clubbing in Sydney, read 3D World or The Drum. Both are free newspapers about the club scene and are available at trendy cafes and record stores. The 3D section Who's Who and what they are wearing is a must read for those who want to match the latest club attire.

The main club scene is centered on Oxford St., Darlinghurst, although there are some other clubs located at the Cross and in North Sydney. Listed here are some of the more popular clubs. Most of the clubs have an entry fee of $5 to $10, unless you have a special membership card. To get these, you have to know the right people. On special nights, as in Ladies Night or Gay Night, the entrance fee is reduced.

KINSELAS, 383 Bourke St., Taylor Square, Darlinghurst, 331-6200. Formerly a funeral parlor, Kinselas is a three story club that appeals to almost anyone. Downstairs is a casual pub (no entry fee) that is used by the ordinary masses for drinking and playing pool. The third floor has live, in vogue bands and comedians, while the middle bar is for members only—those people who have a special key ring or know someone. Even the second and third floor dress scene is pretty casual, with a lot of lycra bike shorts and tight tops. The preferred color of dress is anything black, but jeans and white t-shirts fit in fine. Entry upstairs is around $10.

DCM, 33 Oxford St., Darlinghurst, 267-7380. Once strictly a gay/lesbian bar, Don't Cry Mama now has a mixture of all types. This is the place to go to watch serious exhibition dancing. Anything tight and black fits in. Entry ranges from free to $7.

THE FREEZER, 11 Oxford St., Paddington, 332-2568. Very loud, very crowded (even with two levels), and very hip. This is where the Aussie stars go when they are in town (as in Michael Hutchence from INXS). Popular on Friday and Saturday nights. Expect a line, all the favorites and stars get in first, and if the bouncer doesn't like the way you look, forget about it!

THE CAULDRON, 207 Darlinghurst Road, Darlinghurst. Where the beautiful people go to see and be seen. Popular with corporate executives and their young dates and slick Eurotrash. A membership badge allows for free entry without any wait. Both sexes sport lots of gold jewelry, while women wear tight dresses and the men trousers or even suits—as long as you don't look like you have just come from the office.

ROGUES, 16 Oxford St., Darlinghurst, 332-1718. Depending on the night it can either be a young, private school crowd or a Mediterranean, gold-chained, suited crowd. Membership badges provide VIP treatment.

METROPOLIS, 99 Waller St., North Sydney, 954-3599. If you're 20 or over, you're definitely Over The Hill for this club. This is a place to get hot-n-sweaty and dance, dance, dance! Wear sneakers and shorts or the heat will make you melt.

Metropolis has membership for its special night, LUNACY, which more than lives up to its name. Free entry on Monday and Wednesday. The rest of the week is $10. Closed Sundays.

STUDEBAKERS, 33 Bayswater Road, Kings Cross, 358-5656. A new entrant to the club scene, complete with a Studebaker in the front window. The strict dress code (trousers or a suit for men; dresses, skirts or dress trousers for women) is rigidly enforced. This means no jeans, t-shirts, shorts or ripped clothes. If you are a single male or a pack-male, then look very respectable or you may not get in. Single men after 9 p.m. have a very tough time getting admitted. Expect long lines and preferential treatment for regulars and the right look. The place is very much like a club in the U.S. and plays a lot of Madonna and funk/ disco/ rap music. Entry ranges from $5 to $10.

THE EXCHANGE/THE VAULT, 34 Oxford St., Darlinghurst. More of a pub than a club (this means free entrance), but its two popular dance floors and great music give it a club atmosphere (this means expensive drinks). Formerly a gay pub, the crowd is now crossover, both gay and straight. Dress is casual, the music loud, and the dancing fast and furious.

THE TAXI CLUB, 40 Flinders St., Darlinghurst. The late night club to go to after clubbing. You'll see it all here, black tie, transvestites, old pensioners playing the slots, and the trendy crowd. No dancing, but a great place to relax over a capuccino, and a shot of Zambuca after a night on the town.

PUBS

A book on Sydney would not be complete without a section on pubs. Actually a whole book could be devoted to Sydney pubs! The Aussie lifestyle still centers around pubs, thanks in part to their British heritage and in part to Aussie mateship (Good on ya, mate). Before you go to a pub read page 51 to make sure that you know all the rules on shouting, ordering, and tipping.

Until the 1950s, Australia's "blue" laws outdid even the most fanatical American laws. Pubs had to close at 6 p.m. Since most people had to work until 5 p.m., the pubs became a madhouse for the last hour. Pub owners didn't mind, because people drank as much in one hour as they otherwise would all night! In the early 1960s the laws were relaxed and pubs were permitted to stay open until 10 p.m. Currently, after another change in law, pubs can be open until midnight (for a hotel license) or later if the bar has a special license (usually entertainment is provided at these pubs). Under special licenses, pubs can even stay open 24 hours a day. As a general rule, hotel pubs close at midnight and others at 3 a.m.

Pool and darts are two popular pub sports, although pool is the more popular. Pool competitions (comps) are offered by many pubs, especially hotel pubs, usually from Mondays to Thursdays. Comps are cheap to enter, about $5, and the prizes range from $80 on up, depending on the number of people in the competition. Pool comps tend to attract a lot of regulars, although competitions with the higher prizes can attract pool hustlers. Most of the time, though, people are just there to play pool and to have a good time. Comps usually start around 7 p.m. so get to the pub early and don't drink too much before playing.

Below is a list of some of the pubs that provide fun, entertainment, and great beer. The best way to sample Sydney pubs is to stop in as many as possible for a middy of beer (about half a pint) or a lemon, lime, and bitters, which is a thirst quenching drink for those who are not drinking alcohol. At the end of this section is a detailed pub crawl, which visits about a dozen pubs.

PUBS WITH LIVE ENTERTAINMENT

Live entertainment is usually offered on Thursday to Saturday nights. Most of the entertainment is local bands, although even popular, professional bands still play in small, local pubs to keep themselves close to the Australian public. If you are not familiar with the band that is playing, call up the pub and ask what type of music they play. Guitar-thrashing bands are very popular in Sydney. Remember, some publicans (people who own pubs) still believe the louder the music, the more people the music attracts! If a band is playing expect a cover charge, ranging from $3 to about $10.

HAROLD PARK HOTEL, 115 Wigram Road, Glebe, 692-0564. There is always something happening at the Harold Park. Monday and Friday nights, after 9 p.m., is "Comics in the Park" ($5 entry), where stand-up comedians amuse the crowd. Tuesday night's "Writers in the Park" ($7) presents readings by contemporary writers. Wednesday nights are Improvisation

Nights ($5) with comedy improvisation. Anyone can get up and tell a joke or two, even you! Every week on Thursdays "Actors in the Park" ($9) presents a play, with a new one shown every month. "Politics in the Pub," a satirical comedy show, is the free early Friday night entertainment. Saturdays and Sundays feature live bands. The Harold Park charges $6 to $10 cover charge; for the quality of their entertainment this price is a good value.

The front bar is free to everyone and it's a great place to play pool and listen to the music from the back bar. The crowd here is blue collar and student mix. A schooner (about 3/4 of a pint) costs $2.30. Pool comps are Wednesdays at 7:30 p.m. and Sundays at 4 p.m. Happy Hour is from 5 p.m. to 6 p.m. and schooners are reduced to $1.50. If you're hungry, stop in at Harold's Bar & Grill. The grill has a Happy Hour from 8 p.m. to 9 p.m. Monday to Friday, when cocktails are two for one.

THE ROSE, SHAMROCK & THISTLE, 193 Evans St., Rozelle, 555-7755. There are two pubs of the same name, but only the one in Rozelle is affectionately nicknamed the "Three Weeds". This is a large pub (space for 400 people), which provides ample room for the great bands that the pub attracts. A schooner costs $2.20. Live entertainment is presented Thursdays through Sundays and the cover ranges from $3 to $20. The Male-Bonding-Crowd is the dominant group, especially during Tuesday night Pool Comps. Thursdays and Fridays, the most popular nights, attract a few more females.

If you go to the restaurant for a meal, you don't have to pay to get in to hear the bands. The restaurant has inexpensive pasta, cheap beer, and you are guaranteed a good seat for the shows.

MARLBORO HOTEL, 145 King St., Newtown, 519-1222. A medium-sized pub situated in the heart of Newtown, the Marlboro has a small stage for the bands that play popular, not guitar thrashing music. They also have a restaurant out back that serves pasta for about $6 to $10. Live entertainment plays on Thursdays to Sundays until 1 a.m. The bar gets very crowded on weekends, so get there about an hour before the entertainment starts. Wednesday is Karaoke night. Schooners range from $2 to $2.50 and the crowd is a mix of students and locals.

THE BRIDGE HOTEL, Victoria Road, Rozelle (corner of Wellington). The Bridge Hotel is a pub which attracts professional, alternative-style bands, such as Gondwanaland (who played the music for the movie Mad Max) and other bands who have moved up from the local pub scene. The dress code is very casual, mainly Levi's or anything black, t-shirts especially. Entry is a bit pricier than elsewhere $8 to $15, depending on the bands, but it's generally worth it. The main acts usually don't start until midnight, after a local band has played, and the music goes until 3 a.m.

HENRY THE IX, 259 Pitt St., 266-0610. A good place for after-work drinks. A small English style pub with Guinness on tap and dart boards in the back. Folk or classical rock bands play Tuesdays to Saturdays, later in the evening after the bulk of the Happy Hour crowd leaves (6:30 to 7:30 p.m. 1/2 price drinks, Tuesday to Thursdays $2.50 for a pint of Guinness, and Mondays 7 p.m. to Midnight low price drinks). Mondays and Saturdays (Karaoke) are the busiest nights. The pub closes at midnight.

HOTEL PUBS

Most Aussie hotel bars are small, mellow places where the local mates go to drink schooners and play a little pool or darts. Every neighborhood has its own local pub. The following is a list of typical hotel bars that have live bands, entertainment, and usually an active, late night crowd. Unless you are going in the dance club part of Hotel bars, the dress is very casual.

COOGEE BAY HOTEL/SELINAS, 253 Coogee Bay Road, Coogee, 665-0000. Located directly opposite Coogee beach, the Hotel offers a choice of five bars, pool hall, three restaurants, a disco, and DJs or live bands. The sports bar has nine pool tables, videos, air hockey, and TAB (Off Track Betting). Pool comps are held on Monday nights. A schooner costs $2.50 to $2.75. One man bands play on Friday and Saturday nights from 8 p.m. to Midnight. The crowd in the bar is mainly young. The beer garden is open on weekends from Noon to 5 p.m. The garden bar attracts locals and business people during the day and the nightclub crowd in the evenings. Every night one of the bars has Happy Hour from 6:30 to 7:30, and another bar holds the "Toss The Boss" drinking game. If you win, you get a free drink. Selinas Night Club, which holds 3000 people, attracts top local and international groups who perform live Friday and Saturday nights. Tickets cost about $20, a can of beer $3.50, but from 8 p.m. to 10 p.m. drinks are only $1. (the bands start after 10 p.m.). If you want to do some heavy dancing, arrive early to get a good spot up front. The back area is quieter.

HOTEL BONDI, 178 Campbell Parade, Bondi Beach. Hotel Bondi has every type of entertainment available for the beach bum. Located across the street from Bondi Beach, the Hotel has six bars and 25 pool tables. The Lounge Bar is decorated in art deco style and serves cold beer and ale on tap. The 1920s is a cocktail bar that attracts a mixture of tourists and locals. The City to Surf Bar (also an annual running race that finishes outside the Hotel) has slot machines and free bacon, egg and tomato breakfasts from 8 a.m. to 9:30 a.m. every day.

The Beach Club Disco is the nightclub part of the Hotel Bondi. On Mondays to Thursdays between 7 and 9 p.m. movies are shown. Tuesday is karaoke night. Wednesday is the 31 club, with a $5 cover and $1 drinks, Thursday has a $2 cover, and Sundays have a $7 cover, but English DJs and Club Africana are featured.

The Players Room has six pool tables. The Champions Bar only has four pool tables and attracts a young blue collar crowd. The upstairs pool hall has 15 tables. Pool comps are held once a week, usually Mondays, and the entrance fee is $5.

AUSTRALIA YOUTH HOTEL, 63 Bay St., Glebe. This hotel, built in 1867, is more of a typical Aussie Hotel bar that gets a regular student crowd mixed with some tourists. Fridays are the big nights and the crowd usually ranges in age from 19 to 31. The beer patio has schooners for $2.20 and pitchers for $8. The restaurant at the back serves hearty meals, while up front people relax at small tables or play the pokies. The "100 percent Aussie Youth" t-shirts make great souvenirs.

AUSSIE PUBS

If you want to meet Aussies of all ages, but want more excitement than what is offered in the local hotel bars, head down to the following pubs. Aussie pubs are very similar to British pubs in that people of all ages tend to mix in the same pub.

FRIEND IN HAND, 58 Cowper St., Glebe, 660-2326. Although this has been voted the "Best Tourist Pub in Sydney", Aussies far outnumber tourists. It's a fun and lively pub that has lots of entertainment and promotions that keep the pub interesting: crab racing (that's hermit, not people), free wine or champagne for the ladies, Happy Hours, etc. Plus the pub is loaded with pokies and has a TAB (Off Track Betting) service.

Attached to the pub is No Names Restaurant 2, the more refined version of No Names 1 (page 57). Upstairs from the pub is a coffee, wine and dessert bar.

THE OAKS, 118 Military Road, Neutral Bay, 953-5515. Consisting of four bars and a beer garden, this huge pub is probably the most famous on the North Shore. A schooner of beer costs about $2.50. Thursday nights are the big nights here, when the youngish crowd comes out.

The large bar at the front is situated next to the indoor barbecue. Order a piece of raw meat and the chef cooks it up right in front of you. The beer garden towards the back surrounds an oak tree that was planted in 1939. From the garden walk up into the John Million bar, and then continue into the Governor's bar, a pub for the older generations.

Finally, walk into the Palace bar, which has an open fire and two television sets. The Palace is popular among the English tourists who sit around the tvs and yell about soccer.

THE HERO OF WATERLOO, 81 Lower Fort St., Millers Point, 252-4553. Built from sandstone that was brought from the Argyle Cut in 1843, the Hero of Waterloo is an Aussie pub in every sense of the word, from the beer ($2.75 a schooner) to the music (old time and folk) to the people (Ocker Aussies to the Max!).

On Saturdays and Sundays from 2:30 p.m. to 7 p.m. the old-time bands play and the crowd is middle age and up. Then folk music is played from 7:30 p.m. to close (11:30 p.m.) and a younger crowd strolls in to join in the fun. The pub has Guinness and Bass, as well as a number of other beers on tap, and 50 types of bottled beer. Don't forget to see the Cellar Museum, full of memorabilia from colonial days.

THE LORD NELSON, 19 Kent St., The Rocks, 250-4044. The Lord Nelson was built in 1841 and is the oldest continuously operating pub in Sydney. The Lord Nelson has a bar, restaurant, accommodations ($60 per double room), a wood-burning stove, and a brewery with glass windows so you can watch the boutique beer being made. The staff is very friendly and is willing to explain the brewing process to you.

Early Thursday and Friday nights are the big nights for city workers, and later in the evening a younger crowd comes in to buy pints of beer ($4.50). The decor is a history lesson on Sydney, with artifacts, memorabilia, and newspaper clippings from 1805.

PUBS WITH LIVE JAZZ

Sydney has a handful of pubs that are either dedicated to jazz playing or sponsor special jazz nights. Don't be surprised if a jazz "Great" suddenly jumps on the stage to join in the fun. Many of these pubs are well known worldwide.

REAL ALE CAFE AND TAVERN, 66 King St., City, 262-3277. This underground tavern is probably the best known jazz spot in Sydney. Live music is played almost every night. The cover depends on the entertainment, and ranges from $5 to $20. Diners must pay the cover charge as well. The guests have a choice of 183 different types of bottled beer as well as pints of draft ($5), daiquiris ($7), and more. The cafe is open 8:30 p.m. to 1 a.m. Wednesdays and Thursdays. On Fridays and Saturdays two bands play and Real Ale stays open until 3 a.m.

SOUP PLUS, 383 George St., City, 297-728. If you can't live without jazz, then you'll be happy to know that this restaurant has jazz bands six nights a week. The weekday cover is only $5 and the show starts at 7:30 p.m. On weekends, the cover is slightly higher and the entertainment varies: Western Swing Arm during the day and Jazz at night. There is no entertainment on Sundays.

STRAWBERRY HILLS HOTEL, 453 Elizabeth St., Surry Hills, 698-2997. The music here is very hit or miss. If you hit a good night, it can be amazing. This classic jazz venue has a small, crowded, smoky room, with a stage that is not much higher than the floor.

Go to the hotel if you want to listen to music, but don't bother to try to talk, the noise is too loud!

PUBS WITH DJ'S / AMERICAN - STYLE BARS

If you are not much into the pub scene, which means sitting around a bar stool, being mellow, and drinking a lot, then the solution is to go to one of the following pubs. They offer entertainment, good dance music, and great free Happy Hour Food. The bartenders work hard for their money, make incredible cocktails, and deserve a tip.

BOBBY MCGEES, Darling Harbour, southern end of shopping complex (nearest the Chinese Gardens), 281-3944. This is our personal favorite. The Happy Hour between 5 p.m. and 8 p.m. offers delicious and abundant food, but get there early before all the white collar office workers shovel down the grub! Every night has a different theme, and Bobby McGees tends to be crowded all night long. There is no draft beer, and bottles start at $4, unless it is Happy Hour and then beer is half price.

The DJs make you feel as if you were at a college fraternity party where they teach the Aussie crowd how to dance to Hawaii Five O and other American dances. Every night games are played and prizes are offered. If you win enough McGee Money you can qualify to win suspenders, hats, t-shirts, and more. The dress code is strictly no shorts, unless you come in for dinner or before 5 p.m. This is a bit of a nuisance during Sydney's hot summer months.

Cover is charged on weekends and ranges in price, from $10 and up depending on the entertainment. Don't be surprised if they ask for $15 or more. On these special nights, they usually serve huge buffets for free.

JAMES CRAIG BREWERY, Darling Harbour, northern end of shopping complex (across from the James Craig Ship). Another great Happy Hour place, but louder and more casual than Bobby McGees. The crowd is young and single and the dress is jeans with anything. Pints of draft beer cost $4. There is a cover after 7 p.m., unless you are having dinner, specifically the $6.90 barbecue dinner. Beware, the salad and potato cost extra, but nobody tells you this! The Craig is very busy on Sundays when people gather to play pool, shoot darts, and dance to live entertainment.

PUMPHOUSE, Darling Harbour, extreme southern end near the Entertainment Center, 299-1841. A fully restored pumping station (hence the name), this pub has been restored as a tavern and mini-brewery. Tours of the brewery are available on Mondays to Fridays at 11 a.m. or 2 p.m. and by appointment.

The downstairs bar is for eating or sampling their boutique beers (pricey at $4.50 to $6.50 a pint). The Thunder Club is held on Friday nights from 6 p.m. to closing. A $10 glass (that you keep) of beer gives you a free refill of Thunderbolt (8 percent alcohol) or Brewer's Draught. Upstairs is a night spot for dancing. Live entertainment is showcased on Fridays to Sundays from 10:30 p.m. to 2 a.m. and Sundays from 2:30 p.m. to 5 p.m. Both the upstairs and downstairs crowd can get very touristy.

IRISH PUBS

The Irish make up a large percentage of the population of Sydney. Quite a few pubs have been created to cater to this crowd. Go in any of the following and you may feel as if you were in Ireland! These pubs are for serious drinkers only, who like to weep into their Guinness while they listen and sing along to Irish ballads.

THE MERCANTILE, 25 George St., the Rocks. This Irish pub is known for its lively Saint Patrick's Day celebrations, but it's also a good weekend pub, even on Sundays. The inside gets too hot and crowded, so people usually spill out into the surrounding streets. Irish bands play on Wednesdays and Sundays from 7:30 p.m. Schooners of beer cost $2.50 and Guinness costs $2.75.

KITTY O'SHEAS, Oxford St., Paddington. The pub is located just across the street from the church where the Paddington Village Bazaar is held every Saturday, so it gets pretty crowded on Saturday afternoons and evenings. The crowd ranges in age from 25 to 40 and the dress is casual, but neat. Schooners cost $2.50 to $3, depending on whether the entertainment is playing. Live music is featured every night.

HONEST IRISHMAN, Parramatta Road, corner of Booth St., Glebe. Known as "the Home from Home for Sydney's Irish." This is a late night pub (open until 4 a.m. or sometimes 5 a.m.), and the place where most people (or at least the Irish) go after the Mercantile closes. Food and live entertainment are available, but most of the people stand outside on the sidewalk spinning yarns until the wee hours of the morning.

PUB CRAWL

If you don't have much time to spend in Sydney, and you want to visit as many pubs as possible, there's always the Pub Crawl. Even if you are spending a long time in Sydney, you are bound to get caught up in a crawl or two.

There are many types of crawls. Occasionally RSLs have some or you can join up with Aussies who have their own favorites, or design your own!

Remember Aussie beer has an alcohol content of 5 percent or as high as 9 percent for boutique beers. You may want to alternate schooners with middies or have light beer (Tooheys 2.2 percent or Swan Light 0.9 percent). A light beer means low alcohol, not low in calories. Or have a non-alcoholic beer, a lemon squash or a lemon, lime and bitters, just to make sure you're not crawling, at least not until the last pub is in sight.

Described below is one of our favorite crawls. Some of the pubs have already been described in detail above, others are as reported below. Cheers, Mates!

The Aussie Youth Crawl

This pub crawl takes you through pubs that attract a young, student crowd (19-30). The dress is casual, jeans and t-shirts, and don't forget to bring extra money for pool, food, the pokies, and a taxi home at the end of the night.

Start the crawl at the University of Sydney's bars. There are three: Wentworth, Manning, and the Grandstand. Pick up a couple of Aussie students to show you the way. An offer of free beer usually helps.

Exit "Uni" via Parramatta Road and head over to the Sydney Saloon, 92 to 94 Parramatta Road. The Saloon is a big playhouse with video games, pokies, pinball and a "Jack Daniels' Old Number 7 Pool Hall." Live country music is on Sunday afternoons, Wednesday is Karaoke, Thursday is Carnival and a cover from $2 to $5, and live bands on Friday and Saturday nights; cover varies.

A few doors down is The Student Prince, 82 Parrammatta Road. Because of it's location close to the "Uni," the Student Prince attracts a young crowd. Here you have a choice of either drinking in the dark back bar, reminiscent of a small German Beer Hall, or dancing in the disco to 70s music (not much of a choice really!). Head toward the city and make a left onto Ross St., a right onto Saint John's Road, and enter The British Lion,

178 St. John's Road. This is a well-lit, casual bar which serves free food at 6 p.m. and has live jazz bands from Thursday to Sundays. The Lion serves boutique beer, try the Dogsbolter (9 percent alcohol).

Make a right out of the pub and go down a few buildings, until you reach the next stop, The Nag's Head, 162 St. John's Road. Although it advertises itself as "The Posh Pub" (see the writing above the entrance), it still gets its fill of backpackers and students. The Nags Head has a small, public bar, a lounge bar with a grand piano, and a quieter drinking room toward the back. Wednesdays to Saturdays feature live entertainment and occasionally a Billy Joel-type character on the grand piano.

Your next stop is about a 15-minute walk away. From Nag's Head, make a right and follow St. John's Road toward the City, then a left on Glebe Point Road and a right at the next traffic light onto Pyrmont Bridge Road. Further down on your left, on the corner of Pyrmont Bridge Road and Bridge Road is the Excelsior (101 Bridge Road). If you haven't eaten dinner yet, the fare here is filling and cheap. You can eat in the restaurant or at the bar. Try the buffalo, which is farmed in Queensland.

Wednesday night is the big night at the Excelsior, with free champagne between 7:30 p.m. and 9 p.m. Trivia Night is on Tuesdays, Karaoke Wednesdays, half price cocktails Thursdays, and Happy Hour Fridays. Small bands usually play at 8 p.m. on Thursdays through Saturdays.

Walk carefully out the door and beware of the blind corner as you make your way to the next stop. Cross the road and walk back toward Glebe Point Road until you reach Gottenham St. Follow this street across St. John's Road, where it becomes Glebe St. At the intersection of Glebe and Cowper streets, look straight ahead and you are at your next stop, The Friend In Hand, 58 Cowper St. If you still haven't eaten, either forget about it, or stop at No Names (attached to the pub) for a huge portion of spaghetti for $5.50. (See page 57).

When leaving, make a right onto Glebe St. and walk down to Bay St. A right onto Bay takes you to the Australian Youth Hotel, 63 Bay St. Make sure you get here before midnight when the pub closes. Relax a bit in this quieter pub (See page 57) before heading off to the next, noisier stop. From the hotel, make a right and walk back towards Parramatta Road on Bay St., at Parramatta Road cross over to the Landsdowne Hotel, 2 to 6 City Road (corner of Parramatta Road) and follow the music. If you are staying in the hotel above ($11 per person, per night), you might as well stay and party here until the loud and alternative bands finally stop playing.

You have just made a circle from City Road and back again and have covered 11 pubs! Along the way are just as many more. If you have the strength and endurance, then modify this tour to suit your tastes. The Landsdowne is probably the best ending point because it is open the latest and the music can guide you home.

RETIRED SERVICEMEN LEAGUES (RSL)
AND LEAGUES CLUBS

RSLs and Rugby League Clubs are private clubs that serve beer and meals at a discount and operate pokies. Since these clubs are nonprofit, all the money that is made has to be put back into the club. Some of the clubs have movie theaters, discos, and large snooker and game rooms. Most facilities are free to members, and guests only pay a nominal amount.

Some of the larger RSLs, such as St. George and South Sydney Junior, have large auditoriums and feature extravagant entertainment and Broadway style productions. Clubs are open 10 a.m. to midnight Sunday to Thursday and until 1 a.m. Friday and Saturday.

Although RSLs were actually started for servicemen, membership is now open to everyone. The same goes for Leagues' clubs. The profits from these clubs go into the rugby league team of the same name.

If you are a tourist, "No Worries, Mate!", you can become an honorary member for the day or even for your whole stay in Australia.

All RSLs require that you stand and give two minutes silence in memory of the fallen soldiers. At 6 p.m. the lights dim, heads are bowed, and silence prevails.

When travelling, especially in boring Bush towns, RSLs are the best places to go for entertainment, to eat a hearty, filling, hot meal for only $6 to $7, and to drink schooners of beer for $1.50 to $2.

Most of the clubs tend to have the same facilities, although some are larger than others. Below are two popular clubs.

PANTHERS LEAGUE/WORLD OF ENTERTAINMENT, Mulgoa Road, Penrith 1800-024-911. A massive complex with a hotel, two restaurants, a disco, and a venue for live entertainment. Start by playing some of the games available outside: aqua golf, clay pigeon shooting, cable skiing, golf or tennis. Next, have a break for dinner: salad, bread, drink, lamb chops, potatoes, and two vegetables for under $8.

After dinner, head over to the pokies or sit at the bar and play Keno. Later, enjoy the cocktail bar, night club or live entertainment at The Reactor. Entry to Panthers is free, but the outside entertainment and live entertainment does cost.

Dress is casual for dinner and the pokies, but dress up for evening entertainment. Panthers is an interesting place to go to see the difference in dress, manner, and accent between the "Westies" and Sydneysiders.

BALMAIN LEAGUES, 138 Victoria Road, Rozelle, 555-1650. The orange-and-black colors of the Balmain rugby team are worn here by the loyal supporters. Balmain has cheap meals, movies, live entertainment, pokies, and a night club. The atmosphere is casual, jeans, and t-shirts, but wear neat jeans and a shirt with a collar for the nightclub or evening entertainment.

MOVIE THEATERS

Movie theaters that show the latest releases are abundant in Sydney. Unfortunately, tickets for a first run movie cost around $12 at downtown theaters, and around $9 to $12 in the suburbs. Luckily, Monday and Tuesday nights are cheap nights and tickets cost only $5.50 to $6.50.

Another option, with certain theaters, is to purchase a pack of four or more tickets at a reduced price. You can split the tickets among your friends, or use them on different nights.

These tickets need to be purchased at least one day before you go to the movies. Read the Special Entertainment Section of the Sydney Morning Herald on Friday for time schedules and movie reviews.

A handful of movie theaters offer alternative, foreign, old, second-run, and/or artsy films. The Valhalla is the best known of these, but the Mandolin, Dendy and the Australian Film Institute are other popular, alternative movie venues.

ALTERNATIVE THEATERS

VALHALLA, 166 Glebe Point Road, Glebe, 660-8050. Tickets are regularly $9 or $7 with an International Student Identity Card (ISIC) or you can purchase a special pass for $20, which has four fully-transferable tickets. These tickets cannot be used on the day of purchase.

Weekends are the best time to see a movie and take advantage of the discounted prices. The Saturday matinee is only $6, which includes a drink and a cookie. At noon on Sundays, special interest films, ranging from Jung to sex, are shown for $6. Sunday evening is two for one double feature night.

After the movie, stop in at the Craven Cafe next door. The service is slow, the place a bit of a dive, but they serve good, strong coffee. Take a look at the modern and abstract paintings that decorate the walls. They're for sale!

AUSTRALIAN FILM INSTITUTE (AFI), Town Hall, Oxford and Oatley Streets, Paddington, 361-5398. The AFI features Australian and International experimental films. Tickets are a bit pricey, $10, but most movies shown at the AFI are not shown elsewhere.

MANDOLIN CINEMA, 150 Elizabeth St., the City, 267-1968. The Mandolin shows mainly off-beat and alternative films as well as a lot of music and concert films. Monday and Tuesday nights are the cheap nights; tickets are only $6.

THE DENDY, Martin Place, the City, 233-8166. This small, cozy theater used to show only porno flicks. Now it shows artsy, alternative, and occasionally a more mainstream film. Tuesday night is cheap night, only $6 for a ticket.

MAINSTREAM THEATERS: Along George St., between Goulburn and Bathurst Streets are three huge cinema complexes: HOYTS (267-9877), GREATER UNION (267-8666), and the VILLAGE CITY (2641694). Each has about seven screens. Tickets cost about $12, except on Tuesdays when tickets are only $6.50. Hoyts is the largest of the three, with a McDonald's, Baskin Robbins, bar, restaurant, candy shop, videogames, and about 15 televisions showing upcoming movie previews.

The Inner City has many smaller theaters. STANMORE TWIN, on Parramatta Road, Stanmore, is probably the largest theater.

In Cremorne, the ORPHEUM on Military Road is a famous art deco theater that shows both alternative and first run movies. It's worth seeing a movie here, just to look at the architecture.

THEATERS

Sydney does not have a theater district, such as New York's Broadway, but it does have a wide variety of theaters sprinkled around Sydney.

The following theaters specialize in both fringe and mainstream shows. Theater restaurants are also a popular alternative, although many of these are geared toward tourists and Sydneysiders usually shy away from them.

THE SEYMOUR CENTER (City Road, corner of Cleveland St., Chippendale 692-3511) is one of the most popular mainstream theaters, while the BELVOIR STREET and the WHARF theaters have outstanding "Off Broadway" style productions and even modern dance recitals.

Since ticket prices can be quite expensive, take advantage of some of the lesser priced options. Half Price Tix, a small ticket booth located in the middle of Martin Place, between Elizabeth and Castlereagh Streets, sells half price tickets (plus commission) for that evening's performance. Tickets are available from noon to 6 p.m. Half Price also sells bargain tickets for other attractions, including cruises and Explorer passes.

Otherwise, look in the Sydney Morning Herald under theater listings. Special priced tickets are available for matinees, previews, and last week performances. Students, with valid identification, usually can get cheap tickets. The smaller, alternative theaters normally cost much less, only $15 to $25 for tickets.

OFF BROADWAY STYLE

BELVOIR STREET THEATER, 25 Belvoir St., Surry Hills, 699-3444. The Belvoir has two small theaters that are decorated inside in solid black. Funny, alternative, and political satire shows are presented. They occasionally attract big name actors, writers, and producers. Tickets are $15 to $20.

THE WHARF AND WHARF STUDIO, Pier 4, Hickson Road, The Rocks, 250-1777. Home to the Sydney Theater Company, Sydney's top mainstream theater group. The Wharf Studio shows alternative productions and modern dance recitals, while the Wharf presents mainstream productions. Tickets are $27 to $37.

ENSEMBLE THEATER, 78 MacDougall St., Milsons Point, 929-0644. The oldest running professional theater in Sydney is located just over the Harbour Bridge. It is housed in an old boat shed and has a waterfront restaurant and bar. Special preview price tickets are available. Most productions are alternative, or artsy and dance shows. Tickets start at $21.

BAY STREET THEATER, 75 Bay St., Glebe 692-0977. Alternative, comedy shows, and experimental theater are featured here. The theater is housed in a converted church.

NATIONAL INSTITUTE OF DRAMATIC ARTS (NIDA), 215 Anzac Parade, Kensington, 697-7600. The productions are presented by third year students, many of whom go on to bigger and better theaters.

ABORIGINAL AND ISLANDER DANCE THEATRE. Contemporary Aboriginal dance is performed in a variety of venues. Phone 660-2312 for more information.

COMEDY

COMEDY STORE, 278 Cleveland St., Surry Hills, 319-5731. Unlike Melbourne, Sydney has only one major comedy revue. Besides the Comedy Store, only the Harold Park Hotel has a regular comedy night (page 122).

The dinner shows at the Store on Wednesdays and Thursdays cost $20, while the show itself is only $5. The Friday and Saturday Talent Night shows vary in entrance fees.

CHAPTER 15:

SHOPPING

Sydney is not the place to go to increase your wardrobe. Prices for clothes are high: Levi 501s cost $100, Reeboks $100 to $200, and name-brand, imported clothes are about twice as expensive as the U.S. However, depending on where you look, you'll find many locally-made Aussie clothes selling at bargain prices.

As an alternative to shopping in pricey department stores, you can shop in the suburban indoor malls, the off-price shops in Redfern, or in local markets, if you need t-shirts, dresses, and casual wear. Local specialties and Made-in-Australia clothes, such as Driza-Bones (Australian bush coats) and Bush or Akubra hats are bargains.

Most shopping takes place in malls, but these are not the same as American malls. The term mall usually refers to a pedestrian shopping street. Most of the stores have awnings so that you can shop rain or shine. Once you get out into the sub- urbs, you will find real malls filled with department stores, specialty shops, restaurants, and usually hot bread shops, a butcher, a health food shop, and a supermarket.

Sydney shopping hours are convenient for the traveler and the people who work in the shops, but not so for the average, employed Sydneysider. Most stores are open 9 a.m. to 5:30 p.m., Monday to Saturday and are closed on Sunday. More and more stores are starting to open later and on Sundays, especial- ly in the tourist areas, such as Bondi, Kings Cross, and Darling Harbour. On Thursdays stores stay open until 8 p.m. or 9 p.m. for late night shopping. Try not to shop during this time unless you have to because the stores get very crowded.

On a humorous note, up to a few years ago only stores that sold food were able to open on Sundays. An enterprising owner of a furniture store wanted to sell his wares on Sundays. So, he offered a special: $1,000 to $2,000 for a pound of carrots and he threw in a couch and two chairs for free!

Sydney stores have horrendous return policies. Although by

law they must offer either your money back or an exchange, some stores still refuse to do this. The larger stores and chain stores, such as Targets, Dymocks, and Sussans, allow returns with your money back, but most stores only allow exchanges. At all times you must have your receipt, or forget it!

Instead of concentrating on the common touristy areas to shop, check out the stores listed below by neighborhood to purchase trendy, unique, and less expensive clothes. A description of some of Sydney's markets is also included.

Specialist and alternative bookstores are also discussed in this section, as are camping supply stores.

NEIGHBORHOOD SHOPPING

OXFORD ST., PADDINGTON. A place to shop if you like boutique stores, cafes, and street sellers. Weekends can get very crowded, especially Saturdays when the Paddington Village Bazaar is open. In this neighborhood it isn't unusual to see a Volkswagen parked next to a Mercedes.

The Croissant Show, Hot Gossip, and Cafe Paddington are small cafes where you can sip capuccinos, eat wholesome sandwiches and salads, and have the best croissants in Sydney. Cafe Paddington also has a deli/bakery where you can buy cheese, pate, bread, salads, meats, and anything else required for a picnic in Centennial Park, which is just down the road. They will even make you up a picnic basket, if you are too lazy to do it yourself!

If you want to purchase clothes for the club scene (page 119), stop in at "Dotti's", where the women's clothes are short, sexy, fun, and not overpriced. Most of the other clothes stores are trendy and a bit pricey, but window shopping is a must. On the other side of the road, next to the Church market is the Hattery. Since the sun gets so hot in Sydney, hats are a major fashion statement. The Argentinean owner makes her own hats, from floppy fabric to summer rattan. Prices range from $15 to $80.

Further down Oxford St., toward Darlinghurst and the City, the clothes stores get very funky, especially during the Gay and Lesbian Mardi Gras season. Most of the stores cater to a Gay crowd, and the styles are always up-to-the-minute.

KING'S ST., NEWTOWN. The stores here match the locals: funky, ethnic, and down to earth. Prices here tend to be lower than in Paddington and the City, mainly because there are

many second-hand book and record stores and second hand
and inexpensive ethnic clothes stores.

Drop in at the "Greed Sisters Emporium", and see their
selection of weird gift items and sexy greeting cards. Or, look
into one of the dozen stores that sell Indonesian, Indian or
Asian clothes and accessories.

If you need a book or two while travelling, Newtown has
more than half a dozen second hand book stores, including
Goulds, the immense new and secondhand bookstore. You
have to see Goulds to believe it! They are not computerized
and have little rhyme or reason to their bookshelves. Plan to
get lost here for at least an hour.

King St. is also full of health food stores, cafes, and restaurants, as well as family-owned fruit and vegetable shops
(that seem to be perpetually open), butcher stores, and hot
bread shops.

REDFERN. Previously a poor, inner city neighborhood, Redfern is gradually changing. New restaurants and pubs are
opening, while Regent and Redfern Streets have become the
center for shops selling seconds, samples, irregulars, discount
designer clothes, and originals.

Mambo, a popular Australian brand name of t-shirts and
beach wear, Stussy, Reggae style clothes, Billabong (a popular
Aussie t-shirt brand name which means "watering hole" in
Aboriginal), and JAG are sold at a discount at many of the
stores. This is also one of the few areas where stores are open
on Sundays.

DARLINGHURST ROAD, KINGS CROSS. An adults-only
shopping area, except for the tourist shops on street level.
Climb a flight or two of stairs or descend into a basement and
you will enter the "World Of Kings Cross," where all the
magazines, books, videos, and live shows are located. Some of
the bookstores charge as much as a $2 "looker's fee." The
stores are not as raunchy as New York's 42nd St., although the
live shows are!

The stores at the Cross are open Sundays and stay open all
week until about Midnight. It's a good place to get the Sunday
paper late Saturday night! The Boomerang School (page 80), located near the Cross at 138 Williams St., sells the least expensive boomerangs in town. The tourist shops along Darlinghurst
Road sell items ranging from kangaroo scrotum bags and skins

to aboriginal style earrings, t-shirts, and stuffed wombats, kangaroos and koalas.

The Cross also has a good selection of restaurants and pubs, including the American favorite Tony Roma's Ribs and the Aussie OZ Rock. Both New Zealand and Haagen-Dazs Ice Cream shops are on Darlinghurst Road.

END OF PITT ST., NEAR CENTRAL STATION. The Pitt Street Mall is a huge pedestrian shopping plaza filled with both locals and tourists. Toward Central Station, however, is a Pitt Street few people know about. The street is packed with secondhand record, book, CD and tape stores, along with the odd "Adults only" shop. The secondhand stores will purchase or exchange books, CDs, and tapes.

CHATSWOOD. Located north of the Harbour, Chatswood is the suburbanite's mall Heaven! Take a train to Chatswood, five stops north of the city, and immediately outside is a pedestrian mall, while two other major malls are only a short walk away. Westfield Plaza is the largest of the two, while Chatswood Chase has some expensive stores on the upstairs floor. If you are in the former, check out the Harley Davidson shop with an incredible Harley in the front window.

THE QUEEN VICTORIA BUILDING (QVB). George and Park streets, next to Town Hall, the City. These two areas are the main shopping centers for tourists and city shoppers. The metro level and ground floor shops are somewhat affordable, with stores such as Just Jeans, Portmans, and the Ink Spot, while the top floor is carpeted and geared towards wealthier shoppers. If you are in town at Christmas, stop by the QVB to see their enormous, distinctively decorated Christmas Tree.

PITT STREET MALL. Pitt St., between Market and King streets, the City. This is a pedestrian walkway mall lined with stores and shopping arcades. Centrepoint is the largest arcade and boasts the Sydney Tower as well. The Tower is overpriced at $8 entry, but the view is superb. The top shopping level is carpeted and contains David Jones, the expensive British, Harrod's-style department store that sells any item you might require to pamper yourself.

The Strand Arcade has been open since 1892 and is the oldest arcade in Sydney. The shops are small, quaint, and expensive. The Imperial Arcade has over 100 shops that sell all types of fashions. All along Pitt Street are shops that sell clothes for the nightclubber (Dotti's) or the officeworker (Country Road).

INDIVIDUAL STORES

Although it's more fun to shop in neighborhoods to get the full flavor of the shops and people, there are a few local stores that definitely deserve a mention because of their Aussie style.

AUSTRALIANA

GOWINGS, corner of George and Market Streets, the City. This Sydney institution has a sign above the door that proclaims "Walk Through, No One Asked To Buy". Gowings is a mellow store that looks like an old Sears, Roebuck and Company and sells all of the basics: underwear, socks, flannels, jeans, shirts. This is the shop where visitors from the Bush to the "Big City" used to go to get their clothes, because the items were of good quality and priced right. Nowadays, Gowings has become a bit more modern and sells rugby shirts, jeans, and t-shirts.

The store also stocks traditional Bush supplies for Jackaroos (cowboys), Jillaroos (cowgirls), and farmers: Akubras, Squatterhats, Drizabones, and moleskin pants. For those of you unfamiliar with these items, a Drizabone is an oilskin jacket (either long or short) that was developed to keep horse riders dry while they rode in the pouring rain. Special leg slits, sleeve snaps, and protective flaps are all part of the design. These cost $200 to $400 (U.S.) in the U.S., while they can be bought in Gowings for $60 to $100 (U.S. dollar equivalent).

Akubras are the hats (made of rabbit skin) that are used by everybody to the west of Sydney. Australian golfer Greg Norman is never seen in public without one. The Squatter's hats are worn by all the farmers in Australia (see them at the Easter Show).

OZFURS, on Bourke St. at the corner of Foveux St. A bit pricey, but when they have sales you can get cheap "UGG" Boots, sheepskin gloves, hats, coats, wool sweaters, and more. They have a factory at the back so they have loads of samples and seconds at cheap prices. As the story goes, UGG boots were created by a surfie whose feet got cold after surfing. He wrapped his feet in sheepskin and sewed a pair of soles to the bottom. His friends all said, "Oh, what 'UG'ly boots!" And the name stuck!

THE STRAND HATTERY, the Strand Arcade, Pitt Street Mall, the City, 231-6884. A bit pricier than Paddington, but the service and the wide range and quality of hats make this store a gem. The Hattery will form fit your hat to your head by steaming and stretching and help you pick out the proper feather to wear in the brim.

THE AUSTRALIAN WINE CENTER, 1 Alfred St., in Goldfields House behind Circular Quay, 247-2755. Over 100 different varieties of wine from all over Australia are available here. Try a cabernet, merlot or one of the other fabulous varieties of red or white wines! Open Monday to Saturday 9:30 a.m. to 6 p.m. and 10 a.m. to 4 p.m. There are occasional tastings on Friday and Saturday.

ABORIGINAL ARTIFACTS

While you're in Sydney, you should definitely pick up some Aboriginal items. If you are planning to travel to Alice Springs or Darwin, you may want to wait until you get there to make your purchases, because prices will probably be cheaper. The prices in Sydney are a bit more expensive and the stores more touristy, but there is a wide range of items to choose from. Below is a brief description of Aboriginal items you might want to look for, as well as a dictionary of commonly used terms. Following that are a number of Aboriginal galleries and shops. We have included the stores that I felt have either the best value for money, the widest variety, or that buy directly from Aboriginal artists.

Term Dictionary

DIDJERIDOO - A musical instrument made from hollowed tree trunks. In order to play these you must master circular breathing, taking air in through your nose and out through your mouth at the same time.

BULL ROARERS - These are used to call men to tribal ceremonies. Made from an oval length of wood with a hole in one end to which long strands of human hair are attached, the

Bull Roarers are swung above a man's head. They then emit a spooky, roaring sound that is supposed to scare off both evil spirits and women. A great idea for male bonding nights!

CLAP STICKS - Musical instruments that are beaten together during "Corroborees" to produce a rhythmic beat.

BARK PAINTINGS - Only select Aboriginals from certain tribes can paint, using a feather or twig brush, their special "Dreamtime" drawings onto sheets of prepared bark.

BOOMERANG - Boomerang throwing is the world's oldest sport. Aboriginal cave drawings, dating back 18,000 years ago, document the use of the boomerang. The returning boomerang was rare, as most were used for hunting game. The Aboriginals did not call them boomerangs. This term was introduced by the British in 1820, and came from a similar sounding Aboriginal word.

CORROBOREES - A men-only sacred tribal ceremony which featured talks, dancing, and music. Bull roarers and clap sticks are also used during the ceremonies.

DREAMTIME - The very distant past when the land was formed and huge mythical beasts wandered the plains.

KOORIE - The term used in New South Wales to refer to Aboriginals, who prefer to be called this instead of "Abo," which carries a negative connotation.

ABORIGINAL ITEMS

THE BUSH CHURCH AID SHOP, 37 York St., the City, 262-5017. Arts and crafts and other items made by Aboriginals from communities all over Australia.

HOGARTH GALLERIES, 7 Walker Lane, Paddington, 357-6839. An Aboriginal and Tribal Art Center that displays artifacts from different Aboriginal communities. Open Tuesday to Saturday 11 a.m. to 5 p.m.

COO-EE ABORIGINAL ART GALLERY, 98 Oxford St., Paddington, 331-4477. The gallery specializes in limited editions prints by Aboriginal artists. Open Monday to Saturday, 10 a.m.

to 6 p.m. and Sundays 1 p.m. to 5 p.m.

ABORIGINAL ART GALLERY, Level 1, Argyle Center, the Rocks, 247-1380, and 7A Liverpool St., Paddington. The galleries have beautiful and expensive bark painting, didjeridoos, statues, and other artifacts. Open 9:30 a.m. to 5:30 p.m., seven days a week.

ABORIGINAL AND TRIBAL ART CENTER, First Floor, 117 George St., the Rocks, 247-9025. Expensive bark paintings, posters, and huge fishing nets.

BOOKSTORES

Alternative and specialized book stores abound in Sydney. Unfortunately, new books in Australia are incredibly expensive. The best place to purchase an ordinary fiction book is in one of the many secondhand shops in Newtown or at Goulds Bookstore. However, the following stores sell specialized books that are rarely available in secondhand stores. For more specialized books you may want to consult "The Bookshops of Sydney," which is a guide to all the bookstores in Sydney and the surrounding suburbs.

TRAVEL BOOK STORE, 20 Bridge St., the City, 2413554. The best thing about this store is that you can trade or sell your old travel guides. A 10 percent discount is offered to Youth Hostel Association (YHA) cardholders. They have books on everything you need to know about anywhere in the world.

REX MAP CENTERS, 42 Castlereigh St. (corner of Martin Place), 235-3017. Stop in here before you head outside of Sydney to pick up your maps and travel books.

LANGUAGE BOOK CENTER, 131 York St., the City. Located behind the Queen Victoria Building. This is where to shop if you want to learn to speak any exotic, or even ordinary, languages.

BUDDHIST INFORMATION CENTER, 20 Victoria St., Lewisham. Open Tuesdays, Saturdays, and Sundays from 2 p.m. to 5 p.m. only. This is a library and resource center run by Chi Kwang, one of the only two Buddhist nuns in Australia.

GALAXY BOOKSHOP, 222 Clarence St., the City, 267-7222. This bookshop carries books on science fiction, fantasy, and horror.

SYDNEY ESOTERIC BOOKSHOP AND CENTRE, 475 Elizabeth St., Surry Hills, 319-4224. Thousands of rare, out of print, and hard-to-get books sit next to New Age music and audio tapes, CD's, videos, tarot cards, crystals, and more.

LIFEFORCE BOOKS AND GIFTS, 253 Oxford St., Bondi Junction, 369-1009. Over 2,000 books on self help, body work, metaphysical sciences, and mysticism are sold along with crystals, essential oils, and jewelry.

FEMINIST BOOKSHOP, 59 Orange Grove Plaza, Balmain Road, Lilyfield, 810-2666. Books and information on, about, and by women. The bookshop also coordinates a women's library.

AUTOMOTO BOOKS, 154 to 156 Clarence St., 299-2248. Everything you need to know about motoring and aviation. Try this bookstore before you go to the Australian Motor Museum or for the handbook on your recently purchased Aussie car.

BOAT BOOKS, 31 Albany St., Crows Nest, 439-1133. Hundreds of books on everything that moves in the water, from canoeing to maxi-class yachting.

NATIONAL PARKS SHOP, Cadmans Cottage, 110 George St., the Rocks, 247-8861. This shop has all the information on Sydney's national parks, including maps, hikes, and bushwalks. It's located in the oldest house in Sydney (page 88).

SYDNEY BOOK EXCHANGE, 16 Goulburn St., the City, 267-9656 and GEORGE STREET BOOK EXCHANGE at 601 George St., the City, 261-2360. Both places make it cheap to buy a book or two to travel with by accepting exchanges and selling cheap secondhand books.

DYMOCKS, 424 George St., the City, 224-0411. Neither specialist nor an alternative bookstore, Dymocks deserves a mention because it has a massive selection of new books: fiction, nonfiction, language, travel, study aids, and more. Dymocks also has one of the best return policies in Sydney.

CLOSING DOWN SHOPS

Located all over the City, these stores are perpetually popping up around town and then closing down. A Pommie with a cockney accent is usually standing outside yelling into a microphone while advertising the bargains.

These stores are not a bad place to go for inexpensive t-shirts, stuffed animals, sweatshirts, and other Australian novelties, as well as a lot of junk. The prices here are cheaper than at the Cross.

FOR THE KIDS (OR THE KID IN YOU)

THE ROCKS PUPPET COTTAGE, Kendall Lane, the Rocks. Puppets and marionettes are available to play with, and, of course, purchase. Free exhibitions, shows, and workshops on puppetry are offered from Wednesdays to Sundays.

THAT'S ENTERTAINMENT, Shop 513, Pitt and Alfred Streets, Circular Quay, 241-2369. Welcome to the store where Bugs Bunny is King. Every item in the store, from statues to t-shirts to jeans to toys, has a cartoon character emblazoned on it. A bright, cheery store guaranteed to put a smile on your face, even if you can't afford the prices!

CAMPING SUPPLY STORES

If you are planning to go out into the Bush to do some hiking, you can wait until you get to Sydney to buy some of your camping needs. Backpacks will cost much more in Sydney than in the U.S, but Swiss Army knives, tents, and odds and ends are just as cheap.

Parramatta Road, between Missenden Road, Camperdown and Northumberland St. in Stanmore; Kent St., the City; and the bottom of Pitt St., the City, are all good places to shop. Give the following stores a try. They are pretty reliable.

MITCHELL KING CAMPING AND DISPOSALS, 323 and 327 Pitt St., the City, 283-2979. A small store full of camping gear, tents, crockery and clothes. Slightly damaged Swiss Army knives are a good buy.

MOUNTAIN DESIGNS, 494 Kent St., 267-8238; THE SOUTHERN CROSS 493 Kent St., 261-3822; PADDY PALLIN 507 Kent St., 264-2685. These three stores are within crawling distance of each other. All three stock equipment for bushwalking, camping, climbing and skiing, and also sell clothes, tents, sleeping bags, and shoes.

REBEL CAMPING WAREHOUSE, 119-125 Parramatta Road, Camperdown, 557-3865 and SYDNEY CAMPING CENTER AND DISPOSALS, 148 Parramatta Road, Stanmore, 519-9457. Two huge warehouse stores that are open seven days a week. If you can't find what you are looking for in either of these two stores, it may not exist in Sydney. They both have a huge range of equipment, supplies, and clothes for all types of camping, walking, and skiing.

MARKETS

Sydney has become a real market town. From handmade original items to trash-n-treasure markets, Sydney has over a dozen markets. We always purchase clothes, jewelry, and other collectibles as we travel so that we can sell them in other countries and make extra money. Sydney is the perfect place to do just this. We were quite successful selling Guatemalan clothes to Aussies. One of our pairs of pants even made it on national tv!

If you have anything worth selling, or if you can make some type of handicraft, such as paintings, carvings or jewelry, then try the weekend markets. Some of them are quite easy to get into and charge between $15 to $30 for a stall for one day. Below is a description of, and information on how to get into, Sydney's most popular markets.

PADDINGTON VILLAGE BAZAAR, 395 Oxford St., Paddington. Open from 10 a.m. to 5 p.m. (to 4 p.m. winter) on Saturdays only. With 250 plus stalls, "Paddo" is the largest and best outdoor market in Sydney. The majority of stalls feature handmade original Australian or ethnic items. The bazaar is a great place to buy hats, crystals, jewelry, clothes, bags, t-shirts, plants, paintings, beads, and handmade wood briefcases, paper, and books. In the center playground are handmade toys and games, a giant bubble maker, and women who braid hair in the Brazilian style. At the other end are buskers, musicians, clowns, and bands. Inside are trained shiatsu and remedial masseurs, a foot reflexologist, and a delicious, ethnic take-away food counter. It's very difficult to get a stall in Paddington Market, even if you have something unusual to sell. If you have jewelry, crystals, or retail clothes, don't even bother. But, there is a lot of money to be made here. If you have something unique, show up at the Church by 9 a.m., sign up, and wait. It's almost impossible to get a stall between October and Christmas.

BALMAIN, Saint Andrew's Church, Darling St., on the corner of Curtiss Road, Balmain. Open 7:30 a.m. to 4 p.m. Saturdays only. A small, crowded market that combines new clothes and handmade crafts with secondhand books and clothes. The market has a lot of loyal customers who come as much for the delicious Indian food as for the colorful stalls. There is a chance you can get into this market by calling 810-3712 by Thursday of each week, although the proprietor of the market can be a bit difficult. This is a good alternative to Paddington.

GLEBE, Glebe Public School, Glebe Point Road, Glebe, 660-6667, open 9 a.m. to 5 p.m., Saturdays and Sundays. Glebe started as a small, Sunday market, and has expanded into a huge weekend affair. The market has an eclectic mix of the new and used and the handmade and manufactured. Buskers and musicians perform in the area that is encircled by food stalls. A good place to while away a few hours. It used to be relatively easy to get a stall, but as Glebe Market has grown it has become increasingly difficult to get one. Check the information booth near where the entertainers perform for information on the new rules.

OPERA HOUSE MARKET, Forecourt of the Opera House, Circular Quay. Open 10 a.m. to 5 p.m. (4 p.m. winter) Sundays only. Most of the stalls here can be found at Paddington on Saturdays, but the view of the Harbour and Opera House still makes the market unique. Entertainment is usually playing on the steps of the Opera House which keeps the pace lively and attracts a diverse crowd. The proximity of the Botanical Gardens and Circular Quay make this market a must to visit.

Unless you have goods that are handmade in Australia, and are unique, then it is impossible to get a stall. Plus, the stalls cost $50 for a full table, which is a relatively high price to pay for a market that does not attract a lot of sales. Information on the Market can be obtained at Paddington Market.

ROCKS MARKET, George St., the Rocks. Open 10 a.m. to 6 p.m. weekends. Based on London's Portobello Road, this market contains more than 90 stalls under all weather, old-fashioned canopies. A lot of the stall holders here have shops elsewhere in Sydney. This is definitely a place for browsing, unless you have a lot of money to purchase the antiques and other selections. Have a drink at the cafe tables at the Mercantile or a coffee and cake at Bar Rokka and watch the throngs of people. At Campbells Cove, just around the corner from the Rocks Market, local artists gather to sell and create their masterpieces.

PADDY'S MARKETS, Parramatta Road, Flemington (Friday 11 a.m. to 3:30 and Sunday 9 a.m. to 4:30 p.m.) and Redfern next to the Railway Station in the Old Railway Sheds off Regent St. (Saturday and Sunday 9 a.m. to 4:30 p.m.), 764-3522. An experience in loud, large (1,000 stalls) crowded market shopping. All types of retail goods are sold here at a discount, from Australiana to stuffed toys. Music plays in the background, food is sold, and the atmosphere is fun. Next door to Flemington is the car market (page 32) where cheap cars to drive you out of Sydney are sold, and the vegetable and fruit market, which gets going at 5 a.m. Flemington is currently the larger of the two, but when Redfern Market moves back to its original site at the back of Chinatown it may take the top honors.

PARKLEA MARKETS, Toongabie Road, Toongabie, 629-1058. Very similar to Paddy's, with even some of the same stalls. This market is too far from the city for a casual visit, but if you are in the neighborhood, then stop by for cheap clothes, fruits, and vegetables. Even this short distance west of Sydney the accents and styles of the people change.

MARRICKVILLE (018 460-954) and ROZELLE (818-5573) are more casual, local markets that are worth stopping in if you are in the area, and much easier to get a stall to sell from. These markets are a mixture of trash and treasure, but the prices are right for the budget traveler.

CHAPTER 16:

ANIMAL
& PEOPLE
PARKS

ANIMAL PARKS

Don't call a koala a bear in Australia! Even a five-year-old would look at you strangely. Koalas are marsupials, because they carry their young around in pouches. But it just sounds too strange to say "koala marsupials." The Ex-Australian Minister of Tourism once remarked that koalas were "pissy, flea-ridden creatures." This is far from the truth. However, when koalas wake up from a nap, they have to go to the toilet. The Minister was handed a koala who was awakened from a recent nap, and well, you can guess the rest!

The diet of the koala is eucalypti leaves from the eucalyptus tree. Unfortunately, these leaves can make them sleepy and somewhat drugged, so they occasionally fall out of their trees!

Kangaroos are another favorite Australian marsupial. When the babies, or joeys as they are called, are born they are about two inches in length. They then crawl into their mother's pouch, where they stay for several months and suckle until they are fully developed.

The "Big Red" kangaroo can grow up to six feet high and leap 25 feet and longer in one leap. Wallabies are smaller, less menacing kangaroos, and tree kangaroos and kangaroo rats are even smaller. Some species of kangaroos are endangered. This may make you think before buying a kangaroo skin or scrotum bag.

Wombats are cuddly-looking, solid marsupials. They are nocturnal and sleep all day in the holes that they have dug in the wild or in their cradles that the zoos have provided for them. Wombats usually don't bite, so it is pretty safe to reach over and feel their coarse hair and firm back.

The tasmanian devil, as made famous by Disney, is a fierce creature with a red nose and vicious-looking teeth. Do not try to pet these otherwise adorable looking animals. Just like "Taz" the Disney devil, their diet includes anything they can get their teeth into!

Dingos were made popular by the movie in which Meryl Streep played Lindy Chamberlain, the woman whose daughter allegedly was eaten by a dingo. They are fierce, Bush predators. Although they look like dogs, they can't bark and can only howl like a coyote. When dingos get together in packs, their howl sounds really spooky. Because they hunt and kill sheep for food, they are enemies of Aussie sheep farmers.

The emu, which is similar to the ostrich, shares the Australian coat of arms with the kangaroo. It has a brain the size of a pea. This animal must be one of stupidest birds in Australia. Although zoo emus are mild-mannered creatures that will eat out of your hand (if they can find it), wild emus are much shyer, can run as fast as 30 miles per hour, and can destroy a farmer's entire crop.

The echidna (pronounced eh-kidna) is the Australian version of the porcupine and anteater. This small animal is very cute, but don't try to pet one! They have long noses, funny feet with extremely long claws, and they eat ants.

The kookaburra has been immortalized in an Aussie children's poem.

The kookaburra sits in the old gum tree.
Merry, merry King of the Bush is He.
Laugh, Kookaburra, Laugh.
How gay you're life must be. HA! HA! HA!

The bird is much loved among Australians who imitate the high piercing laugh it emits when calling to another bird. They are often found sitting on telephone wires out in the Bush.

The white cockie (cockatoo) is another favorite. These birds are found all over Australia, even in the parks of downtown Sydney. They are the same birds that sell for around $1500 each in the pet shops of America. The cockies have all white plumage with a yellow crest and are usually found hanging about in flocks or eating a Sydneysider's cedar house.

Wild camels live in Australia. "Fair Dinkum!" They were brought to Australia by Afghan camel drivers who used them in the early 1900s to trek their goods from Adelaide to Alice Springs, and then up north to Darwin. When the railway was finally finished it was named "The Ghan" after the camel drivers and it linked the three towns. The camels were no longer needed and they were let loose in the Bush where they continued to breed. They still thrive today. Alice Springs even has camel races!

Sydney has five zoos and parks within the city limits, while a short drive takes you to half a dozen more. Most of the smaller parks have the same animals, along with petting zoos and places to take pictures with koalas, but unless you have grown up in OZ, it is really difficult to get tired of seeing sleeping koalas, hopping "roos", and spooky devils. Make sure you bring at least one roll of film per park or you'll be sorry. Don't forget to buy some food to feed to the kangaroos. They like peanuts, not meat pies!

PARKS WITHIN AN HOUR FROM SYDNEY

TARONGA PARK ZOO, Bradley's Head Road, Mosman, 969-2777. Open 9:30 a.m. to 5 p.m. daily. Entry is $14. The Sydney Public Transport System offers a zoo package called the Zoo-Pass which includes the ferry, bus, zoo entry, and safari. The pass is $17/$8.50 children and cheaper than buying all the tickets separately. When you get off the ferry either jump on bus #238 or take the aerial tramway ($2.50) up the hill to the main entrance. Ferries depart Circular Quay every half hour from 7:15 a.m. on weekdays, 8:45 a.m. on Saturdays and 9 a.m. on Sundays.

Taronga has 3,500 native and exotic animals. They also have a special enclosure to see koalas in the trees, an underwater platypus house (only open 11 a.m. to Noon and 2 p.m. to 3 p.m.), a rain forest aviary, a Friendship Farm where you can pet the animals, sumatran tigers (don't pet these!), a seal show, an Australian Rain forest, and an Animals of the Night exhibit (open 10 a.m. to 4 p.m.) which is an underground building filled with flying foxes.

FEATHERDALE WILDLIFE PARK, Kildare Road, Doonside, 671-4984. Open 9 a.m. to 5 p.m., daily, except Christmas day. The park is a one-hour drive or train and bus ride from Sydney. Catch the train to Blacktown and then bus #725 from the station.

Featherdale is the home of the Quantas koala, who as a true star is a bit of a loner. The koala sanctuary opens from 10 a.m. to 11:30 a.m. and 2:30 p.m. to 3:30 p.m. You can take pictures of all the sleeping koalas and for a small fee have your picture taken with one. Frillynecked lizards and large exhibits of birds (rozellas, cockies) are featured with the regular animals.

KOALA PARK SANCTUARY, Castle Hill Road, West Pennant Hills, 484-3141. Open 9 a.m. to 5 p.m. daily except Christmas day. A half-hour car ride from Sydney or a 45-minute train ride to Pennant Hills Station and buses 661 to 665 to the park. The 10 acre park has been open since 1930. Entry is $8/$4 children.

The main theme of the park is the preservation of the koala. Pictures with koalas can be taken at 10:20 a.m., 11:45 a.m., 2 p.m., and 3 p.m. The first Aussie koala hospital for sick and injured koalas is located within the park. Entry is $8/$4 children.

WARATAH PARK, Namba Road, Duffy's Forest, 450-2377. Only a 40-minute drive from Sydney or take a train to Chatswood and then the Forest Coach Lines bus. This privately run bus leaves at 11:05 a.m.(call 450-1236 for updated prices).

Waratah is the home of "Skippy, the Bush Kangaroo", who was the star of the famous 1960s television show of the same name. The park is a beautifully landscaped animal reserve and most of the animals roam freely. While you are there, tour on the Little Bush Railway, a 15-minute ride that passes through the park.

PARKS MORE THAN AN HOUR'S DRIVE FROM SYDNEY

SYMBIO KOALA GARDEN, Laurence Hargrave Drive, Helensburgh. Open from 9:30 a.m. to dusk every day. The main attraction of this park is a special nocturnal house that has flying foxes and other night creatures.

NOWRA ANIMAL PARK, Kangaroo Valley Road, Nowra. Open daily except Christmas day and entry is only $5/$2 children. This small animal park is a two and a half hour drive from Sydney. The family-run park does not receive any aid from the Government to operate. Personal care is accorded to all the animals. If you are in the area, definitely visit this park. The park has all the usual animals, plus a large kangaroo feeding area, complete with huge, aggressive big reds and a place to get up close to, and take photos of, koalas.

AUSTRALIAN PARK (EL CABALLO BLANCO), Camden Village Way, Catherine Field, 606-6266. Open 10 a.m. to 5 p.m.

daily and costs $15/$8 children. An hour's drive southwest of Sydney, this big time tourist park has Spanish dancing stallions, sheep shearing, sheep dogs, a small wildlife park, and demonstrations. You can get around the park via horse drawn omnibus. Not my favorite park, but if you are bored and in the neighborhood, then it might be worth a visit.

PEOPLE PARKS

You could visit one park a day for a month and still not see all that Sydney's parks have to offer. The Royal Botanical Gardens, Hyde Park, and Centennial Park are the three major parks in Sydney. Then there are Harbour parks, gardens, sports parks, and even a Chinese garden.

HARBOUR PARKS

BALLS HEAD RESERVE. Located on the north side of the Harbour to the west of the Harbour Bridge, Balls Head Reserve attracts people who want to see Aboriginal rock paintings and carvings. Picnic and barbecue spots, walks, and picture perfect Harbour views make this park an attractive place to visit.

ASHTON AND NIELSON PARKS. Both of these are covered more in depth on page 89. They have picnic and barbecue spots, beautiful views, walks, and trails. Ashton Park has historic forts, gun pits, cannons, and tunnels. Nielson Park has historic Vaucluse House, a shark-netted beach, and good rock fishing.

CITY PARKS

TUMBALONG PARK AND THE CHINESE GARDENS. Unfortunately, most of the people who take advantage of these areas are tourists. Both the park and gardens are toward the south of Darling Harbour, near the Pumphouse Brewery. All through the summer and occasionally in winter, jazz players, dancers, buskers, clowns, and wandering minstrels liven up the park. The atmosphere is lively and fun.

Across from Tumbalong Park are the Chinese Gardens. These gardens, which are the only authentic Cantonese-style gardens outside of China, include a Courtyard of Repose, a three-tiered pagoda, waterfalls, a waterside pavilion, a rock garden, statues, and rambling passages. Take a rest and sip some tea on the balcony of the treehouse. The gardening philosophy is Tao based and the results are fabulous. Entry is only $2.50/$.50 concession, free with an Explorer pass.

CENTENNIAL AND MOORE PARKS. Adjacent to Moore Park Road and Oxford St., Paddington, Sydney's largest park is a short walk from the city center. Centennial Park was actually supposed to be a tunnel, designed to bring water from the swamps on the outskirts of Sydney to Hyde Park. Governor Bourke began this project in 1824. However, an alternative water supply was found, and the grounds were turned into a park. Work was completed in 1888, in time for Sydney's Centennial Celebrations.

Many people hire bicycles (398-5027) or horses (332-2770) to tour around the two and a half mile track, which passes by lakes, tame birds, and joggers.

Moore Park is connected to Centennial Park. The former park is mainly used for sports and contains a championship par 70 golf course, clay tennis courts, basketball courts, hockey fields, softball diamonds, the Sydney Cricket Ground (where cricket is played), and the Sydney Sports Stadium (where rugby and Australian Rules football are played). The park was originally the source of Sydney's fresh water supply and for 40 years it was a zoological garden. Moore Park is also the home of The Royal Agricultural Society's Show ground, where the Easter Show (page 169), Craft Show, and other events are staged.

HYDE PARK AND THE DOMAIN. Between Elizabeth and Park Streets, the City. Hyde Park is flanked by Saint Mary's Cathedral on the east and the Great Synagogue on the west. The park was formerly used as a cricket pitch and a race course. In 1810, Governor Macquarie renamed the park after London's Hyde Park.

The business crowd likes to lounge around and eat lunch in this park, since it is so close to the City center. Hyde Park is covered in detail on page 103.

Directly to the northeast of Hyde Park is the Domain, set aside for public recreation. The Palm Sunday Peace March finishes at the Domain. It is a also a popular area for free concerts and the "Opera Under the Stars" held during the Festival of Sydney. Every Sunday the park becomes a free speech forum. For more information on the Domain see page 81.

THE ROYAL BOTANICAL GARDENS. 231-8111. Open 8 a.m. to dusk. The 74-acre garden stretches from the Harbour and merges into the Domain. The Garden Palace gates (at the Opera House entrance) are all that are left from an international exhibition building that was burned down in the 1800s. The gardens were established in 1816. The upper garden, to the south, is used for research. The herbarium, built in 1899, houses some original plant and tree specimens.

Walking through the gardens, you will see a glass pyramid. This houses a tropical display of plants and flowers. Admission is $5; open from 10 a.m. to 4 p.m. (6 p.m. Summer), every day. The middle garden has a memorial pond, a kiosk, and winding walks that pass by flowers and various native Aussie trees.

A giant Moreton Bay fig tree and a Port Jackson fig tree (lawn #44) are located near the walkway of Farm Cove. The lower gardens stretch down to the Harbour and Mrs. Macquaries' Chair (page 102). A Queensland Bottle Brush Tree (the leaves look like a bottle cleaner) is on lawn #29.

Free guided walks are offered at 10 a.m. on Wednesdays and Fridays. The walks start at the Visitors Center, near the Art Gallery. Or pick up a self-guided tour pamphlet at the center.

PARKS OUTSIDE OF SYDNEY

MOUNT TOMAH, Bells Line of Road between Richmond and Bell (about an hour and a half drive from Sydney). The Mount Tomah Botanical Gardens are the cool climate annex to the Royal Botanical Gardens. The gardens are open 10:30 to 4 p.m. (6 p.m. summer) and entry is $6 per car.

LANE COVE RIVER, Off River Road, Lane Cove. This is a State Recreation Area (SRA) that is run by the National Parks and Wildlife Service (NPWS). There are over 1000 acres of bushland to hike through and beautiful spots along the river to have a picnic. If you feel like exploring the long, lazy river, rowboats and canoes are available for hire.

DAVIDSON PARK. Another SRA run by the NPWS. Although this park with 3,000 acres is larger than Lane Cove, the attraction here is the Bantry Bay Explosive Complex. The park also has bushwalking, views from the sandstone cliffs, a beach with shark netting, fishing, boating, and horse riding.

KU-RING-GAI CHASE PARK. Over 37,000 acres of Bushland are contained in the park. If you drive, you can enter through one of four entrances: Mount Colah and the Pacific Highway in the west, Turramurra in the southwest, and Terry Hills and Church Point in the southeast. By car, entry is $6 for the carload. A daily ferry runs between Palm Beach, to the north of Sydney, and Bobbin Head. The price is $10 each way. Call 918-2747 for ferry timetables. The Historical Society (457-9322 weekdays and 457-9310 weekends) can provide you with information on the park.

The 90-foot-high America Falls is at the end of America Falls Track, while the 30-foot Duck Hole Falls is near the entrance to the Park on McCarr's Creek Road.

KU-RING-GAI WILDFLOWER GARDENS, 420 Mona Vale Road, St. Ives, 440-8609. The garden is a short walk from the park. Take a train to Pymble station, then bus #191 to St. Ives, and walk north along Mona Vale Road to the gardens. The best time to visit is in August and September, when the spring wildflowers are in bloom. Walking tracks meander through the gardens. They are suitable for the elderly, wheelchair users, and the blind. The gardens are open 10 a.m. to 4 p.m. daily and there is a small entrance fee.

ROYAL NATIONAL PARK. Situated to the extreme south of Sydney, this is the first Aussie national park and the oldest national park in the world after Yellowstone. The park can be reached by car ($6 per carload), by train to Audley, or by train to Cronulla and then a ferry from Port Hacking to Bundeena (523-2990 for ferry information).

Developed in 1879, the park has a beautiful coastline, a 40,000-acre sanctuary of flowers, over 200 bird species, and bush walking, fishing, canoeing, and climbing. Some of the paths were made by Aboriginals, while others were made by cattle and deer. Wallabies, echidna, and deer are sometimes visible. Many natural sights are located in the Royal National Park, including several waterfalls along the coast track from Port Hacking Road and from the towns of Otford and Curracurrong Falls, which are over 210 feet high.

Both camping and bush camping are allowed within the park. The official campsite is in Bonnie Vale and free permits are available from the Visitor's Center (542-0648), near Audley train station.

CHAPTER 17:

SPORTS

Sydney has sports for every spectator and participant, from abseiling to zen tennis. Because the climate in Sydney is more or less mild during the day all year round, most sports are played outside. Call Sports House (241-2311) for information on participation sports in Sydney.

NATIONAL SPORTS

These are the sports that get all the Aussies out cheering and a good many out training: cricket, rugby, soccer, swimming and of course, gambling.

CRICKET. The cricket season runs from October through March. If you happen to be in town during a match, absolutely go and attend a game at the Sydney Cricket Ground, as much to watch the fans as the players. Try to get a reserved seat, $25 to $30, as opposed to a non-reserved, $20. The crowd in the unreserved area, especially the crowd in front of the score board in the area that was once "The Hill," is exceptionally rowdy. Watch out for "The Wave" which is when bottles, cans, and food go flying!

Cricket is played in all countries that have ties to Great Britain and the Commonwealth. It is taken very seriously in Australia, although it is not the "Gentleman's Game" that it still is in Britain.

Thanks to Kerry Packer, an Aussie millionaire, there is now One Day (nicknamed Pajama) Cricket. These games are much more exciting than the five day Test Matches. The rules are essentially the same for both, with the exception that you can have a draw at a Test Match, but need a winner at the Pajama Games.

The rules are complicated to explain to non Aussies, but in short they are as follows: Each team has 11 players and they wear white during the Test Matches (and colors during Pajama

Games, hence the nickname). The team that's not in has to get the team that's in out. When the team that's in goes out, then the team that's not in goes in, and so forth.

When the little red ball (that's the one the bowler rubs against his crotch) knocks over the wickets (those are the three poles behind the batsman) then the batsman goes out and another one comes in. If the batsman hits the red ball and if the ball gets caught without touching the ground by the team that's not in, then the batsman is out. However, if the ball doesn't get caught and hits the perimeter (the boundary) then the team that's in gets four runs. If it goes over the perimeter without touching the ground (a home run) then they get 6 runs.

In One Day Cricket each team has 50 overs. An over is finished after the bowler makes six throws. At the end of 100 overs (50 overs per team) the team with the highest number of runs win. One-day cricket games last from 12 p.m. until they finish, usually about 9 p.m., and there's a break at 4 p.m. for tea. That's it in a nutshell. Just grab a meat pie, a schooner, and some chips, and cheer when everyone else does!

RUGBY. In 1823 William Webb Ellis was playing soccer at Rugby School in England. In the midst of the game, he bent down, picked up the ball and ran into the goal. Rugby was born! There are three types of rugby (commonly referred to as football) played in Australia: League, Union, and Aussie Rules.

Aussie Rules is mainly played in Victoria, South and West Australia. The Sydney Swans were introduced into Sydney to try to make Aussie Rules more popular in New South Wales, although most of the original players were from other States. The attempt more or less succeeded. Two teams of 18 players each confront each other to play a fast moving game with an extremely confusing scoring system. Players can catch the red ball, but they can't pass it with their hands. Instead, they have to make a fist and punch the ball. Points are scored when a player kicks the ball through the goal (the poles that look like American goal posts). The easiest way to tell Aussie Rules Players from Rugby and League players is that Rules guys have much tighter uniforms than everyone else: tank tops and itsy bitsy shorts.

Although most Aussies play Rugby League and Americans play Union, the Aussies were still the 1991 Rugby Union Cup champions. Union and League are very similar, except that there are 15 men on a Union team. The object in both games is to advance the football over the goal and score the highest number of points. Any player can run, pass or kick the ball. Play continues after the tackle and there are few stoppages. The 15 players stay in the field for the entire fast paced game.

The Union players are also bulky guys. The forwards are big and strong and much more mobile than your average American football player. That's mainly because neither Union nor League players wear the amount of padding that American football players wear. The backs are similar to running backs, wide receivers, and safeties. The players move around the field very fast and have outstanding ball handling and kicking skills. Union players wear those really cool "Rugby Shirts" made out of durable cotton with rubber buttons.

In New South Wales, League is the game. On a League team there are 13 men on each side. League rules keep changing as the officials try to make the game safer and flow smoother. The players tend to be bigger and bulkier than Aussie Rules players. Maybe that's why they don't wear such tight uniforms. Instead they wear short sleeve shirts with v-neck collars and boxer style shorts. The major League teams are the Souths, Easts, and the Penrith Panthers. The All Blacks are the creme de la creme of Rugby League teams. Too bad they're from New Zealand!

GAMBLING. This is one of the largest participant sports in Australia. It has been said that Australians will "bet on two flies walking up a wall." Betting is legal only at race tracks, TABs (this doesn't mean Totally Allowed Betting, as we thought. It stands for Totalizator Agency Board), or in officially recognized casinos.

Jupiters in Surfers Paradise, Queensland is one of the most popular casinos. A casino is being planned for Sydney at the Old Pyrmont Power Station site on Darling Harbour. It is expected to bring in millions of dollars, mainly from Asian tourists. There has been much debate over the development of the casino, because everyone is worried that there will be serious corruption. For the first five years, revenue from the Casino will be dedicated to the national health budget.

At the TABs people bet on horses, the "Trots", greyhounds, and footy (Rugby League). TABs are usually found in shopping centers or on the main street of every suburb or small town. Poker machines and keno are legal in registered clubs, but roulette, blackjack, and other casino games are legal only in registered casinos.

Two-up, an Aussie coin throwing game, is semi-legal on Anzac Day. Every other day it is illegal, except in casinos. Two-up is also becoming popular in casinos in Las Vegas and Atlantic City. A thrower holds a small wooden board with a handle that holds two old English pennies. The official calls, "All bets, all ready, come in Spinner." The thrower is called the "Spinner." The coins are launched in the air, and you bet on heads or tails. Someone in the circle of players has to accept and match your bet with an opposite bet. If the coins fall as one head, one tail than it is a re throw.

SWIMMING. If you can't swim, or you can but are not a very strong swimmer, then you may want to consider one of the adult swim courses offered by the NSW Department of Sport, Recreation and Racing (923-4234). The beaches of Sydney have very strong riptides and a number of people drown each year.

Most beaches and communities have fresh or saltwater pools that cost between $1 to $2 per visit. Pools usually open at 6:30 a.m. to allow for early morning workouts. The Bondi Iceberg Pool ($1, for cold-water lovers only) attracts many year-round early morning swimmers.

The Leichhardt Pool ($1.30) is heated, 50 yards long, and is situated right next to the Parramatta River. The Andrew Charlton Olympic is at the Domain and is open 6:30 a.m. to 7:15 p.m. (358-6686). Balmain has a saltwater and tidal pool on Fitzroy St. It's open from 7 a.m. to 5:30 p.m. (810-2183). Or try some of the free saltwater pools open at Cronulla, Coogee and other local beaches.

THE A TO Z OF SPORTS

ABSEILING. At Stanwell Tops, south of Sydney. Call 583-1543 for information on the $65 fees.

BALLET. Modern ballet is taught at the Rozelle School of Visual Arts, 57 Nelson St., Rozelle, 388-7652. The cost is $25 for 10 lessons.

CABLE SKIING. Penrith Leagues Club, Penrith, 047 321-044. One hour of skiing for $9 from Monday to Friday, 11 a.m. to 4 p.m., and weekends to 7 p.m. Rides on the giant waterslides cost $2.50 per hour and the slide is open from 11 to 5:30, daily.

CROQUET. Thanks to the pommies, croquet is played in Australia. Classes are offered at Marrickville, 579-5417.

DIVING. A few companies offer certificate courses, dives to local wrecks (Dee Why Beach), and reef dives up the Coast. It's a bit boring to dive in Sydney compared to the Great Barrier Reef. But try Deep 6 (977-5966) or one of the local beach dive shops if you're interested.

GOLF. Moore Park is a Championship 70 Par and is the easiest place to get to in town, although there are dozens more around Sydney. The cost is $20 and the course is open from 5:30 a.m. to 9 p.m. during the week and to 8 p.m. on weekends. For further information call 663-3960.

GYMS. Sydneysiders are finally getting into the exercise craze. This trend took about 10 years longer to arrive in OZ than it did in the States. In response, many new gyms have opened. Try the following:

The Sports Pit, Parramatta Road, Petersham. A no-nonsense workout gym managed by Adrian Batho, a former Mr. Australia, and Mandy, a former bodybuilding champion. Great aerobics classes, good free weights, and so-so machines. Open 6:30 a.m. to 10 p.m. (9 p.m. summer).

Broadway Gym, 160 Broadway, 211-5068. Another no-nonsense gym with an accent on free weights. Big, muscular men tend to be the main customers. Open 7 a.m. to 9:30 p.m. Monday to Friday and 9 a.m. to 6 p.m. weekends.

The City Gym, 107 Crown St., Darlinghurst, 360-6247. Bruce Springsteen worked out here! This is a big flashy gym, with modern machines, good free weights, and picture windows to watch people sweat. Mainly frequented by a gay and small crossover crowd. Open 24 Hours a day Monday to Friday and 9 a.m. to 7 p.m. weekends.

HANG GLIDING. Call Chris Boyce (042 942-545) for information on a variety of flights. A two day course costs $180 and includes a tandem flight and one day on the sand hills. A six day course costs $525 and includes two days on the low hills, one instructional tandem, two days on higher hills, and two high glides. Tandem flights without lessons cost $95.

HARNESS RACING. At Wentworth and Harold Park the "Trots" are on Friday nights. Call 660-6964 for other nights and entry fee.

HORSE RACING. Randwick is the most prestigious racetrack (663-8400). Canterbury (799-8000) and Warwick Farms (602-6199) are two smaller racetracks. All newspapers have a racing section with a racing card for that day.

ICE SKATING. Situated very close to town is the ice skating rink in Prince Alfred Park, located behind Central Station. The park is bordered by Chalmers and Cleveland Streets. Take a train to Canterbury to get to Canterbury Olympic at Tasker Park on Phillips Avenue, Canterbury (789-4044). Or take a bus to Narrabeen, 18 Lagoon St. (913-9595).

KICKBOXING. The Newtown Police Boy's Club, 17 Erskineville Road, 982-5742, sponsors kickboxing classes Mondays to Thursdays at 5 p.m.

PARAFLYING. For $39 cable winch parasailing on the Harbour, phone 627-3831. The company also offers champagne breakfasts, and lunchtime, party and twilight group parasailing.

PARAGLIDING. Phone 042 674-570 or write to P.O. Box 22, Bulli, New South Wales, 2516 for more information. Bulli is about an hour's drive south of Sydney. A one day introductory course costs $120, which includes use of equipment, insurance, transportation to local flying sites (usually outside Sydney), and an information package. Tandem flights with instruction cost $70.
Active Air Sports (042-942-584) offers hangliding and Paragliding lessons from Stanwell Tops, about one hour's drive south of Sydney.

RACQUETBALL. This sport is slowly growing in popularity in Sydney. Unfortunately, there are no racquetball courts. You'll just have to take your chances and play on a squash court. With most courts, the ball will keep flying out the back. Just ring up one of the dozens of squash clubs in your area for times. Some clubs will rent racquetball rackets and balls.

ROLLERBLADING. Blades can be hired or bought from 44 Pittwater Road, Manly (976-2058), open 9 a.m. to 7 p.m. daily. Good places to rollerblade are the Corso at Manly or at the beachfront.

RUNNING. There are a number of running clubs throughout Sydney. The City to Surf Race held in August is a popular but difficult race that is the equivalent of the San Francisco Bay to Breakers. The race attracts celebrities from all over the world and has big prizes for the winners. For more information on races and places to run call the following: NSW Athletic League, Harry Stanley at 669-2983; Sydney Marathon Clinic's Trevor Long at 481-0354; and Sydney Striders' Jon Marsden at 428-2001.

SAILBOARDING. Known as windsurfing in the U.S., sailboards can be hired from 7317 Spit Road, Manly (968-1044). Classes are also offered. Many people head up to Narrabeen Lakes (across from the beach), Pittwater (Dee Why Beach), and other Northern Beaches. Check out the local surf shops for more information.

SAILING. The Australian Sailing School and Club (960-3077) is located at Middle Harbour at The Spit, Mosman. The club offers sailing lessons. Northside Sailing School (969-3972) offers lessons, day trips, and day hires. Sailing party boats are available for hire from 018 278-511. The six-and-a-half hour cruise costs $39 and includes a barbecue lunch and wine (bring your own beer and champagne).

Boats depart from Campbell Cove, the Rocks from Thursday to Sunday at 9:45 a.m. and return at 4:30 p.m. These party boats can be heard noisily sailing around the Harbour. Don't forget to make a reservation.

SOCCER. Australia is still not very keen on soccer. They call it soccer and not football. The sport is mainly kept alive by European immigrants. The World Cup attracts a team from Australia and manages to keep enthusiasm going for a while every year.

SQUASH. The individual clubs in Sydney are too numerous to mention, but almost every neighborhood has at least one squash club. You don't need to be a member to play. Look under squash courts in the phone book, and call to reserve a court for 30 minutes or one hour. It's much cheaper to play before 5 p.m. Rackets, balls, and towels can be rented at the clubs. Prices vary from $12 to $17 an hour during peak time.

SURFING. Another major Australian sport. Shops near and even on most beaches usually will rent or sell boards and surf wear. The Surf Safari (043 841-413) hires boards, arranges classes and offers surf tours to other key surfing areas. Call The Surf Travel Company for information on surf adventure tours to Fiji and Indonesia.

TAI CHI. This sport is growing in popularity in Sydney. A number of places offer lessons and one even offers outdoor courses. Call Tony Ward (389-2930) to get information on the 7 a.m. class in Centennial Park.

ULTIMATE FRISBEE. Go down to Gore Hill Oval, Pacific Highway, Saint Leonards on Mondays and Wednesdays from 7 p.m. to 10 p.m. to watch the Aussies at play and find out how you can join a game. Or call 416-3801 to find out how you can join a game at Centennial Park.

YOGA. Individual programs are offered at Bondi Junction. Call 369-4982 to speak with a "yoga consultant."

ZEN TENNIS. Call 365-7795 for more information on how to learn to be a Zen Master while playing tennis.

EQUIPMENT AND ADVENTURES

RECYCLED SPORTS. Located on 228 Oxford St., Bondi Junction (369-2867), this store sells used surf skis, water skis, and other gear. They will buy and sell your equipment on consignment.

MILD TO WILD ADVENTURE CENTER, 111 Lawrence Hargrave Drive, Stanwell Park (042 943-606). This company arranges abseiling, hangliding, and paragliding courses and day adventures.

WILD PERSPECTIVES. This company (988-4778) offers bush walks, abseiling, courses in bush craft and survival, and sea kayaking.

THE WILDERNESS SOCIETY. An arm of The Wilderness Shop (92 Liverpool St., the Rocks), the society organizes bush walks and environmentally aware activities. Call 267-7525 for information.

WORLD EXPEDITIONS. Call Andrew (264-3366) to plan day and evening photo courses. The cost starts at $60 for an eight hour course.

CHAPTER 18:

FESTIVALS
AND
SPECIAL EVENTS

Sydney is never boring. Every month, festivals and special events are being held somewhere in town. Pick a month to visit, and enjoy the fun. The largest events are the Festival of Sydney (January), The Easter Show (April), and the Sydney Film Festival (May/June), but there are dozens of smaller festivals that provide just as much excitement and entertainment. Below is a description of events by month.

JANUARY

Festival of Sydney (267-2311, fax 261-3014) is a month-long celebration that culminates on Australia Day, January 26. January is not the month to do business in Sydney, because everyone is too busy taking advantage of everything the festival has to offer. Nightly theater, opera, dance, and music programs are presented in different locales around town. The Bacardi Festival nightclub opens up for weekend outdoor entertainment at the Hyde Park Barracks, while the Coca Cola Bottlers Dance Hall opens up for five days of samba, jive and cha-cha. Events for kids and adults alike are spread all over Sydney. Cartoon characters, clowns, and aliens wander the streets.

Australia Day is an outrageous day with a Ferry-a-thon (a race in which all the Sydney Harbour Ferries take part), boat races, a reenactment of the Rum Rebellion and fun, fun, fun for everyone.

Taronga Park Zoo and **All That Jazz.** January is the perfect month to visit the zoo and catch the live jazz entertainment, from 2 p.m. to 5 p.m., every Sunday, free with Zoo admission.

FEBRUARY

Gay and Lesbian Mardi Gras (332-4088, fax 332-2969) The wildest festival of the year began in 1975 as a protest march. Now it features one of the largest nighttime parades in the world and rivals Brazil's Mardi Gras Parade. After the three hour long parade that marches down Oxford St., a wild party for 30,000 people is held in the Horden Pavilion, in the Showground. Tickets cost $50 and are extremely hard to get, but if you can get your hands on one then go party! The dance lasts from 11 p.m. to noon the next day. During this same week is the Gay and Lesbian Film Festival.

Surf Carnivals. The carnivals take place at different beaches throughout the summer. On the day of a carnival, there is a parade featuring individual lifesaving clubs, then demonstrations of skill and competitions. Carnival days are exciting action-packed days that makes you feel like going out for some exercise yourself!

Chinese New Year. The New Year festivities are held throughout Chinatown and include a parade, traditional dancing, and a giant dragon. Most restaurants offer special discounts on meals.

South American Festival. For only $10 you are welcomed to South America and a mini Brazilian Mardi Gras. Have fun doing the lambada, cha cha, and salsa to live music. The festival is held in the Bondi Pavilion.

Grass Skiing. The Kurrajong Heights Grass Ski Championship is held at Kurrajong at the same time as the Dual Slalom Mountain Bike Championship.

MARCH

Leichhardt Festival. Celebrate Little Italy's Annual Party on Norton St. with rides, entertainment, a pasta eating competition, live entertainment, comedians, celebrities, dance competitions, a market, and food, food, food. Go for breakfast, lunch and dinner!

International Jazz Festival. Eleven days of classical and modern jazz. Concerts are presented all over Sydney, at hotels, shopping centers, tourist sites, jazz clubs, and elsewhere. Both domestic and international jazz greats are featured.

International Women's Day. Parades, speeches, demonstrations, and workshops are held in different locales in the City. The parade culminates in a small section of Hyde Park, where the people gather to listen to the speakers.

NSW Barefoot Waterskiing Championships. Just like its name. The championship is held a little north of Sydney in Moorehead.

APRIL

The Royal Easter Show. The Sydney Showtime Easter Parade, with 400 farm animals marching through George St., starts the fun. During the next 12 days the show is held at Moore Park's Sydney Showground. What began as an agricultural show in 1824, has now turned into an action packed couple of weeks for farmers, tourists, and city folk. Thirty-five thousand cows, pigs, sheep, dogs, and cats are judged and tons of farm equipment and machinery is bought and sold. Competitions of sheep shearing, sheepdog trials, rodeo riders, and more take place within a special outdoor arena. International visitors just need to show their passports to the information booth, or talk with a "foreign" accent, and they may get prime ringside seats. Meanwhile, fashion and flower shows, a carnival, marching bands, and a children's theater line Side Show Alley. Don't forget to pick up a show bag, loaded with manufacturer's samples of teeth-decaying candies and toys.

Nighttime entertainment includes fireworks, human cannonballs, the Dinkum Dunny Derby (Port-a-potties towed along a race track), stunts, and concerts. Tickets cost $13 for all day entertainment, 9:30 a.m. to 9:30 p.m. Rides, show bags, and special concerts cost extra.

Anzac Day. A day to celebrate and remember the soldiers of the Australian and New Zealand Army Corps. On the solemn side, there are prayers and services in memory of the soldiers. These events commence at 5:30 a.m. with a march through the town center to lay a wreath at the War Memorial.

On the fun side, pubs and RSL clubs open as early as 6 a.m. and people really do start to drink this early! Two-Up is legal and played all day.

Motorcycle Grand Prix. Held at Eastern Creek Raceway in mid-April, the world's motorcycle greats come out for the 500 CC races. Tickets are $15 Friday, $25 Saturday, and $40 Sunday. The City Rail Link offers a special train/bus/entry ticket for $7 more than the admission price.

Peace Parade. Every Easter Sunday, a parade marches through downtown Sydney to celebrate Peace. Starting at 12:30 p.m. from Belmore Park near Central Station, the parade then winds its way through the City and finishes at the Domain. Here the crowd is addressed by speakers and local activists. A band provides entertainment, while stalls offer food, clothes, and information.

Dinosaurs Picnic. A fun day at The Australian Museum for dinosaurs of all ages. Prizes are awarded for dinosaur models and costumes, and music and entertainment is scattered around the museum. The picnic is open from 10 a.m. to 2 p.m. Museum entry is at children's prices, for all ages, all day.

MAY

Sydney Film Festival (660-3844, fax 692-8793) For the movie aficionado, this two week film extravaganza is a must see. Movies are screened in the State Theater (which looks like something out of a Cecil B. DeMille epic film). You can purchase one of several types of passes (day, evening, or unlimited) and see dozens of movies from around the world. At the end of the two weeks, the spectators get to vote on the best overall film and other categories.

Dragon Boat Festival. Held in late April or early May, the Dragon Boats go racing down the Harbour. With racers dressed in traditional Chinese costumes and drummers marking the stroke, the boats start and finish at Darling Harbour. According to legend, the racing boats would sail blind, if not for the help of a Buddhist Priest. Therefore, before the races, a Priest paints eyes on the bows of the boats. The Chinese Gardens are open free to the public and various celebrations take place in Chinatown.

Power Boat Race. The annual Bridge to Bridge Power Boat Race is held on the Hawkesbury River at Windsor. The race starts on the river at Governor Phillip Reserve.

Music in the Zoo. Concerts are played at the Zoo every Sunday throughout May. The entertainment is free with your ticket to the Zoo.

JUNE

Zoo Ball. An animal masked ball, where people dress as animals and dance the night away with Sydney celebrities. All the proceeds go to an animal related charity. Tickets are $75 each, but if you have some extra cash, it's a unique time to see the Zoo and the money goes to a worthy cause. Call the Zoo for more information.

AUGUST

City to Surf Race. One of the hardest and most popular running races in Sydney. The race begins at Park St., the City, and goes through the wealthy suburbs of Sydney, up long "Heartbreak Hill," which is through Rose Bay and Vaucluse, and down to Bondi Beach, finishing at the Hotel Bondi.

SEPTEMBER

Festival of the Winds. A one-day festival held at Bondi Beach Pavilion. This is a time of kite flying and exhibitions of new, old, traditional, stunt, and bizarre kites, to sample and buy. Hundreds of amateurs and professionals show off their kites. Bands play, stalls serve food, and there's live entertainment inside the Pavilion, while outside the kites fly.

Teddy Bear Picnic. Anyone with a teddy bear can ride free on the train! Fair Dinkum! Head down to the Rocks where the young and old are out with their bears. Exhibitions, bear sales, information on the history of teddy bears, competitions, prizes, and Teddy Bear food are featured at the picnic.

Carnivale. A multicultural festival unique to Sydney. Different nationalities present plays, dances, and shows in different venues in Sydney. The event lasts for the entire month.

NOVEMBER

Glebe Festival. The festival and Sunday market combine to make this event crowded and lively. The numerous restaurants on Glebe Point Road make the neighborhood party a great place to sample some good food. Almost all of the restaurants put cafe tables on the sidewalk.

Kings Cross Carnival. Yet another of Sydney's neighborhoods to have its own one day fair, but since it is the infamous Cross, the fair is a bit wilder and more colorful than the others. The carnival is held up and down the length of Darlinghurst Road and has live entertainment, food, market stalls, and giveaways. Some years there is a famous stars look alike contest with Madonnas, Elvises, and even Leslie Nielsens competing for prizes. Just be careful you know which sex is in the Madonna costume!

The Bed Race. Held the Saturday before the Kings Cross Carnival, the race gets everyone excited for the party weekend. Male and female nurses race old hospital beds on wheels. Two people push, while one sits on the bed and attempts to steer.

Water Ski Classic. The Bridge to Bridge Water Ski races are held in Windsor on the Hawkesbury River. The races start from Governor Phillip Reserve.

DECEMBER

Sydney to Hobart Race. An annual yacht race held on Boxing Day, December 26. All classes of yachts, from the maxi to the mini, battle to arrive first in their class in Hobart, Tasmania. To get a great view of the race moving from the Harbour to the ocean, head over with a picnic early in the morning to South Head. The race takes from three to five days, depending on winds. Competitors celebrate at a huge New Years' Party in Hobart.

Craft Show. Every December a major craft show is held at the Sydney Showground. You can see many of the same vendors at Paddington Village Bazaar and other markets, but here they all come together under one roof. Unfortunately, you have to pay to see them. The cost is about $4.

Christmas at the Opera House. During December, the Opera House presents plays, musicals, and concerts with a Christmas theme. They also have carol singers on the steps. Anyone can join in!

CHAPTER 19:

DAY TRIPS
FROM
SYDNEY

Now that you've had your cuppa, shouted schooners for your mates, learned the difference between "Coming the raw prawn" and "Fair dinkum" and can appreciate bugs and rockies, it's time to say "G'day" to Sydney and travel into the Bush to meet a few Ocker Aussies.

Actually, these trips are mainly one day adventures, but it's quite easy to pack a tent and do some overnight camping or to find a cheap hotel.

The following places are as close as a half-hour drive and as far as a one-and-a-half hour drive. We've put in some of the typical tourist areas (the Blue Mountains), some Aussie tourists areas (Berrima), and some places for bushwalking, swimming, and shopping that are not really well known even to Sydneysiders. Most of the places can be reached by train or bus, or you can rent a car with a few friends for the weekend. "G'day and see you at the Back of Bourke!"

BOBBIN HEAD AND BROOKLYN

How about a day on the water? If you're in the mood to sit on the deck of a boat, to explore some small islands or to do a bit of fishing, then head over to Bobbin Head on the Hawkesbury River. It takes less than an hour to get here, and you will be surrounded by the National Forest.

How to get there

Head north over the Harbour Bridge and follow the signs for Pacific Hwy. #1. Get onto the highway and drive north through Pymble where you will see a sign on the left of the road directing you to Bobbin Head. Continue on this road and the populated areas will eventually thin out. At the end of Bobbin Head Road you'll be there.

BOBBIN HEAD The Bobbin Head section of Kur-ing-gai Chase National Park is very tranquil. If you'd like to stay for more than a day, Halverson's will rent you a four, six or eight berth cruiser. Prices are around $120 per day for an eight berth, plus gasoline. You need to supply your own food, although the boats are well stocked with utensils. Take your own barbecue and moor on the banks of the river for a picnic. Weekends in this area start on Friday afternoon and last until Sunday afternoon. It's best to hire a boat on Friday, so that you can find a secluded cove in which to lay anchor for the night.

The river at Bobbin Head is actually part of the Hawkesbury River estuary, which in turn flows into the Pacific Ocean at Palm Beach. We don't recommend going into the ocean because the boats are flat bottomed and can turn over in waves. Instead, miles of creeks are yours to explore. Maps of the creeks and waterways are available at Halverson's.

If you stop by for the day, there are some great bushwalks, both long and short. The walking track to the town of Berowra is a little over four miles long. The walk is easy and passes near the river and near Waratah Bay to the little highway town. The track to Cowan Creek is shorter at two miles. These walks and others start at Apple Tree Bay which is to the west of Bobbin Head, about a quarter of a mile down the road.

BROOKLYN When you're done exploring Bobbin Head, drive into Ku-ring-gai Chase National Park via Bobbin Head Road, and drive out of the park on Ku-ring-gai Chase Road until you reach Mount Colah. From Mount Colah go north on the Old Pacific Hwy. #1 and before the Mooney Mooney Bridge turn right at the sign for Brooklyn.

If you decide to go straight to Brooklyn from Sydney, follow the directions to Bobbin Head as above, but when you get to Pymble continue on the Pacific Hwy. (don't turn on Bobbin Head Road) to Wahroonga where you will see a sign for the Newcastle Freeway. Turn left onto the freeway and travel for about 10 miles until you see an exit for Berowra.

Turn off the freeway and continue north through Berowra on the Old Pacific Hwy. Before you get to Mooney Mooney Bridge turn right to Brooklyn, and drive until you get to the boat yard and the pub.

Don't worry if you miss the turnoff to Berowra on the freeway, just continue north. When you go over the Mooney Mooney Bridge you will have to turn around and come back over the bridge to enter Brooklyn. The only turn off from the freeway to Brooklyn is going south. Another option is to take the Gosford train from Central Station.

The tourist masses have yet to hit Brooklyn, so the area is still relatively unspoiled. From Brooklyn you can go for a two hour walk on Dangar Island, which is located in the estuary. The ferry times are 6:35 a.m, 7:20, 7:55, 9, 10:45, 2 p.m., 3:30, 4:30, 5:30 and 6:30. On weekends the hours vary: Saturday 8 a.m, 12 p.m., 2, 3, 4:15, and 5:15; and Sunday 9 a.m, 10, 11, 12 p.m., 1:45, 2:45, 3:45 and 4:45.

The ferry stops at two points on the island. Stop on one side, bushwalk and picnic in the middle, and catch the ferry on the other side to go back to Brooklyn. Also in this area, the Department of Sports and Recreation has recently opened a camp at Broken Bay. You can only reach the campsite by a twice daily ferry, 1:30 p.m. on weekdays and 11 a.m and 1:30 p.m. on Saturdays and Sundays (and all week long during the summer school holidays December through January). The camp has gas barbecues, a swimming area, and bush walk trails. The ferry fare is $10 return/$5 concession and stops first at Patonga Beach, which is a little beach for swimming. After Patonga the ferry continues on for 15 minutes to Broken Bay. Both of these stops are on the Gosford side of the River.

Another possibility is the Lunch Cruise, which is a bit pricey at $30, but it includes the ride, lunch, and afternoon tea. The cruise leaves Brooklyn at 11 a.m, heads upstream under the Mooney Mooney Bridge, and stops at McClure's Kitchen Eatery for a lunch of hamburger, fish, chicken, or vegetable pie, all served with the mandatory chips and salad. Book ahead of time for the cruise, because they need a minimum number of passengers before they can leave. Call (02) 985-7566 to make a booking.

By far, the best deal is a trip on the River Postman. As you may have guessed by the name, this is a delivery service which ferries an assortment of necessities to the people who live along the river, such as newspapers, groceries, and, of course, the mail. People can pay for a ride, but the boat sails regardless of passengers.

The skipper is an amiable character who has been plying the river for a number of years, and he has many interesting stories to tell. If you make only one trip, be sure it's this one.

The 8:15 a.m train from Central Station in Sydney gets you to Brooklyn in time to catch the riverboat. On Mondays, Tuesdays, and Thursdays, the River Postman leaves Brooklyn at 9:30 a.m returning around 1:15 p.m. On Wednesdays and Fridays, the mailman leaves at 1:30 p.m. and returns around 4:15 p.m. (closed public holidays). The cost is $20, but it includes morning tea. Call (02) 985-7566 for more information.

Other options from Brooklyn are ferries to Dangar Island, Wobby Beach, Kangaroo Point, Bar Point Estate, Glenwood, Marlow Creek, Fisherman's Point Estate, and Sunny Corner. They leave 9:30 a.m (returning 1:15 p.m.) on Mondays to Fridays, as well as 1:30 p.m. (returning at 4:30 p.m.) on Wednesdays and Fridays. Call (02) 985-7566 for more information.

THE HAWKESBURY RIVER

The Hawkesbury is the name given to the collection of small towns that sit on the banks of the Hawkesbury River, which is to the west of Sydney. This area is a great place for a day trip to go grass or waterskiing or to explore one of the earliest farming areas of New South Wales.

How to Get There

Head west on Parramatta Road and get on the F3 Freeway at Strathfield. Continue heading west for a few miles and turn off at the sign for James Ruse Drive and Windsor. As you drive north along James Ruse Drive you will cross over Rydelmere Road where James Ruse Drive becomes the Parramatta Bypass.

Continue on and follow the signs for Windsor. After you pass under two bridges, the bypass changes its name to O'Briens Road and finally to Old Windsor Road. This road passes through Kellyville and Vineyard. About an hour after you leave Sydney you will arrive in Windsor.

GRASS SKIING IN KURRAJONG HEIGHTS. If you want to go grass skiing before you do anything else, pass through Windsor and follow the signs for Richmond. Drive through Richmond and follow the signs for North Richmond. Continue straight through North Richmond into Kurrajong Heights. On the right hand side of the road you will see signs for grass skiing at 1376 Bells Line of Road.

Lessons and the rope tow cost $18 for a full day, plus the area has barbecues and picnic tables. Beware of this sport! It requires some care. Unlike snow skiing, edging does not slow you down. In order to stop, turn up hill. You can pick up megaspeed on these skis, so unless you feel confident or suicidal, stay on the baby slope.

RICHMOND. When you've finished grass skiing and touring Kurrajong, head back to Richmond the way you came. Richmond was established by Governor Macquarie. About all that it has to offer are some interesting small town shops which line the main street.

AUSTRALIAN PIONEER VILLAGE. From Richmond head in the direction of Windsor. At the junction of Windsor Road and Macquarie St. turn left over the bridge. The road will continue to Wilberforce.

The Australian Pioneer Village is located on a 30-acre site of park land in Wilberforce. You can hire paddle boats, watch sheep shearing demonstrations, and experience life in the 1800s. It costs $8/$2.50 children/$15 family to enter and is open daily from March 1 to January 31. Telephone 045 741-457.

WATER SKIING ON THE HAWKESBURY. From the Pioneer Village drive south toward Windsor and turn left in the direction of Sydney. Take the first turn on your left, which is Pitt Town Road. Continue for six miles until you reach Pitt Town, a picturesque small town which has been in existence since the 1800s.

If you fancy some more skiing, except this time with a softer landing, try water skiing. The Water Ski and Caravan Park is at 505 Pitt Town Bottoms Road. If you are an experienced skier, you can use the slalom course and also the ski jump. If you are not, then stick with taking the lessons that are offered. On the weekends spend the night in their rental caravans or at their tent sites, but call ahead for availability, 045 723-769.

In late November a must see is the Bridge-to-Bridge Water Ski Classic. It's held on the stretch of the Hawkesbury that runs through Windsor. Super fast power boats pull the dozens of entrants up the river. The speed of the boats that pull the waterskiers is terrifying to watch!

WISEMAN'S FERRY AND HILLBILLIES. Leaving Pitt Town, continue north on the Cattai Road, which changes its name to Wiseman's Ferry Road after the town of Cattai. If you love to golf, then stop in at the public golf course at Riverside Oaks on O'Briens Road, which is off Wiseman's Ferry.

The drive passes through the Cattai State Recreation Area, which has bushwalks as well as the usual barbie/picnic areas. About a half hour north from the Recreation Area you will drive into Wiseman's Ferry, another early Bush town that dates back to the 1800s. A statue of the city's founder, Mr. Wiseman, is on the main street, although the statue of his ferry is not!

The town sits on the banks of the Hawkesbury. The main reason to visit the town is to cross over the river on the car ferry and head to Saint Albans via the town of Central Mc-Donald. The car ferry operates 24 hours a day, every day of the year.

Once you are on the other side of the river it is a half hour drive to Saint Albans. All this town has is a pub, called the Settler's Arms Inn, and a few convict-made houses, but the whole area is full of history. Many of the folks here have never been to the "Big City" of Sydney.

The Saint Albans Valley, which runs north from the pub, is a little like your average West Virginian Appalachian town, complete with Aussie hillbillies.

Most people live in little convict-made houses hidden up in the Bush. Don't be surprised if you catch gramps hanging about on his porch smoking a corncob pipe!

When you are finished exploring this bizarre little town, cross over the river on the Saint Albans Ferry, and return to Wiseman's Ferry via Webb's Creek. Continue on the Wiseman's Ferry Road east and within 20 minutes or so you will connect with the F3 Freeway which gets you back to Sydney in under an hour.

BERRIMA

This old fashioned town is the perfect place to get away from Sydney. Go during the week so that you don't get hassled by all the Aussie tourists.

The town has historic old buildings, some of which have been renovated, a sandstone jail that is still in operation, and lots of antique and craft stores. The surrounding bush countryside makes the drive down south quite a pleasant experience. Unfortunately, the area's prices cater to the tourist crowd, so bring your own food, buy a counter lunch in the pub, or split a Ploughman's lunch between two people.

How to Get There

First head out toward Liverpool by driving west on Parrammatta Road, and when you get to Ashfield, about seven miles from the City, turn left onto the Hume Hwy. (well signposted). Drive through Enfield, Chullora, Yagoona, Bass Hill, Liverpool, Mittagong and finally Berrima.

Your first stop when you arrive should be the Court House. For $1.50/$0.50 concession you will be treated to an audiovisual presentation on the history of Berrima. The area was quite rough and tumble: sheep and cattle stealing, drunkenness, lynch murders, and sleazy affairs.

After the show, wander around the rooms filled with relics. The Jury Room reenacts the case of Lucretia Duncan, who killed her husband to live with her lover, Martin Beech. This was in the 1800s, not the present time, although some things never change! She and her lover were caught and eventually hung. The Court Room has a figure of Lucretia pleading her case, while poor Martin sits in solitary in the Male Cell.

Across the street is the Berrima Gaol (pronounced jail). The sandstone block building is so solid that it is still in operation today. Unfortunately, no tours are permitted.

Around the corner is Harpers Mansion. This building is in the midst of being renovated. The outdoor dunnies and stoves are in shambles and cannot be repaired, although the rest of the house is in marginally better shape. It's worth the small entrance fee to get a look at what the house was like before renovations, and what has been done to restore it to its original grandeur. This includes hand-painting the wallpaper to match the earlier design. The Surgeon General on Hume Hwy. is the oldest, continuously operating hotel in Australia. The place gets jam packed on weekends when locals from all over the area, as well as Sydneysiders, come to relax at the outdoor tables or have lunch inside.

Next door is a cafe serving ploughman's lunches and other light fare, and an expensive craft store filled with antiques and modern bric-a-brac.

Ploughman's lunches are very popular in this area, even though they are an English tradition. Although they vary in content from place to place, expect a big slab of cheese, a hunk of bread, sweet pickles, hot mustard, fresh butter, and either sausages, dry meat, or salami.

The best place for lunch is The Loft (owned by American and Australian opera singers). The ploughman's lunch is large enough to be shared between two people with room for one of their delicious Devonshire Teas, piled high with fresh cream or their homemade pies and cakes, which are sinfully rich.

Next door is a candy shop that makes its own fudge, hard candies, jams, and other sweet items. Along the rest of main street are antique shops that sell 18th and 19th century furniture, as well as paintings and modern fine art.

Near the Village Square is a large nursery that sells hand grown herbs. Or, stop down the road and fill up on peanut brittle and other country treats. Across the road and to the left is another historic building; this one filled with antique typewriters, garden and kitchen equipment, and with a room that has been transformed into a hospital room from the 1800s. Keep wandering around, enjoying the atmosphere, and looking at the old buildings. If you keep your eyes open you may even come across an old pub, built with sandstone and convict bricks, that has been converted into a craft and glass shop.

GOSFORD - OLD SYDNEY TOWN

In the mood for a short drive out of Sydney and into the year 1788? Then join the rest of the tourists, mainly Aussies, who head down to Old Sydney Town to experience life as it was when the First Fleet arrived.

How to Get There

Go north over the Harbour Bridge and continue on the Pacific Hwy. #1 until you get to the F3 Expressway at Wahronga. Turn north onto the F3 and follow the signs for Old Sydney Town. After about 30 minutes you will turn off at the Gosford exit towards Old Sydney Town. Rail packages plus entry are also available. Call 02 219-4544 for more transport information.

Entry is a bit pricey at around $14.50, but with a student card and a nice attitude you may get a concession even though this is not advertised. The town is open from 10 a.m to 4 p.m Wednesdays to Sundays and Public Holidays. Call 043 401-104 for more information.

The entire place looks as Sydney Cove did in 1788, complete with redcoats, old British accents, scruffy convicts, bums, and an authentic bullock cart. The townspeople are willing to chat with you as they go about their everyday affairs, but don't try to get them to act as if this is the 20th century. We're certain some of them actually believe they are living in the 1700s.

As you enter the town, you will walk through a row of shops, including a craft store, a leather store, a blacksmith's, and other typical shops. The shopkeepers are all busy hand crafting items. Demonstrations of candle and tool making, boomerang throwing, and mead tasting are featured throughout the day.

Further down the road you can take a tour of the harsh looking gaol which is joined to the Magistrate's Courts. If you are lucky you may even see some convicts being tried and punished, either by being put in the stockade and/or by being whipped! Boxing matches and pistol duels take place all around the town.

If you're not careful you may be dragged into the crowd and married by the local pastor! When the cannon goes off, don't worry, a revolt hasn't started. It's just the equivalent of the noon-time whistle. Make sure you stop to listen to the Town Crier when he tells his stories across from the pub.

On the lake is a replica of one of the Tall Ships that sailed from England to Sydney Cove. You can explore the ship and see the small area in the hull that was designated for convicts.

Stop in the pub restaurant for some authentic Aussie damper bread and other typical edibles of the late 1700s. Before you leave, take the bullock cart around "Sydney Cove" over to the Petting Zoo and feed the kangaroos, emus, and other animals that are wandering about.

If you leave near the end of the day, you will get to see the redcoats marching toward the flagpole where they conduct the flag lowering ceremony, complete with cannon salutes.

THE BLUE MOUNTAINS

Tired of the heat of summer or feel like going somewhere to bush walk and watch the leaves change color? Then head out to the Blue Mountains, about 60 miles away from downtown Sydney.

The mountains are actually blue! The secret is the hundreds of eucalyptus trees that release drops of oil into the atmosphere, which in turn reflect the light rays of the sun and create a blue mist over the entire mountain region.

BLUE MOUNTAINS

PICNIC TABLE

GOLF COURSE

Blackheath

GRAND CANYON

Katoomba

Leura

Wentworth

Lawson

Hazelbrook

N

GREAT WESTERN HIGHWAY

JAMISON VALLEY

1/ Pulpit Rock
2/ Govetts Leap Lookout and Walking Track
3/ Blue Gum Forest
4/ Hydro Majestic Hotel
5/ Three Sisters
6/ Sublime Point Lookout

This trip takes you from Sydney to Leura, for a bushwalk, to The Three Sisters at Katoomba, and out to Govett's Leap at Blackheath.

How to Get There

Head west on Parramatta Road, and take the F3 Freeway at Strathfield. The road goes as far as Penrith where signs will direct you to the Blue Mountains. (A new highway is being built from Penrith to Glenbrook. Completion is scheduled for 1997.)

GLENBROOK. As you ascend the mountains, look back to see some stunning views of Sydney. The road twists and turns its way up toward Glenbrook. Once in Glenbrook, turn left at the traffic light in the middle of town, and follow the brown colored signs which direct you to the National Park. The drive is only about three miles.

When you get into the park follow the road that leads down to the river and to some great swimming holes. Park your car in one of the two parking lots and follow the trails to the river swimming holes surrounded by massive boulders.

LEURA TO THE SCENIC RAILWAY BUSH WALK. From the swimming holes, drive back the way you came and get on the highway at Glenbrook continuing west to Leura. From Leura you can hike two and a half hours into the Megalong Valley.

If you are going by train to the Blue Mountains, get off at Leura and take the bus (or walk for 20 minutes) to the Kiah Lookout. If you are driving, make a left from the highway at the sign for Leura onto the road which goes over the railway tracks, then turn left again onto Railway Parade, a right onto Grose St., another right onto Megalong St., and a left at Wascoe Road, which becomes Jersey Avenue.

At the bottom of Jersey Avenue is a "T" Junction. Turn right onto Borden St. and follow the road to Leura Cascades and the Kiah Lookout.

At the lookout take the 1,330 steps down to the valley and make a left where you will begin the Federal Pass Bush Walk. Keep following signs for the Scenic Railway which, at this point, is about two and a half hours away.

This is a very scenic, easy stroll through rich, green vegetation. You will pass by all kinds of gumtrees (watch out for koalas) as well as Linda Falls. You will see the turnoff for the

Three Sisters (see below) when you are about two thirds done with your walk. The sisters are three huge pinnacles of rocks that stretch up from the valley floor to the cliff top. Don't attempt to walk up the stairs at this point. There are more than 1,000 very steep stairs to climb.

The last stop is Katoomba Falls, near the bottom of the railway. The Scenic Railway (about $3) goes almost vertically up the cliff for 450 yards, but the distance from the valley to the top of the cliff is only 250 yards. It is supposedly the steepest railway in the world. The seats face down the mountain so try to get a back seat, because the backwards view is unbelievably scary! Even though we knew the railway works on a counter balance system, we still couldn't understand why we didn't fall over! Look to your left on the way up and you will see the balance coming down.

From the top of the lookout you can get a panoramic view over the whole valley, including the Three Sisters and the Jamison Valley, where you have walked. Then you can take the aerial skyway (chairlift) from this cliff top to another and then walk (or chairlift) back to Echo Point.

If you want to save some money, walk back from the lookout, which takes about half an hour. Go out of the parking lot and turn right onto Falls Road. Walk along here and turn right onto Birdwood Road, right onto Panorama Road and then the first right into Echo Point at Katoomba.

THREE SISTERS, KATOOMBA. From the parking lot at Echo Point, follow the paths to get a great view of Three Sisters. An Aboriginal legend says that a father turned his three daughters into stone to avoid an evil wizard. The father became an eagle and to this day still flies around the rocks and mourns his lost daughters. The area is somewhat commercialized with greasy spoons and pricey cafes.

If you've left your car at Kiah Lookout, it is only one stop away by bus. The local bus leaves every half hour for Kiah and continues on to the Leura and Katoomba train stations.

THE HYDRO MAJESTIC. This beautiful hotel is an Aussie institution. Sydneysiders head out here all year long for romantic weekends in this grand old hotel, but they come here in droves during winter to sit in front of log fires and drink a glass or two of port. You can't miss the hotel.

Many non-Aussies celebrate Christmas in July in the Majestic. If they're lucky, they may even see snow! The bright pink 1930s style building is on the highway at Katoomba and "stands out like dogs balls." If you feel like a splurge, stop in for a drink. Call 047 881-002 to rent one of their luxurious rooms for $120 and up.

GOVETT'S LEAP, BLACKHEATH. From Kiah Lookout go back to the highway and continue west for about 20 minutes until you get to Blackheath. From the highway turn left onto the main street which is opposite the train station. The main street has a few dusty, old antique shops.

From the shops take your first right, go past the Bowling Club and turn left on Clan Williams St. Follow this street until you get to Govett's Leap Lookout. The view is magnificent. You are looking at the valley which is north of the Three Sisters Valley. In between the two is the mountain range. The Leap is a semicircular cliff face with small waterfalls that drop into the valley below.

If you want to bush walk into the valley, follow the path that is off to the left of the lookout. The trail heads down into the Blue Gum Forest. The walk and hike is a bit difficult, so we would suggest bush-camping at the bottom and saving your energy for the next day when you hike back out. If you want a bit more information on this bush walk or any other in the Blue Mountain Region, the Tourist Association (047 821-348) back at Echo Point, Katoomba will give you maps and grades of all the walks in the area.

BUSHWALKING TIPS

A few tips for safe bushwalking: Be certain that you take more than enough supplies with you, especially water and maps. Let someone know where you have gone hiking and how long you plan to be. Every year bushwalkers lose their way and have to be airlifted out. The Blue Mountains Rescue Unit is so tired of doing this they are contemplating charging lost hikers for their rescue missions. This could cost up to $10,000. Remember, Australia is known as the "Empty Continent." It only takes one wrong turn off the track and you can walk hundreds of miles without seeing anyone. Don't kid yourself, it can happen even this close to Sydney!

WENTWORTH FALLS. On the way back to Sydney, you may want to take a detour to Wentworth Falls. If so, get back on the highway at Blackheath and head east toward Sydney. After you pass Katoomba and Leura you will see signs for Wentworth Falls. Turn off into the town of Wentworth Falls and follow the signs for the lookout. This is another spectacular lookout into the Jamison Valley. Give yourself an hour or so to walk around the trails that lead from the lookout. From the falls head back to the highway, turn right and head home to Sydney!

BOTANY BAY AND LA PEROUSE

Only a 45-minute drive from Sydney is the area where Captain Cook and the First Fleet first landed. On the Sydney side of Botany Bay is the Snake Man and an area with a strong Aboriginal influence.

How to Get There

To get to Kurnell and Inscription Point to see the buoy marking the spot where the First Fleet landed, take Parramatta Road west, turn onto City Road where it runs through Newtown, and follow the road south, until it becomes the Princess Hwy. When you arrive at the suburb of Rockdale, keep an eye out for signs directing you to Taren Point. In Rockdale, you will turn left onto Rocky Point Road, cross the bridge, and continue until Rocky Point Road changes to Taren Point Road. At the big roundabout, make a left onto The Boulevard, which becomes Captain Cook Drive. Follow this road all the way to Kurnell and follow the signs to the park.

THE FIRST FLEET BUOY. The quiet National Park offers an uninspiring view of the buoy that marks the spot where Captain Cook landed in Botany Bay. A small museum featuring the sights and sounds of the voyage of Captain Cook, including parts of the boats, is in the park as well. The exhibits include journals and quotes from Captain Cook, Joseph Banks, and Captain Phillip. The peaceful park is filled with Aussie wildlife. Keep an eye out for cockies (cockatoos), galahs (red chests), and kookaburras (the laughing birds).

LA PEROUSE. Follow the above directions back across Taren Point Bridge where Taren Point Road changes its name to Rocky Point Road. Continue north on Rocky Point Road and turn right onto Park Road. At the end of Park Road turn left and you will be on Grand Parade, passing through the suburbs of Brighton Le Sands, Kyeema, and the airport. Slightly after the airport, turn right onto the small freeway signposted to Port Botany. Continue along the shores of Botany Bay. The freeway will intersect with Botany Road. Make a right onto Bunnerong Road and follow this to La Perouse. Or take bus #394 from Circular Quay or #393 from Central Station to La Perouse.

La Perouse was named by the French explorer Perouse. He arrived around the same time as Captain Cook. But after naming this small section of OZ, he was content enough to leave the real discovering to Captain Cook, Captain Phillip, and the British. The area is a small neighborhood in which Aboriginals who are descended from the original inhabitants still live.

The Community has a distinctive Aboriginal flair. On the corner of Bunnerong Round and Anzac Parade a few Koories sell handmade boomerangs and teach tourists how to throw them. This family has been selling these "rangs" here for generations. Slightly further down on Anzac Parade is the La Perouse Museum (page 117), which commemorates the "discovery" of the area by Perouse, as well as the influence of the Aboriginals on the Europeans.

The Snake Man of La Perouse performs on Sundays and public holidays from 1 p.m. to 4 p.m. His shows last about 45 minutes and are free. The family of Snake Men have been coming to this spot for decades. The performance is fascinating, as the Snake Man pulls out everything from tiny, vicious, poisonous snakes to extra large, shy goannas. Don't try to steal his donations! They are safely tucked away in a bag with the most poisonous snakes he owns.

The larger of the two Botany Bay beaches is across from the museum. Phillip Bay doesn't have many waves, but the calm waters are ideal for windsurfing. Both boogie boards and windsurfs are available for rent along the beach. The smaller beach, Little Bay, is behind the Snake Man. Pull into the parking lot and follow the path down to the water. This is a popular family, weekend picnic beach. Many of Sydney's biathalons and triathalons take place here. If you are in town during one of the races, try to head down early to LaPerouse to watch the events. Bear in mind that Botany Bay has more sharks than anywhere else in Sydney!

WEEKEND TRIPS
FROM SYDNEY

CHAPTER 20:

WEEKEND TRIPS FROM SYDNEY

Now that you've experienced Sydney, as well as some of the outlying areas, it's time to go a bit further out and visit the Aussie bush "Beyond the black stump." You can still use Sydney as your base. Pack a smaller backpack and ask your hostel to watch the rest of your stuff. Most hostels will provide this service for free.

The following areas are as close as 120 miles away (the Hunter Valley), and as far as 240 miles (Dubbo). Many bus and tour companies offer trips to these areas, but the best idea is to buy or rent a car with friends.

If that's not possible, check the hostel notice boards and grab a ride with some other backpackers. Usually, you pay only a share of the gas and other expenses. Make sure you call and meet the people beforehand, so that you know you are compatible.

Detailed directions are given in the following sections. Don't worry too much about losing your way. This is the Bush, not the highways in suburban American! Usually only one road goes between two towns and if there are two roads, chances are excellent that both lead to your destination.

TO DUBBO VIA THE MUDGEE WINE REGION

This trip's itinerary takes you to the Western Plains Zoo at Dubbo, stopping along the way in Mudgee to see the vineyards and to taste some Aussie wines, and coming back via Wellington to see the Wellington caves.

If you are traveling during winter (May through September) take some warm clothes. The temperature is a lot colder (by 8 to 20 degrees) on the Western Plains than in Sydney.

How to Get to Mudgee

The best way out of Sydney is to drive west on Parramatta Road until you reach Strathfield. This wealthy, exclusive suburb with its huge mansions used to be a suburb on the outskirts of Sydney. Now Strathfield is a major train interchange for suburbs that lie outside of Sydney to the west and the north.

From Strathfield, get on the Western Freeway, and go as far as Penrith, the outermost suburb of Sydney. From Penrith you can make a choice: either continue on the F3, which is not a freeway in the American sense because it has traffic lights, or go through Penrith to Bells Line of Road and come back via the freeway. Bells Line of Road is the old highway. It's a two-lane road, with some traffic lights, but it is a much more picturesque and interesting route than the highway. I would suggest the latter option.

If you decide on the old highway, get off the Western Freeway at Penrith and head north to the town of Richmond, which is signposted from Penrith. However, just before Richmond take the left turn that is signposted to North Richmond and Kurrajong.

Kurrajong is a good place to stop and stretch your legs. It's an old settlement town of New South Wales and has many antique shops and little cafes to stop in for a traditional (and pricey) Devonshire Tea, served anytime. These teas include homemade scones, with jam and fresh cream. Ultra calorific!

The road continues on through Bilpin, where Bilpin apples are grown. The stalls along the road sell fresh apples in season and other fruits for very cheap prices. Stock up! Continue to Berambing and Mount Tomah, which at 2,800 feet is one of the highest points on Bells Line of Road.

Further down the road at the town of Bell you will see the Old Blue Mountains Railway that goes to Lithgow and Mount Victoria. A short drive from Bell is Lithgow, where you will rejoin the Western Freeway going west. If you feel homesick after all this Aussie culture, you can stop off for lunch at the huge McDonalds, located at the intersection of Bells Line of Road and the freeway.

A mile or so down the freeway you will pass a sign for Mudgee. Turn north at this exit toward Mudgee. The road lies next to a coal-fired power station that is still in active use today. The old concrete road becomes narrower, but it's still in good condition. Continue for about one and a half hours, or about 72 miles north, until you arrive in Mudgee.

MUDGEE. Mudgee is a pleasant, bush town 150 miles from Sydney. It's hot and dry in the summer, and fairly cold in the winter, especially at night. Mudgee lies in a fertile valley with the ideal climate and soil for the cultivation of grapes.

The valley was discovered by Lieutenant Lawson, who, in 1821, was exploring this region with some convicts and an aboriginal guide. After the landing of the First Fleet everything to the west of Parramatta and Richmond was left undiscovered, largely because the settlers viewed the Blue Mountains as impassable. But in 1813 the Blue Mountains were crossed by Blaxland, Lawson, and Wentworth. Towns have been named in these explorers' honor.

In 1820, a severe drought hit Sydney and massive efforts were made to explore the land further west of the mountains in order to find good grazing lands and supply the rapidly increasing population of Sydney and her suburbs. The Superintendent of Police at Bathurst discovered the Cudgewong River. Lieutenant Lawson and his guide were to push farther afield. They came across the valley in which Mudgee and Gulgong are now situated.

WHERE TO STAY. Accommodation in a motel or pub will cost about $35 to $45 a night. Try a caravan (trailer) park, which costs only about $8 to $10 for a trailer with bed, small fridge, sink, and utensils. There are three in the Mudgee area. The closest to town is Riverside (063 72-2531) at 22 Short St., down the road from the movie theater on Church St. It also has tent sites on the riverbank, free barbecues and an outdoor camp kitchen complete with stove. Cooinda Caravan Park (063 72-3337) is at the intersection of Market and Bell Sts.

MUDGEE'S WINERIES. One of the best excuses for stopping at Mudgee is the wine tasting. Wine has been made in the Mudgee district since the 1850s, when the German settlers established wineries for the thirsty gold miners.

Up until the 1960s, wine was never a profitable way to make a living, but during this decade wine drinking became very in vogue. In the early 1960s, 20 tons of grapes were being crushed each year in the Mudgee Valley. Today, 4,500 tons plus are being crushed!

Grape harvesting in autumn (March and April) is the best

time to visit, but any month is a good time for tasting. Drive up to one, or several, of the dozens of tasting rooms, and work your way through what they have to offer. Remember, you don't have to buy, but if you like something buy a bottle or two for lunch and dinner, since most Mudgee wines are not available in shops in Sydney.

If you plan a picnic lunch of cheese and crackers make sure you buy your food in town BEFORE you go tasting. Food is not available from the wineries. Most of the wineries will have picnic tables and a shady spot for lunch.

TOUR OF THE WINERIES. Here's a suggested circuit of the wineries. From the main street in town, drive north over the river, toward the "airport" (a tiny runway in what looks like an overgrown field), and turn off at Henry Lawson Road.

There are six wineries ((Mudgee Wines, Lawson Hill, Knights, Amberton, Montrose, and Miramar) on Henry Lawson and two more (Craigmoor, Seldom Seen) very close by on the branch roads.

At this point, you may want to pick a designated driver. Each winery usually gives you about three half filled wine glasses, so watch out! If you make a right at the top of Henry Lawson, at the Clydesdale Stud Farm, you can come down Cassilis Road.

On your way back toward town, make a left at the sign for Botobular Winery. All the wines here are made using special techniques from organically farmed grapes. Take an organic lunch to go along with the wine!

HOW TO GET RICH BY GOLD FOSSICKING. Ever dream of being in a small dusty town and stumbling over a gold mine worth millions of dollars? Then Mudgee is the place for you! Small gold mining towns are scattered all around this area. The gold boom lasted only 20 years, from 1853 to 1873, after which the thousands of miners, many of whom were Americans, drifted back to the Bush and their home towns and created virtual ghost towns out of the once thriving miner's towns.

The road to the ghost towns is part gravel, but very well maintained so it is possible to get to these towns from Mudgee in an hour. From Mudgee, take the road to Gulgong. Stop in at St. Vincent Meadery, where they make sweet wine, and Honey Haven, which makes delicious varieties of honey, and afterward turn left toward Cudgegong Park.

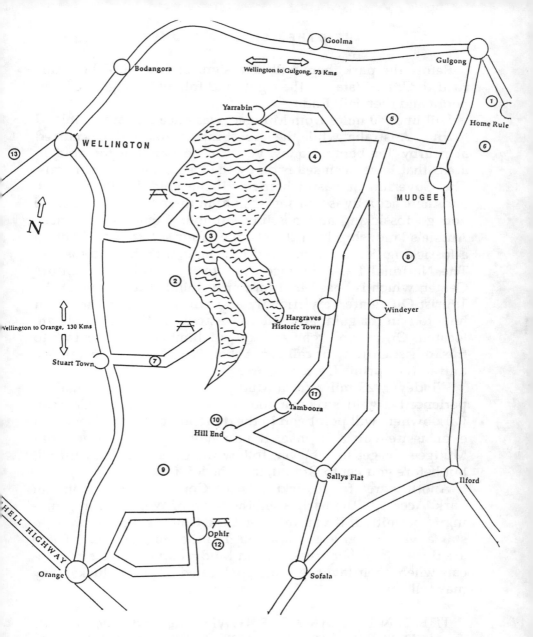

CENTRAL WEST GOLDFIELDS

1/ Glassblowing
2/ Burrendong State Recreation Area
3/ Lake Burrendong
4/ Cudgegong River Park
5/ Winery
6/ Winery

7/ Scenic Drive
8/ Avisford State Forest
9/ Mullions Range State Forest
10/ Mine Shafts
11/ Ghost Town
12/ Early Gold Discovery
13/ Wellington Caves

Before the park there will be a sign for Grattai. Follow this road to Grattai (stay to the right) and follow the signs to Tamboora and then Hill End.

Hill End, 40 miles from Mudgee, was once the largest inland town in Australia, while the largest inland gold strike occurred at nearby Tamboora. Today, you can go panning for gold in areas that have been set aside by the Department of Minerals. The Government hasn't horded all the gold for themselves, and there actually is still some "gold in them thar hills." Before you go fossicking and possibly stumbling onto some ornery Aussie's land, stop in at the Mudgee Tourist Office and obtain a fossicking license, a pan, and information on how to fossick. The National Parks Service operates the Hill End Visitors Center, which is based in a former hospital. The people at the Tourist Office are very friendly and will be glad to show you how to pan for gold, and tell you where the "good" spots are located. Or, try an organized tour of Tamboora. Either talk to the Tourist Officers or call Ted Abbot (063 378-251) to arrange a tour of the "prime fossicking areas."

Windeyer, 25 miles from Mudgee, is another town that experienced a gold strike in the 1850s. The Bushland Caravan Park owners will point you in the direction of Merro Creek and even issue you a license, if you haven't gotten one from Mudgee. To get to Wineyer, follow the directions to Hill End, but before you get to Grattai, take the left fork.

Another area for fossicking is the Goulburn River National Park. Access to the park is via the town of Wollar. Bush camping is permitted, if you really get the Gold Fever and want to stay a week (or at least until you find the "big nugget.") There are dozens of other areas around Mudgee. Ask some of the locals where their favorite spots are located. If you're lucky, they may tell you!

THE TEN DOLLAR NOTE TOWN. The next day, on your way to Dubbo, stop off at the small mining town of Gulgong 18 miles to the north of Mudgee. Much of the historic town is still as it was in the 1850s. It hasn't been rebuilt, but has been preserved by the townsfolk.

Take a $10 Aussie note out of your pocket. The design on the back is of a part of Gulgong, taken from an 1850s photograph of the town. Australia's most famous poet, Henry Lawson, lived here at one time. A memorial to Henry Lawson is located back in Mudgee on Henry Lawson Drive.

HIGHWAY ABORIGINAL ART. If you have the time to back-track, go east from Gulgong along the road to Cassilis and Muswellbrook. After about 20 miles you will come to a sign for "Hands on the Rock", an Aboriginal historical monument. You'll have to bushwalk for about half a mile to get to the site. There are signs along the way to direct you.

This site features ancient stencil impressions of Aboriginal hands that are thought to have been made by Aboriginals who placed their hands on the rocks and then blew paint from their mouths, leaving the stencil impression.

On your way back to Gulgong, about one mile from the hands, you'll see a sign for "The Drip." This is a slow dripping waterfall. It's not much to see as waterfalls go, but you can swim in the river at the bottom of the falls.

How to get to Dubbo:

From Gulgong take the road to Dunedoo (pronounced Dunny Doo). In the middle of Dunedoo turn left onto the road that goes to Ballimore.

Drive straight through Ballimore and into Dubbo through the back door. And don't worry too much about getting lost. Remember this is the Bush — there's only one road between towns!

WHERE TO STAY AND EAT IN DUBBO. Most of the accommodations in Dubbo are in motels or pubs. There are dozens of $30 to $40 and up hotels along Mitchell Hwy. Try one of the caravan parks instead. The closest one to town is on Bligh St., overlooking the highway. Caravans are $10 for two people or you can camp for $8.

For food, entertainment, drinks, and "night life" (what little there is) head over to Dubbo's RSL on Brisbane St. on the corner of Wingewarra St. The cafeteria charges about $6 for a hot dinner of steak, veal or lamb with two vegetables, potatoes, etc. The fancier restaurant has table service, slightly more variety, and a higher price.

THE OLD GAOL. The Old Dubbo Gaol (Jail) is on Macquarie St., the main street in town, near the corner of Church St. Entry is only $2 and you can easily spend an entertaining hour or two exploring the jail.

At the main entrance is an animated Robot Guard who gives you a brief description of the inside. Pick up a free brochure and follow the suggested tour. In our opinion, the best sight is Cell #6, where the condemned awaited execution. The robot replica of Thomas Moore, a murderer who was hanged, will tell you his gruesome story. Next door is the graffiti cell where you can check out the names and add your own.

In the tool shed outside in the exercise yard is a pushbutton story on the history of the gallows and the eight murderers who were hung there. The last hanging took place in 1904, and the jail was officially closed in 1966.

WESTERN PLAINS ZOO. Follow the road to the airport, make a left on Whylandra St. and follow the signs for the three-mile drive to the zoo.

The zoo is situated on 720 acres of good grazing land. Moats, not bars or cages, separate the animals from the visitors. The open bushland territories complete with watering holes are beautifully landscaped.

The zoo is home to 2,000 animals. The vicious, rare, and exotic animals are kept away from visitors, while emus, kangaroos, and peacocks roam freely inside the zoo.

You can explore the zoo by walking, biking or driving. The cheapest way is by foot, but the best way is by bike because you can double back to see the animals being fed. It takes about four or five hours to see the entire zoo on foot. Bicycles cost $16 for a whole day or $8 for a half a day.

You can also bring in your own car or hire a minimoke, which is a small, open topped vehicle capable of holding four people comfortably. If you are carrying food for a barbecue (barbecues are located on the grounds of the zoo and are free to use), you'll probably want transport. Pricey refreshment areas are located inside the zoo.

The zoo's planning makes it a unique place to see animals from all over the world (including North American deer and turkey). Because the zoo has a commitment to the breeding and rearing of rare and endangered species, many of the animals here are not found in other zoos in Australia. White rhinos, Galapagos turtles, and African elephants are among the animals on exhibit.

The Friendship Zoo, a section of the Western Plains, has kangaroos, emus, llamas, donkeys, and other young and orphaned animals. The Cobb and Company Stables are in this area.

The famous Outback Stagecoach Company, the equivalent of the American Wells Fargo and Company, housed their horses in these stables. The building was donated to the zoo, moved from its former site, and reconstructed here.

The area that is now the zoo was formerly an army training camp, so years of landscaping and rejuvenating of the soil were needed to bring the zoo up to the level of excellence required to maintain the animals. Today, it is also a garden of native Australian plants, which include the many varieties of wattles, flowering grevilias, and eucalyptus trees (crush a leaf in your hand and smell).

Before leaving the zoo, be sure to check out the gift shop. If you're lucky they'll have a sale on their animal t-shirts. The zoo is open from 9 a.m. to 5 p.m. Entry is $14/$7 for children.

WELLINGTON CAVES. Now that you've seen all there is to see, at least in this area, head back to Dubbo and turn onto the Mitchell Hwy., the main road to Sydney. The town of Wellington is about 30 miles down the highway. Continue for about five miles past Wellington until you see the sign for Wellington Caves, which is half a mile from the main road.

The two show caves are the Cathedral Cave, with one of the largest stalagmites (that's from the bottom) in the world, and the Gaden Cave. Besides these two, there are many other smaller caves. The Water Cave was found 20 years ago, after it was lost. (Don't ask where it went!) The River Cave is magnificent, but it's only open to certified scuba divers who are able to dive in deep cave waters.

Wellington Caves were discovered in 1828 by Hamilton Hume, and in 1830 George Rankin and Thomas Mitchell discovered thousands of fossil bones in the caves. The most famous of these were the bones of the Diprotodon, a huge prehistoric animal.

Apart from the caves, there is a golf course, a barbecue area, a few domesticated emus and kangaroos wandering around, and a camping and caravan park.

BURRENDONG DAM. On the Mitchell Hwy. toward Sydney, you'll see a sign for the Burrendong Dam (which is 12 miles off the main road). It's certainly worth a detour to see this magnificent expanse of water out in the middle of the dry, dusty bush. If you keep a careful lookout you may see some giant red kangaroos on the horizon or even a confused emu or two. As we found out, the emus in the wild are much different from zoo emus and will run incredibly fast to avoid people.

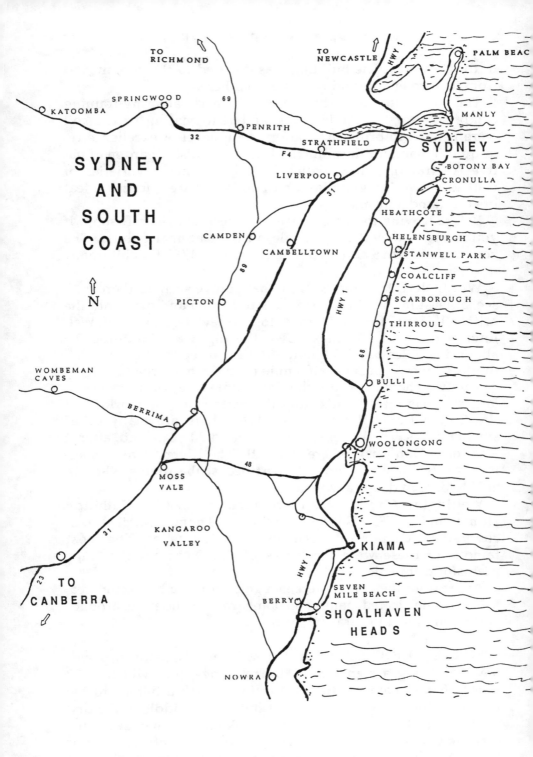

Back on the highway, head toward Orange, and then continue east toward Lithgow (and the McDonalds). From Lithgow drive up to Blackheath, Medlow Bath, Katoomba, Leura, Springwood, and then finally back down to Penrith. From here rejoin the F3 to arrive in Sydney in an hour. For an in-depth tour of the Blue Mountains see page 181.

SHOALHAVEN HEADS AND KANGAROO VALLEY

This trip heads south along the coast road and passes through Stanwell Tops (the central location for hangliders), the blowhole at Kiama, and Shellharbour (which has a lake and three beaches) to Shoalhaven Heads and returns to Sydney via Berry (an old Bushtown loaded with antique and craft stores), the Kangaroo Valley, Bowral, and Mittagong.

How to get there:

Leave Sydney via Parramatta Road west and then turn south (left) onto City Road (which is off Parramatta Road at the Landsdowne Hotel). Follow the signs for Princess Hwy., since City Road eventually turns into the highway. Until you get way out of Sydney, the highway is just another road.

Drive south through Newtown and then past the suburbs of Tempe, Rockdale, and Blakehurst. You'll drive over a river bridge that is known as Tom Ugly's, although no one seems to know from where the name originates.

After the bridge, the road becomes more like a highway, although there are still numerous traffic lights. The last suburbs that you'll pass are Sylvania, Southerland, Loftus, Engadine, and Heathcote. At last, the road looks like a real highway! Continue for a few miles until you see a sign for the freeway (even though it costs to drive on the "free"way). Take the turnoff just before the freeway, which has a sign that directs you to the Old Princess Hwy. #1. At the "T" junction make a left turn and you'll be on your way to Woolongong via the back road.

Stay on the #1, go under the freeway, down and up a small hill, past a gas station on the left, and after the crest of the hill there will be a small road to the left with a sign that says "Stanwell Park." Take this road to the coast and you will be rewarded with staggering views of the beaches down below and a superb view of Woolongong (which looks much better from the Coast Road than it does up close).

You will come to a major fork, with one road leading to the south along the coast (follow the sign to Woolongong). Stay to the left for about one quarter of a mile.

A parking lot on your right will let you know that you have arrived at Stanwell Tops. The view here is magnificent. On any given day (especially weekends), you should see hangliders jumping off the cliff and landing on the beach below.

Go back the way you came (toward the fork) and this time head south along the Coast Road.

THE COAST ROAD. The road veers sharply downhill to Coalcliffe, the first town on the coast. This whole area is used for coal mining, although the pit heads (or entrance to the mines) are way off the road to the right on the face of the cliff and are difficult to see. Some of the mines go out under the sea for three to four miles where the coal seams are located.

Next you'll drive through Scarborough, which has a few shops and a local pub named The Scarborough Hotel, which serves lobster lunches for $10. The road meanders around the cliffs and every few yards there are signs warning drivers to beware of "Falling Rocks - Do Not Stop!"

The Coast Road is very popular among bikers who love the thrill of a long, winding road with sharp corners and few police.

Down the road is Wombarra, where at low tide you can explore the large rock ledge with lots of rock pools. To get there by foot, take the path past the cemetery.

Continue driving south to Austimer and the larger community of Thirroul, which has quite a nice beach backed by Norfolk pine trees. These come from Norfolk Island off the New South Wales coast.

The beach is popular among surfies, because the surf is consistent. Farther south the coastal road ends and you intersect with the main Woolongong road, which is the Princess Hwy.

Continue along the main road for approximately a half of a mile until you get to Bulli. The architecture of Bulli is very typical, historic Bush town style, and utilizes lots of wood, balconies, and awnings. The town contains many antique stores.

WOOLONGONG. As you continue south you will start to go through the northern suburbs of Woolongong.

The next towns are called by names only Australians could dream up: Bellambi (which is the name of a town and a large coal company), Balgownie, and Fairy Meadow.

There is not too much of interest in the northern suburbs or even Woolongong. The latter is home to the large steel mill of Port Kembla, which is located in the south of Woolongong.

If you like steel mills, and feel like taking a detour, you can actually have a tour of Port Kembla Steel. Otherwise, bypass Woolongong by continuing south and following the signs for Port Kembla and Shellharbour.

SHELLHARBOUR. This is a small seaside resort mainly patronized by locals. It has three beaches and a lake. From Port Kembla, continue south on the main road and you'll cross over Windang Bridge and Lake Illawarra. On the other side of the bridge turn right onto Reddall Road, along the shores of Lake Illawara.

All along the lake are kiosks that will rent windsurfs, surfboards, canoes, catamarans, small fishing boats, small sailing skiffs, and water skis (talk to the members of the Water Ski Club).

If you land in this region during the summer months, get a scoop net and fish for the sweet lake prawns. Otherwise you can try for some other lake fish such as bream, blackfish, and flathead, and during the summer months, whiting. The bait and tackle shops will hook you up with everything you need. Try your luck and maybe you'll be able to "Throw another shrimp on the barbie!"

If you prefer ocean fishing, you can fish for jewfish, snapper, mackerel, kingfish, and tuna. The bait and tackle shops will tell you where to go outside of the Heads.

Drive back toward the Windang Bridge, and turn right onto Shellharbour Road. If you want to scuba dive, go to Coastwide Diving Services on Addison St. They are very friendly and can recommend snorkeling and diving spots and arrange boat dives. The Marine Reserve at Bass Point has some good diving spots as well.

Another option for snorkeling and ocean fishing is to follow Shellharbour Road one mile south and take the turn off to Killalea State Recreation Park. This national park charges a small entrance fee. The most popular beach among the surfies, known as the "Farm" or "Mystics," is also located in here.

Shellharbour has four golf courses in the area as well as an 18-hole golf course at the back of town.

WHERE TO STAY AND EAT IN SHELLHARBOUR. If you want to spend the night here, the Caravan Park on John St. rents caravans and has room for camping. The Warilla Hotel Pub is about $35 and up a night and the Blackbutt Hotel is even pricier.

Shellharbour has its fair share of clubs, including the Worker's and the Golfer's (Addison St.) clubs. Both serve the usual Chinese fare, but for something a little bit different, try the Albion Park Hotel where you can buy a raw steak and barbecue it yourself in the back garden! Or, if you're desperate for lots of food, the Sizzler on Shellharbour Road at the Warrilla Grove Shopping Center is always good value.

BUSH WALKING AND JAMBEROO. Leaving Shellharbour, go west along Pioneer Road to the Princess Hwy. at the town of Albion Park Rail. Head north (back toward Woolongong) for one quarter of a mile and turn left onto the Illawarra Hwy. A mile or so down the road is a sign for Jamberoo. This is the road you will take to continue south to Shoalhaven Heads.

However, if you want to detour and spend some time bushwalking in the Macquarie National Park, continue along the Illawarra Hwy. for six miles and you will come to the foot of the Macquarie Pass. Picnic areas are located here and on Clover Hill Road. To reach one of the two waterfalls, walk from the northern picnic area, and to reach the other drive up the Macquarie Pass and take the Clover Hill turnoff to the picnic areas. From Clover Hill it's only a short, but rocky, walk upstream to Rainbow Falls and the Balancing Rock, where you can cool off and go for a swim.

Serious bushwalking trails are scattered throughout the park. You can camp at the Macquarie Rivulet Picnic Ground, but take your own water and a shovel for the toilet.

If you don't have the time, take the turnoff for Jamberoo, which is a very pretty way to get to Kiama and where you will see some of the most beautiful countryside in New South Wales. The Jamberoo Recreation Park is also on this road. It is open daily during summer school holidays (December through January), on weekends during the rest of the time, and closed during winter.

The park has a mountain slide which is a summer version of the bobsled run. Can you get to the bottom of the mountain without putting the brakes on? Go-carts, power boat rides, and other activities can keep anyone occupied for hours.

KIAMA AND THE BLOW HOLE. Continue south from Jamberoo and the small road you are on will bring you straight into Kiama.

The most northern beach looks inviting, but don't be tempted to swim. The currents here create dangerous riptides (that's why no locals are out). Wait until you get to Seven Mile Beach, which is farther down the coast to the south of Kiama.

Kiama is a picturesque, small town. The north side of town has Main St., which used to be the main highway before the bypass was built. This area is a bit touristy, but you can still track down a few Aussie souvenirs and a Devonshire Tea.

Laconia, a great old-fashioned milk bar, serves mega-portions of chips, delicious fried fish, and the largest gyro we've ever seen for unbelievably low prices. The Fudge House serves free samples of fudge and sells homemade ice cream. The bakeries sell lamingtons, vanilla slices, and other Aussie delights. Grab some food to feed to the greedy seagulls at the Blow Hole.

To get to the Blow Hole, go south on the main road, pass the traffic light at the post office, and turn left at the end of the road into the car park. The Blow Hole is in the middle of some rocky cliffs, and when there is a high tide or big swell the Hole blows water up to 100 feet into the air. Return to the Princess Hwy. by heading back the way you came, turn left at the traffic light and left again when you see the sign for Nowra.

SEVEN MILE BEACH. From Kiama drive south for about two miles, in the direction of Nowra, to Kiama Bends, which are wild bends in the road. When you get to the bottom of the hill, take the turnoff on the left that crosses the railway line. At this turnoff is an advertisement for Boral Cement products, which has been there almost as long as the Aboriginals have lived in Australia. Well, not really.

Continue on this road until you get to Gerringong, a small town which has a nice beach for swimming. As you drive over the River Bridge, to the south, you'll see a caravan park. One mile or so past here is the sign for Seven Mile Beach. If you want to go to the beach, turn left at the turnoff. Even though you can't see the beach from the road, it's there, about a mile from the road. The beach stretches for seven miles to Shoalhaven Heads. The surf is always good, but there are no Surf Lifesavers on duty.

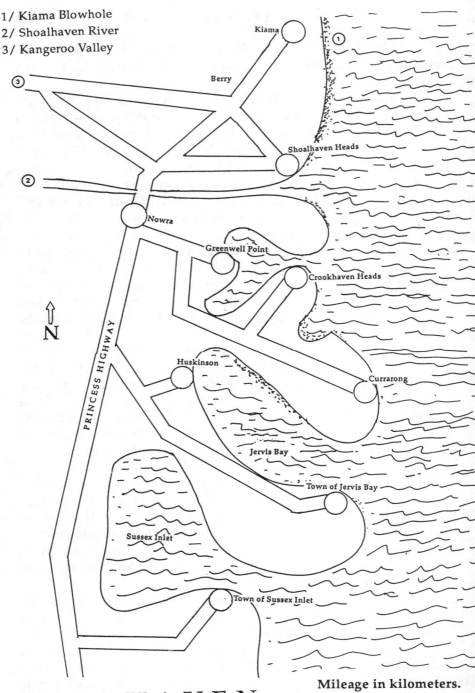

1/ Kiama Blowhole
2/ Shoalhaven River
3/ Kangeroo Valley

Kiama

Berry

Shoalhaven Heads

Nowra

Greenwell Point

Crookhaven Heads

N

PRINCESS HIGHWAY

Huskinson

Currarong

Jervis Bay

Town of Jervis Bay

Sussex Inlet

Town of Sussex Inlet

SHOALHAVEN
HEADS AREA

Mileage in kilometers.
Shoalhaven Heads to Nowra - 19 Km
Nowra to Kangeroo Valley -16 Kms
Nowra to Currarong 27 - Kms.
Nowra to Jervis Bay - 34 Kms.
Nowra to Huskinson - 23 Kms.
Nowra to Sussex Inlet - 41 Kms.

SHOALHAVEN HEADS. Finally, at the seventh mile of Seven Mile Beach and about 120 miles from Sydney is the halfway point of this trip, Shoalhaven Heads.

The local community is rather small during the winter, but during the summer months a lot of Sydneysiders head out this way to enjoy the ocean beach.

Another attraction is the estuary or river mouth. When the tide is out, you can walk for miles on the hard-packed sand. Dozens of birds, including pelicans, hang out in this area and fish in the small pools that have been left by the receding tide. The river mouth also has good swimming channels.

BERRY. Make a right on the main road when you leave Shoalhaven Heads, then make the first left and head straight for about four miles to the Princess Hwy. and Berry. The town is an interesting Bush neighborhood, where the farmers intermingle with the alternative lifestylers.

The shops sell antiques, crafts, and woodcarvings, as well as crystals and New Age music. The restaurants are typical of a country town with home-baked stone ground breads, cakes, and other hearty foods.

The town gets a good crowd in the summer when the city folk come out to the country for the weekend.

NOWRA. Before you leave Shoalhaven for Sydney, stop in at the little town of Nowra. The Aussie folk around here are pretty friendly.

The local Shoalhaven radio station is based in Nowra and it is quite good for a small town. Tune in to 2UUU FM for political commentary, classic rock, Aboriginal music, and blues. The president of the Radio Station, Robert Bell, will gladly give you a tour of the small station or trade some tunes with you. For preferential treatment, tell him you read about the station here.

To get to the station from Shoalhaven Heads, go back to the Seven Mile Beach Road, turn left and continue to Bombaderry. Go through this town, and when the road "T" junctions at the Princess Hwy., turn left, go over the bridge, and enter Nowra.

After the radio station, head north over the bridge outside of Nowra, turn left at the sign for Kangaroo Valley, and head to the Nowra Animal Park (page 153). From Berry head south toward Nowra and turn right, before you enter the town, onto Kangaroo Valley Road in the direction of Kangaroo Valley.

KANGAROO VALLEY. Driving west on Kangaroo Valley road takes you up Mount Cambewarra. The mountain is not very high, but the views from the top are superb. Once you get down the other side of the mountain you'll be in Kangaroo Valley, a small, friendly community.

Unfortunately, contrary to the name, you won't find kangaroos shopping down Main St., but you will find a wide variety of shops, such as Valley Woodcrafts, where everything imaginable is made from wood, a Fudge House, an ice cream shop, and The Friendly Inn Pub, which is true to its name. Order Aussie damper bread along with your counter lunch.

The Glenmark Caravan Park is located in town, and the Hampden Bridge is outside of town. If you want to bush camp, head over the bridge and turn right onto the dirt road that follows the river for about a mile. You can camp on the banks of the river for free. Below the bridge is a good spot for swimming and canoeing.

FITZROY FALLS. Back on Kangaroo Valley road, head up the valley toward Fitzroy Falls and Bowral. Keep watching out the windows, because the drive up the valley affords some spectacular views of the coast.

When you arrive at Fitzroy Falls, park the car and follow the signs which lead you into the Bush and to the falls. Fitzroy was the actual discoverer of these fabulous falls from which water plummets back down the escarpment into Kangaroo Valley.

BOWRAL AND THE BUSHRANGERS. Back in your car, follow the signs for Bowral and you will pass through Bundadoon. When you come to the "T" junction at Sutton Forest, turn right and follow Argyle St. which changes its name to Bong Bong St. and becomes the main street of the little town of Bowral.

This old Australian Bush town, along with many of the other towns in the southern highlands, was once home to the Bushrangers who held up stagecoaches and railroads and robbed people during the gold rush of the mid-1800s. Today, modern Bushrangers (lawyers, bankers, etc.) have their expensive country estates here!

While you are in town, stop at the Blue Boar Pub and Hotel or at the Bowral Cafe, which serves typical Aussie country treats.

The Grand Hotel and Coffee Shop was built in 1888, is still

in impeccable condition, and has been renovated into a classy hotel and coffee shop. Antique shops line the streets, and you can find a lot of old Bush antiques unique to this area. The Past and Present has estate jewelry and silverware, while John Lane's has some old kitchen items and other collectibles from the 1800s.

MITTAGONG AND HEADING HOME TO SYDNEY. As you leave Bowral, head towards Mittagong, where you will join the main Sydney to Melbourne Hwy. As you drive into Mittagong, you will arrive at the foot of the Clock Tower War Memorial. From there turn right and head home towards Sydney.

Now that you're finished with the tour and back on the main road, you should arrive in Sydney in about an hour and a half. You'll arrive via Liverpool and then you will need to wend your way back to the appropriate suburb. Stay on the Hume Hwy. as long as possible, since it's the least confusing route home.

HUNTER VALLEY

Are you ready for some serious wine tasting? With the extensions of the highway, the Hunter Valley is a mere two hours' drive from Sydney. If you don't want to spend the entire time sipping wine, don't worry! Antique shops, craft galleries, an orchid farm, aqua golf, clay pigeon shooting, and champagne balloon flights are all available in the region. This trip concentrates on the Lower Hunter Valley. But, if you have extra time, head up to the Upper Valley.

How to get there

Head north over the Harbour Bridge and follow the signs for Pacific Hwy. #1. Continue through Sydney's suburbs, including Chatswood, Pymble, and Turramarra. When you arrive in Wahroonga, you'll see a sign for the F3 Freeway. Stay on the F3 for two hours and follow the signs for the little town of Cessnock. At the entrance of town is a map and information, which you can use to plan which part of the valley you want to visit.

WOLLOMBI. If you plan to see Wollombi before you reach the Hunter Valley, try the picturesque, alternative route. Turn off the freeway at Peat's Ridge and take the Great Northern

Road, which was built by convicts. The road twists and turns through farmland and into Wollombi, which is only 18 miles from Cessnock.

While you're there stop off at the school, post office, and courthouses to see the original stone architecture. You may want to buy some "Dr. Jurds Jungle Juice" at the old fashioned country pub called the Wollombi Tavern. Ask for a free tasting! It's a mixture of some of the local wines and alcohol. Be careful, because it goes down smoothly but has a kick! Or go to the home of Old Frank's Firewater and enjoy their selections of wine and alcoholic cider.

THE HUNTER VALLEY. The Hunter Valley is located in the district of Cessnock, which was settled over 150 years ago by free settlers and freed convicts. The first vineyard was established by James Busby, who was given 2000 acres. He sailed back to England and returned with 700 vine cuttings, half of which were planted in the Royal Botanical Gardens, and the other half of which were planted on his land.

During this period the government of the new colony was still trying to combat the influences of rum. They decided that table wine would be the answer to diabolical spirits. The government invested in the Pokolbin Lower Hunter area and for a while grape growing flourished.

But the climate of Hunter Valley proved very temperamental. This, on top of the Depression of 1893, almost wiped out the baby wine industry. The Hunter was not a very productive region until the 1960s when wine drinking came into vogue. Today, those 700 vines have expanded into 7,000 acres!

WHERE TO STAY AND EAT IN LOWER HUNTER. The hotels in the Hunter Valley are not only pricey, they are usually filled to capacity. If you want to stay in a hotel, either go during the week and take advantage of their Sunday to Thursday specials or book ahead.

The best option is to stay in a caravan park. The Valley View Caravan (049 902-573) on Mount View Road and the Cessnock Cabins and Caravan Park both have room for camping, a swimming pool, and inexpensive caravans. The former seems to fill up slowly and is on a quiet dirt road, while the latter is across from a restaurant and a paved road and can be noisier.

HUNTER VALLEY WINERIES

1/ Hunter Estate
2/ Marsh Estate
3/ Sutherland
4/ Richmond Grove
5/ Terrace Vale
6/ Sorbells
7/ Littles
8/ Moorbank
9/ Calais
10/ Fraser
11/ James Hunter
12/ Millstone
13/ Honeytree
14/ Scareborough
15/ Oakvale
16/ Chateau Francois
17/ Tyrells
18/ Hungerford Hill
19/ Verona
20/ Robson
21/ Tallawanta
22/ Rothbury Estate
23/ Gateway
24/ Lesnick
25/ Dawson Estate
26/ Brokenwood
27/ Tamberlaine
28/ Polkolbin
29/ Tullochs
30/ Windara
31/ Thalgara
32/ Lindeman's Hunter River
33/ Golden Grape
34/ Draytons
35/ Mount Pleasant
36/ Saddlers Creek
37/ Hillside
38/ Mountview
39/ Jacksons Hill
40/ Peterson
41/ Briar Ridge

If you are planning to eat while you taste (a very good idea), buy all of your food at the supermarket BEFORE you go tasting. One or two wineries provide nibbles, but most don't even provide so much as a cracker to munch on. If you are desperate, the Hungerford Hill Wine Village has a farmer's market that sells fruits, cheeses, and the like, and it also has a kiosk for greasy, takeout meat pies.

At night, dinner pickings are just as slim. The restaurants are either pricey, such as Peppertree's, or serve fried counter foods, as does The Bellbird Hotel. Your other options are the Ex-Services club which serves Chinese and Aussie food, McDonalds, Kentucky Fried Chicken or Pizza Hut. None of these places lets you drink the wine you bought! You may just want to cook up some food in your caravan and drink your wine in peace.

TOUR OF THE LOWER HUNTER VALLEY WINERIES. With 40 wineries in the Lower Hunter Pokolbin Region, you can spend a week sampling wines. We took two days to do the following small tour. It was just enough time and alcohol to make the weekend trip enjoyable. Grab a map at the Visitor's Center on the corner of Mount View and Wollombi Roads and adapt our tour to suit your needs.

Remember that some wineries specialize in mixing certain grapes, others have wine that is available only in the valley, and still others produce wine here that they sell all over Australia and abroad. Most wineries are open 9 a.m. to 4:30 p.m. Monday to Friday and 10 a.m. to 4:30 p.m. Weekends. On Sundays, some of the wineries are closed.

The winemakers in the Hunter Valley have developed their own grading system for their finest wines. "Classic" refers to wines that are mature and ready to drink, while the term "Benchmark" designates younger wines that need further cellaring and have the potential to become "Classics."

After you've arrived in town, picked up the map, bought supplies, and maybe reserved your caravan, head back north on Allandale Road. The first stop is Dawson Estate, which is a small family-owned winery that specializes in chardonnay grapes.

Next, the Lesnick Family Winery is up the road on the right at the corner of Broke and Allandale Roads. The Lesnicks have been making wine for over five generations, both in Australia and Austria. They specialize in blends of semillon, chardonnay, riesling, cabernet sauvignon, shiraz, pinot noir, merlot, and malbec, brut champagne, a variety of port, and liquors.

Make a left onto Broke Road and your first left onto the small road that leads to Debeyers Road, and Tullochs and Lindemanns wineries. Lindemanns, on the corner of McDonalds and Debeyers Roads, is one of the largest wine makers in the Hunter.

Dr. Lindemann was one of the first to grow wines when he opened this winery in 1842, and now the family owns three wineries in the Lower Valley. The wines are available in many stores in Australia and abroad, but they have some good young and classic wines to sample at the wineries.

Turn right at McDonald's Road and visit Tullochs. The winery is named after the founder, J.Y. Tulloch, who was given a parcel of land in repayment for a debt. He planted some grapes and the original 60 gallons sold so well that he never looked back! Cabernet sauvignon and hermitage grapes are used to make red wines.

The grapes are grown on red volcanic hills. The semillons, chardonnay, and verdelhos are used in the making of whites and are grown on sandy creek flats.

The historic Pokolbin Winery is next door. The first owner, John McDonald, started the winery in 1886, but it was sold to Lindemanns in 1912. The original buildings, constructed in the 1880s are still standing and form an active part of the winery.

The next small winery, Tamburlaine, specializes in boutique wines that are unavailable outside of the region. The proprietor loves to talk about the shower of fruity tastes that flow over your tongue while drinking his wine!

If you are in a rush, stop in at the Small Winemakers Center. They represent Veronas, Dawson Estate, Reynolds, and Simon Whitlam (son of ex-Prime Minister Gough Whitlam) wineries, and they have a deli-cafe with pecan pies and pecans. If you have plenty of time, you should visit these wineries on your own.

Across the street from the center is Brokenwood, a very small winery which prides itself on making great reds and explaining its wines to the guests. Brokenwood has won several show awards and even exports wine to the United States and Fiji.

In contrast, the Hungerford Hill Winery is located on a huge complex which includes a gallery, farmers market, kiosk, restaurant, and even an aqua golf driving range! The dark, traditionally styled tasting room is called the Cellar. Limited releases and other wines are available for tasting.

Make a left back onto Broke Road and head over to Tyrells, the winery that put the Hunter Valley on the map. Tyrells 1976 Pinot Noir took first prize in the 1979 Paris Wine Olympiad, and was then declared one of the 10 best wines in the world. Murray Tyrell was the first to introduce home grown Chardonnay to Aussies.

The Long Flat Red and Long Flat White wines are inexpensive wines that are available in your local bottle shop. Since the winery has become so large, it has lost some of its personal touch. If you have the time, stop by. But if not, go to a friendlier winery or buy a bottle of Tyrells in Sydney.

Pace yourself to visit the last three wineries on our tour, which are slightly out of the way, but deserve a visit. The beautiful setting of Richmond Grove Winery, combined with great wines and monthly Saturday evening recitals makes this winery one of the more original ones in the Hunter.

Richmond Grove is mainly known for its red wines, although the whites are delicious as well. To get to Richmond follow Broke Road and make a right onto Hermitage Road. The winery is on your left.

Leaving Richmond, head back down Hermitage Road. At Deaseys Road turn right and continue until you reach Sutherland Wines. This small winery has won more than 100 National Awards. Neil Sutherland's chenin blanc is an unusual wine with a slightly fruity taste. Recently, he has created a chenin cremant by adding the methode champenoise to his chenin blanc. Chardonnay and semillon are other white grapes, while the reds are shiraz, cabernet sauvignon, and pinot noir.

Last is the Rothbury Estate. From Deaseys Road turn right onto McDonalds Road and then a left back onto Broke Road. Rothbury offers guided tours every day at 11 a.m. and 2 p.m. for only $2.

If you have a group of ten or more, an extensive tour and tasting can be arranged at a cost of $4 a person. Rothbury makes wines that are available in specialized bottle shops in Australia. The setting is beautiful and is the perfect place to relax before heading home for some dinner and a nap.

CANBERRA

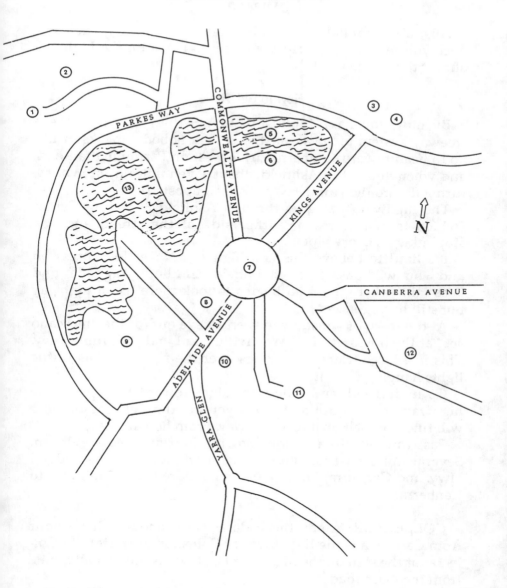

1/ Black Mountain Lookout
2/ Royal Botanical Gardens
3/ Blundell's Farmhouse
4/ Australian American Memorial
5/ Captain Cook Memorial Fountain
6/ Carrillon
7/ Capitol Hill
8/ Foreign Embassies

9/ Government House
10/ Royal Australian Mint
11/ Redhill
12/ National Velodrome
13/ Lake Burley Griffin

CANBERRA

Australia's capital city is only three hours from Sydney and once you're clear of Sydney, you get to drive on the highway almost the whole way!

How to Get There

By now you have found out that Sydney doesn't have a freeway system to speak of (that's why nobody speaks of it!). So to head toward Canberra, drive west on Parrammatta Road, and when you get to Ashfield, about seven miles from Sydney, turn left onto the Hume Hwy. (well signposted).

The highway first goes through Ashfield Shopping Center (which is just stores on either side of the street) and has stoplights on every block.

It's hard to believe this is a highway. Never fear, press on and you will pass through Enfield, Chullora, Yagoona, and Bass Hill, where the road begins to look more like a highway but still has lights.

At the town of Lansdowne keep an eye out for the "meccano set" at the intersection of Woodville Road and the Hume Hwy. This is a large frame that hangs over the road and has traffic lights hanging from it.

Go underneath and follow the signs toward Liverpool. The highway heads south and when you get through Cassula you will find yourself on a real highway. From here it's easy.

Pass through the towns of Bowral, Berrima, and Goulburn. Several miles past Goulburn, take a left turn for the Federal Hwy. and Canberra. From here it's no more than 45 minutes to Canberra.

COLLECTOR. Along the Federal Hwy. about half an hour from Canberra is the little town of Collector. Turn right to Collector at the sign on the highway. The town is only a half a mile from the main road.

There's not much more to Collector than the Collector Tavern. It's an old bushranger tavern filled with Ocker Aussies drinking schooners, playing pool, and acting Aussie. Outside is the obligatory lazy guard dog and cars that look as if they should be in a museum. Pick up a souvenir bumper sticker, "I got held up at the Bushranger Hotel." The menu is hilarious and we dare you to try some of it. Their specialties are:

APPETEASERS
Mortal Bay Bugs

SOUP
Soup du Yesterjour (been soup)
Big Red - Kangaroo Tail (skinned extra)

GAME - FOUL & PALTRY
Pressed Rabbit (straight from the highway)
Spoonbill Surprise (small spoon, big bill)
Savoury Swallow (one swallow's enough)

ONTRAY
Beef Strongenough
Crowquettes
Aussie Snitzel
(a hunk of emu fillet bashed flat with an axe)

CHEF'S SELECTION
Lake George Trout
(tantalizingly teased from the lake by carefully placed hand
grenades. Served with araldite (glue) sauce)
Burymundi (served weekends only)

SWEATS
Fruit Fly Pie

For all you unadventurous types, if the menu is too daring, have plain old counter lunches and schooners of beer or lemon squash.

THE DISAPPEARING LAKE. About 15 minutes outside of Canberra is Lake George. This is no ordinary lake, because sometimes it's there and sometimes it's not! Other times it's partially there and the land turns into grazing pastures and is filled with cows. No one really knows where the water goes. Some people believe it disappears into the limestone and returns when the rock is full.

CANBERRA. This is a young city that has a population of only 900,000 people. Canberra was well planned and designed by a Chicagoan named Walter Burley Griffin, who was an associate of Frank Lloyd Wright.
Griffin's design won an international competition in 1909, but it took over 40 years to get the project moving. The design

is similar to a wheel with many spokes, but it works! The streets are wide, the houses set back, the stores and gas stations hidden, and the lighting perfectly spaced. Many people say that Canberra is boring and lacks character. Unless you keep yourself occupied with the museums, galleries, shopping centers, and Parliament, Canberra can get a bit boring. But as far as character goes, it's just different from the hustle and bustle of Sydney.

WHERE TO STAY IN CANBERRA. Canberra is not a backpackers' center like Sydney, so it doesn't have the same range of accommodations. The prices for hotels are much higher. Slightly upmarket accommodations can be pre-reserved from Sydney. Either visit the Canberra Information Center at 611A, Wingello House, Angel Place, or call at 02 233-3666.
Try the youth hostel or one of the following "cheapies:"

Youth Hostel, Dryandra St., O'Connor, 06 248-9155. The suburb of O'Connor and the YHA are on the opposite side from where you arrived and about five miles outside of town. If you arrived in Canberra by bus, switch to bus #380 which leaves every half hour (weekdays) and hourly (weekends) from the City Terminal to Scrivener St., and from there you can follow the signs to the hostel. The YHA is a bit out of the center of town, but it has a nice green, shady setting. The cost is only $15 per night, plus, if necessary, $3 for a sleep sheet and $5 extra for non-YHA members. The hostel has all the facilities of a YHA, including a notice board with tours of Canberra. The hostel is open from 7 a.m. to 10:30 p.m., but check in can be as late as midnight with advance reservations.

The Chelsea Lodge, 526 Northbourne Avenue, Downer, 06 248-0655. Many hotels are located along Northbourne Avenue as you arrive from Sydney. This hotel is $38 per person per night including a hot breakfast.

The Blue and White Lodge, 524 Northbourne, 06 248-0498. Another cheapie by Canberra standards, $30 plus for double rooms, but a television and tea making facilities are in every room.

Canberra Motor Village, Kunzea St., O'Connor, 247-5466. Less than two miles from the city center, this caravan park charges $18 for a trailer site and starts at $39 for a double caravan. The village has a swimming pool, tennis, and a joint kitchen. Other caravan parks are much cheaper, but they are further out of town. If you have transport, these are a great idea.

GETTING AROUND CANBERRA. If you don't have a car, Canberra has an excellent Public Bus Transportation System (no trains). The fare for most trips is $2. With a Daytripper ($4.80) or a weekly ticket ($18), you have unlimited bus travel. These are available from most newsagents.

The Downtowner, a bus that looks like a tram, provides a free service around the Civic Shopping Mall.

Another alternative is to tour by bicycle. You can hire one at the YHA, the Acton Ferry Terminal, or the Glebe Park Kiosk. Rates start at about $6 an hour or $20 a day. Canberra is very flat and has minimal traffic. This makes bike riding enjoyable and safe. If you need any other information contact the Canberra ACT Tourist Commission on 1800 026-166 (free call from anywhere in Australia) or 06 205-0044.

THE WAR MEMORIAL. Corner of Limestone, Fairbairn, and Anzac Avenues, 243-4211. The memorial is free to visit and it's not quite as boring as other war memorials because of the great variety of exhibits. It even has a section on the Gulf War of 1991, the Vietnam War (with miniature soldiers fighting in foxholes), and World Wars I and II.

The Airplane Hall has old World War I and larger World War II fighter planes suspended from the ceiling, as well as a bomber parked on the floor. The special permanent exhibits on "Women in War" and "Prisoners of War" are especially interesting. Open daily from 10 a.m. to 5 p.m. except Christmas.

OLD AND NEW PARLIAMENT HOUSE. King George Terrace and Capital Hill. The Old Parliament was virtually abandoned in 1988 when New Parliament House opened its doors after almost ten years of construction. Since then, the most exciting event in the Old House was when the Aboriginals took over the building in 1992 and proclaimed the building the Aboriginal Embassy. Notice how similar the Old House looks to a wedding cake?

Go explore the New Parliament to find out what the Australian taxpayers got for $1 billion. When Parliament is in session the public is invited to watch the proceedings from the Public Gallery.

The best spectacle is Question Time. This is when the Government defends itself and its policies from the attacks of the Opposition. These attacks can get very nasty! You can mail away for tickets in advance or ask at the Information Booth. When Parliament is not in session, 45 minute tours of the building are given. They start at 9 a.m. every day and go every half hour until 4 p.m.

The building has a beautiful entrance hall that was designed to resemble a eucalyptus forest. One look at the 48 pink marble columns and stairs and you can figure out where a large portion of the $1 billion went! The Senate has 76 Senators elected for a period of six years. They convene in a pink room. The Lower House of Representatives has members who are elected for three years and sit for only 60 to 70 days each year. The Representatives convene in a larger green room.

Inside King's Hall is one of three surviving copies of the Magna Carta. Next, take the elevator to the roof which is covered in grass for insulation purposes. If you have ever wanted to picnic on the most important roof in Australia, here's your chance! The flagpole on the roof is a landmark that can be seen from almost anywhere in Canberra.

EMBASSY ROW. On the other side of Commonwealth Avenue, across from King George Terrace, is the area that has been set aside for foreign embassies. Many embassies were built in the style of the home country: the American Embassy is an old Virginian mansion (the land was leased the day Pearl Harbor was bombed); the Chinese is similar to a Chinese temple (complete with tennis courts, swimming pool, and other outdoor amenities); the Thai looks like the Thai Royal Palace in Bangkok, and the British has a croquet lawn (while the building looks like a typical, drab London style complex).

LAKE BURLEY GRIFFIN AND THE COMMONWEALTH PARK. The lake is an artificial creation. The Molonglo River was dammed and 22 miles of park shores were created. Paddle boats can be rented at Acton Park to explore the peaceful lake.

On the shores of the lake are gifts that were presented to Australia from various countries. The British carillon is one of the oldest musical instruments and one of the largest of its kind in the world. Tiers of bells are played from an organ-like keyboard. The largest bell weighs more than six tons, while the smallest weighs only 16 pounds. Recitals are every Saturday, Sunday and holidays from 2:45 p.m. to 3:30 p.m. and every Wednesday from 12:45 p.m. to 1:30. You can visit the building from 1 p.m. to 4 p.m. on Saturdays and 9 a.m. to 2 p.m. on Sundays.

The American gift is very easy to spot. It's an eagle on top of a 240 foot pole! The U.S. gave the monument to Australia to commemorate American help in the defense of Australia in World War II.

The Captain Cook Memorial Fountain is the huge jet d'eau that is located in the lake near Commonwealth Park. The fountain only operates from 10 a.m. to Noon and 2 p.m. to 4 p.m., and 7 p.m. to 9 p.m. during daylight savings. Inside the park is a nine-foot globe which marks the routes followed by Captain Cook as he went "discovering" countries.

Blundell's Farmhouse, built in 1858, is in the Commonwealth Park between Commonwealth Avenue and Kings Avenue Bridges. For history buffs, this ancient house is the farmhouse that belonged to the original owner of the Canberra region, William Blundell and family. Three rooms are furnished in old Aussie Bush pioneer style. The lake is artificial, but the house is not. Blundell's is open from 10 a.m. to 4 p.m. and entry is only $1.

THE NATIONAL GALLERY. King Edward Terrace, 271-2411. If you are into art exhibits, this gallery features a wide range of Australian artists, including Aboriginal works and internationally respected artists (even Americans!). Check the newspapers to see which special exhibits are featured. Open every day from 9 a.m. to 4:30 p.m. and costs $3/free with a student card.

THE NATIONAL MUSEUM. Lady Denman Drive, 256-1111. The museum has a comprehensive exhibit of Aboriginal artifacts, a history of the Aboriginals in Australia, and the heart of Phar Lap, the Australian horse that died of mysterious circumstances in California in the 1930s. The museum is open daily from 10 a.m. to 4 p.m. on weekdays and 1 p.m. to 4 p.m. on weekends.

QUESTACON SCIENCE CENTER. Donaldson St., between the High Court and the National Library, 270-2800. If you have time for only one museum, head over to the National Science and Technological Center. You can while away hours playing with the hands on exhibits. Each level offers activities, exhibits, and games to play. Open daily from 10 a.m. to 5 p.m. Entry is $6 and $3 for students with identification.

MOUNT AINSLIE. For a killer bike ride or casual drive, climb the winding roads that lead to the top of Mount Ainslie. The views from here are superb, mainly because Canberra is so flat. You can see how the suburbs of Canberra are now spreading farther and farther out into the Bush. Don't kid yourself, a few miles away is the real Aussie Bush. This is why Canberra has such extremes of temperature.

CIVIC CENTER, London Court. If you wonder where all the people in Canberra disappear to on the weekends, then check out the Civic Center. Monaro Mall, between Petrie and Alinga Streets, has good shopping on three levels. The outdoor plaza has cafes and small restaurants and shops.

THE SIX STORY SHEEP. From Canberra, head north up Northbourne Avenue which becomes the Federal Hwy., rejoin the Hume Hwy. at the south of Goulburn and continue toward Goulburn. Before you come to the town center, you will see a sign directing you to the Big Merino. If you look to the left you won't be able to miss this six-story sheep.

You can't get much more tourist tacky than this, but Australia is known for its overgrown items. In addition to the sheep, Australia has a Big Potato, Big Pineapple, Big Banana, and Big Lobster. Climb up to the top of the sheep to see a history of wool making and then climb even higher to peer out of the eyes of the sheep. On the ground floor is a gift shop that uses every part of the sheep possible to make tourist souvenirs. Even the Ampol gas station has little cars with sheep on the top! If you want to stop for a bite to eat while you are at Goulburn, skip the Big Merino and stop at the Paragon, which is halfway down the main street on the left hand side. The restaurant has good food for cheap prices. Continue north on the Hume Hwy. and you should hit home in about two hours.

BATEMAN'S BAY. Another option from Canberra is to head on down to the sea and Bateman's Bay, which is where the Canberrites head for the weekends. It's a sleepy little town built on an estuary, and it has a few good, uncrowded beaches.

If you like very secluded beaches, follow the road that leads around the south of the estuary and stop at Surf Beach, Morooya, or Guerilla Bay. For the bay, turn off the road at the sign for Guerilla Bay and follow the dirt road until you reach the walking track to the lighthouse. You'll have amazing views up and down the south coast of Australia.

On your way back make a right onto the dirt road that is before the main road. Drive to the end of the road, and from here you will see a path that leads to walks along the beaches, coves, and rocky outcrops.

Also down in this area is Pebbley Beach, which is north of Bateman's Bay on the Princess Hwy. Watch out for the small sign on the right hand side of the road, which directs you into the Bush. On the narrow roads, don't forget to keep an eye out for kangaroos.

The beach itself is home to dozens of kangaroos who have no fear at all of people. They hang around waiting to be hand fed, and they can get pretty aggressive if food is not quickly forthcoming. So be prepared with bread, peanuts or other kangaroo delicacies. The wallabies are cute, but the six-foot-tall big reds can be pretty scary!

CHAPTER 21:

THE
OLYMPICS

The fireworks that lit up the sky above the Sydney Opera House and the Harbour to celebrate Sydney's winning bid for the Olympics were just the beginning of the planning, building, and partying that will last until the year 2000.

Australia first took part in the Olympics in 1896 and is one of only two countries that have attended every single one since. This will not be the first time that the Olympics have taken place in Australia, either.

In 1956 Melbourne was host to the Games, which became known as "the Friendly Games." Australia has yet to perform as well, athletically, as she did that year when she won 35 medals.

Brisbane bid unsuccessfully for the Games in 1992 and Melbourne bid again, unsuccessfully, for the 1996 Olympics. When Sydney won the bid for 2000, there was quite a bit of teasing and jeering since the two cities are known to enjoy a rivalry over everything from fashion to finance.

The theme for Sydney's bid was "Share the Spirit." The cities have put their differences aside, for the time being, and the country is busy coming together to celebrate the Games, which will be held between September 15 and October 1, 2000. Sydney has decided to make ecology a priority and has named these Games the "Green Olympics."

PRE-OLYMPIC CELEBRATION

Since the Aussies love a party, the Olympics are a great excuse to throw one—a three-year long one at that! The festivities will begin in 1997 with a cultural Olympiad and the Festival of the Dreaming. This celebration will focus on indigenous cultures worldwide, with a particular emphasis on the Aboriginals of Australia and the part they have played in Australian culture.

Sea Change will be the theme for 1998. The focal point for the events, which will laud the contributions made by immigrants and explorers (specifically, those from the nearby Pacific Islands), will be the Maritime Museum in Sydney Harbour. In 1999, the international community will be drawn into the festivities with the Reaching the World program. All eyes will be on Australia's performing arts, with a special emphasis on Aboriginal arts and performances.

The Cultural Olympics will conclude with a massive party named the Harbour of Life. Beginning on September 2 (two weeks before the opening of the Games) and lasting until October 7 (one week after the closing ceremonies), this festival will celebrate the world's cultures and express the hope that the new millennium will lead to peace and friendship. A children's choir, with members from every Olympic nation, will close the three years of parties with a Hymn to the Future of the World.

However, will the festivities really end after the Olympics? The following year is the centenary of the declaration of Australian Federation. Stories have been floating around for a long time that the year 2000 will be when Australia decides to declare full independence from the United Kingdom and become a Republic. As soon as Sydney won the bid for the Olympics, these rumors went into full speed. After three years of parties, the Aussies may declare independence and continue the fun!

THE OLYMPIC PLAN

A massive Olympic Park is being built at Homebush Bay, only 9 miles from Sydney. The park will complement the already existing facilities which include sports, hockey and softball centers. Construction will include athletic and aquatic facilities. Included is a new $85 million colosseum in the park, to be used for the opening and closing ceremonies, athletic events and the football finals. Tour operators are already cashing in on the popularity of the Olympics. Tours of the park cost $5/$2.50 children and leave from the north end of Strathfield Train station. Call 735-4800 for reservations and information.

Darling Harbour will also be the focus for some events. The existing 60-hectare harbor complex will be expanded and the current Exhibition Center will also be enlarged. Darling Harbour will provide venues for judo, boxing, table tennis, tae kwon do, weightlifting and basketball.

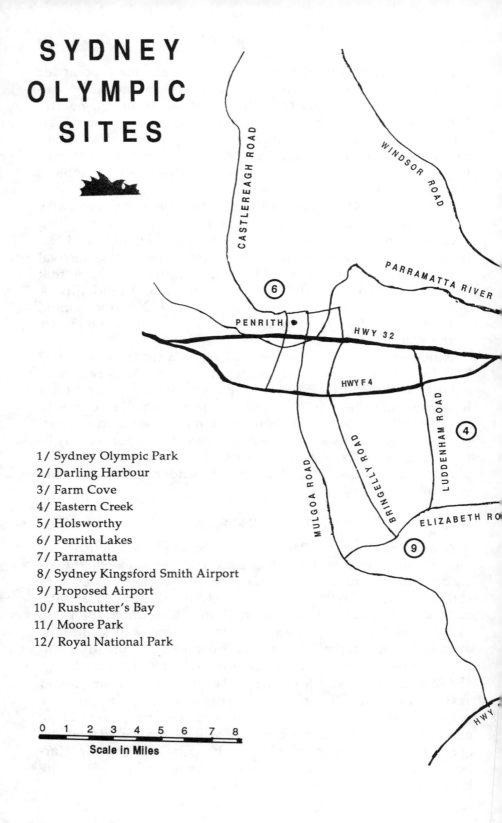

SYDNEY OLYMPIC SITES

1/ Sydney Olympic Park
2/ Darling Harbour
3/ Farm Cove
4/ Eastern Creek
5/ Holsworthy
6/ Penrith Lakes
7/ Parramatta
8/ Sydney Kingsford Smith Airport
9/ Proposed Airport
10/ Rushcutter's Bay
11/ Moore Park
12/ Royal National Park

CASTLEREAGH ROAD

WINDSOR ROAD

PARRAMATTA RIVER

⑥

PENRITH

HWY 32

HWY F 4

LUDDENHAM ROAD

④

MULGOA ROAD

BRINGELLY ROAD

ELIZABETH RO

⑨

HWY

0 1 2 3 4 5 6 7 8
Scale in Miles

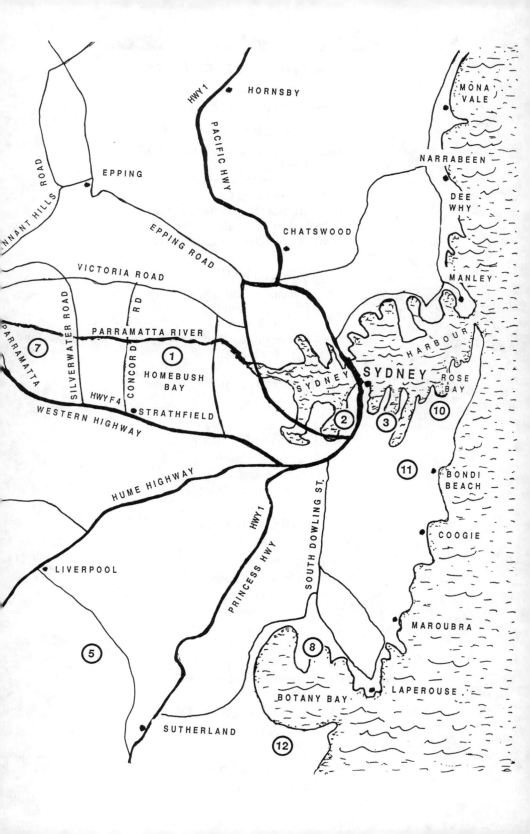

LOCATIONS OF EVENTS

SYDNEY OLYMPIC PARK
Homebush Bay
15 sports, including Track and Field
Hockey   Softball
Aquatic events
Main Press Center
International Broadcast Center
Technical Officials' Village
Opening and Closing Ceremonies

DARLING HARBOUR
Judo   Boxing
Table Tennis
Tae kwon do
Weight Lifting
Basketball

FARM COVE
Triathalon

EASTERN CREEK
Cycling Time Trials
Equestrian
Mountain Biking

HOLSWORTHY
Shooting

PENRITH LAKES
Canoeing
Rowing

PARRAMATTA
Football preliminaries
Waterpolo preliminaries

RUSHCUTTER'S BAY
Yachting events

MOORE PARK
Soccer preliminaries

The marathon will be at Farm Cove, along the Harbour. The soccer preliminaries will be held in Moore Park (where most of the soccer games are already held.) The Commemorative Pavilion, just a short walk away from Moore Park, will hold the wrestling events.

Yachting events will take place on Rushcutter's Bay in Sydney Harbour and in the Pacific Ocean, just beyond the Heads. Rushcutter's Bay is the location for shore-based yachting facilities.

A few sports will take place outside of the immediate city center, but most will be played no farther than 30 minutes from the Olympic Village and about an hour from Sydney. Equestrian sports, road cycling trials and mountain biking will be conducted at Eastern Creek, about 50 minutes from the city center. Shooting competitions will be at Holsworthy, also 50 minutes away.

Canoeing and rowing will be on Penrith Lakes, about an hour from the city. Football and water polo preliminaries will be held at Parramatta (half an hour from the city), as well as in Melbourne, Brisbane, and Adelaide. Some of the volleyball preliminaries may also take place in Melbourne.

A state-of-the-art International Broadcast Center and Main Press Center will be set up in Homebush. Journalists and broadcasters will be connected to all Olympic facilities through optic fibers. The Center will be open 24 hours a day.

Although not part of the Olympics, the Surf Life Saving Association of Australia is planning an international surf life saving tournament at Sydney's Bondi Beach during the Olympics. The lifesavers include some of Australia's best (and best-looking) swimmers.

THE OLYMPIC VILLAGE

For the first time in modern Olympic history, all athletes and team officials will be housed together in one Olympic Village.

The Village will combine architectural design with environmental awareness. Greenpeace Australia has played an important role in the design and implementation of the area's environmental guidelines.

The street lighting, water heating, and air conditioning will be solar powered. Bath and kitchen water will be treated and reused on site for gardens and washing cars and trucks. Buildings will be constructed facing north to maximize warmth in winter and coolness in summer. There will even be a ban on environmentally harmful gases in such items as refrigerators, air conditioners, and insulation. Greenpeace would like Sydney's Green Olympics to be the beginning of environmentally responsible Games. After the Olympics, the Village will become a new affordable suburb.

OTHER CHANGES IN SYDNEY

Sydney has used the Olympics as a reason to upgrade many other facilities. Almost $3 billion (U.S.) has been earmarked to improve the infrastructure of this old city. This is sorely needed.

The first stage of Sydney's second international airport will soon begin. In addition, a controversial third runway at Sydney's current international airport has been completed. Buses and trains and their facilities will be upgraded and roads and bridges will be improved.

The Government is planning to build a bridge to connect downtown Sydney and the Olympic Village, in addition to a new ferry service. All of these renovations will make life easier for the visitor.

DETAILS FOR THE TRAVELER

For those worried that Sydney will be overcrowded and practically unaffordable during the Olympics, there is hope.

Agreements have been signed with the hotel industry which would reserve 80 percent of hotel and motel accommodation for the Olympic Games visitors. All hotel rates, including food and beverage charges, are scheduled to be based (with an inflation percentage factored in) on the average published rate for 1998. With 30,000 rooms currently available, and another 6,000 planned, along with numerous private accommodations, a visit to the Games is not out of the question. Also, visitors should remember that spectator tickets will start at only $10.

During the two-week period of the Olympic Games, the climate should be ideal with temperatures ranging from 60 to 70 degrees. Because the breeze from the Harbour can be cool in the evenings, always be certain to carry a light jacket.

For more information on the Olympics, contact the Sydney Organizing Committee for the Olympic Games, GPO Box 2000, Sydney, NSW, 2001, Australia. (Phone 612 931-2000/FAX 612 931 2020).

NOTES

NOTES

I N D E X

Photo / Carlos Villanueva

Authors Zena L. Polin and Stephen G. Gatward have lived in Sydney, Australia, for a combined total of more than 20 years. They devoted a year to exploring almost every city street, park, beach and neighborhood in Sydney. In their course of their research for this book, they discovered hidden tunnels and created beach and bush walks and even a pub crawl. They have also co-authored another guidebook, The Pub, Club and Grub Guide to Washington, D.C., and have written numerous travel articles. They enjoy traveling around the world and writing about their experiences.